The Archaeology of Refuge and Recourse

ARCHAEOLOGY OF INDIGENOUS-COLONIAL INTERACTIONS IN
THE AMERICAS

Series Editors
Liam Frink
Aubrey Cannon
Barbara Voss
Steven A. Wernke
Patricia A. McAnany

The Archaeology of Refuge and Recourse

Coast Miwok Resilience and Indigenous Hinterlands in Colonial California

Tsim D. Schneider

THE UNIVERSITY OF ARIZONA PRESS

TUCSON

The University of Arizona Press
www.uapress.arizona.edu

We respectfully acknowledge the University of Arizona is on the land and territories of Indigenous peoples. Today, Arizona is home to twenty-two federally recognized tribes, with Tucson being home to the O'odham and the Yaqui. Committed to diversity and inclusion, the University strives to build sustainable relationships with sovereign Native Nations and Indigenous communities through education offerings, partnerships, and community service.

ISBN-13: 978-0-8165-4253-6 (hardcover)
ISBN-13: 978-0-8165-4799-9 (paper)

Cover design by Leigh McDonald
Cover art: *Pomo Indians Camped at Fort Ross* by Carl Von Perbandt 1886, courtesy of The Oakland Museum Kahn Collection, A68.163
Typeset by Sara Thaxton in 10.5/13 Garamond 3 LT Std

Publication of this book was made possible in part by the author's start-up funding from the University of California, Santa Cruz.

Library of Congress Cataloging-in-Publication Data
Names: Schneider, Tsim D., 1979– author.
Title: The archaeology of refuge and recourse : Coast Miwok resilience and indigenous hinterlands of colonial California / Tsim D. Schneider.
Other titles: Archaeology of indigenous-colonial interactions in the Americas.
Description: Tucson : University of Arizona Press, 2021. | Series: Archaeology of indigenous-colonial interactions in the Americas | Includes bibliographical references and index.
Identifiers: LCCN 2021007078 | ISBN 9780816542536 (hardcover)
Subjects: LCSH: Miwok Indians—California—San Francisco Bay Area—History. | Miwok Indians—Colonization—California—San Francisco Bay Area.
Classification: LCC E99.M69 S39 2021 | DDC 979.4/6004974133—dc23
LC record available at https://lccn.loc.gov/2021007078

Printed in the United States of America.
♾ This paper meets the requirements of ANSI/NISO Z39.48-1992 (Permanence of Paper).

For Liz

Contents

Illustrations

Acknowledgments

I AM A proud citizen of the Federated Indians of Graton Rancheria, the sovereign and federally recognized tribe of Coast Miwok and Southern Pomo people whose ancestral homelands and homewaters take center stage in this book. While my views may not necessarily reflect those of other Graton Rancheria citizens, I am deeply grateful to our ancestors and my community, especially members of the Sacred Sites Protection Committee, Tribal Heritage Preservation Office, and Tribal Council who, in one way or another, saw some value in this research, generously shared their time and perspectives, and permitted archaeological study of some of our oldest and most precious places. My field and lab work, community engagements, and interpretations are in part the outcome of many invaluable conversations through the years with Jeanne Billy, Gene Buvelot, Joanne Campbell, Tim Campbell, David Carrio, Joan Harper, Charles Johnson, Matthew Johnson, Buffy McQuillen, Peter Nelson, Frank Ross, Greg Sarris, Annie Swoveland, Ken Tipon, Nick Tipon, members of my immediate family, and several tribal elders who I had the pleasure of interviewing as part of my doctoral dissertation research. *Yawi! Ka molis!*

This book bears my name as author, but it reflects the hard work and thoughtful support of several people, many of whom I've had the pleasure of meeting and working with over the last two decades. Some of them contributed significant time and energy to my field and lab research. Others helped me fine tune the broader arguments of my writing. Here I acknowledge and thank Kent Lightfoot, Meg Conkey, Junko Habu, Kerwin Klein, Steve Shackley, Roberta Jewett, and Ed Luby. Jessica Tudor, Andrea Yankowski, and several student volunteers—Chris Avery, Brady Blasco, Anneke Janzen, Julie Kircher, Devin Landau, Laura Lee, Rachel Marks, Phoebe Peronto, and Megan Sharpless—worked with me at China Camp State Park or helped sort and inventory materials in the lab. Fellow graduate students Liz Soluri, Lee Panich, Kat Hayes, John Matsunaga, Rob Cuthrell, David Cohen, Shanti Morell-Hart, Sara Gonzalez, and Matt Russell also graciously volunteered time to help in the field. Before China Camp, my interests in the Indigenous peoples of colonial-era Marin County were enriched by conversations with Betty Goerke and Sylvia Thalman who I interviewed as part of my master's thesis research—work supervised by Mariah Wade, whose honesty, humor, and seriousness shaped me as a scholar.

I am fortunate to have been able to carry out archaeological field research in two of the most beautiful places in California: China Camp State Park and Tomales Bay (Toms Point Preserve). Research at China Camp was facilitated and enhanced by California Department of Parks and Recreation maintenance workers, rangers, and archaeologists, most especially Breck Parkman, Glenn Farris, and Rick Fitzgerald. This work was funded in part by a William Self Associates Fellowship, the Robert H. Lowie and Ronald L. Olsen Endowed Fellowship (Department of Anthropology, UC Berkeley), and by the Irving and Gladys Stahl Endowment Fund for Archaeological Research (Archaeological Research Facility, UC Berkeley).

Toms Point field and lab research benefited from the energy of students from UC Santa Cruz (GeorgeAnn DeAntoni, Abby Judkins, Alec Apodaca, Maggie Hames, Tate Paffile, and Alyssa Gelinas) and Santa Clara University (Emi Caprio and Ben Griffin), and from the friendly support and curiosity of Audubon Canyon Ranch (ACR) staff and researchers. A special nod of appreciation goes to John Kelly, who initially approved research at Toms Point and opened the stunning Cypress Grove Research Center as a place to camp, prepare meals, and rest after long workdays. Toms Point research was funded by a COR research grant from UC Santa Cruz, a Franklin Research Grant from the American Philosophical Society, and a multiyear collaborative research grant from the National Science Foundation (BCS 1558987 and 1559666). Here, Lee Panich deserves special thanks and recognition as co-principal investigator on the Toms Point project and as a longtime friend and colleague. It was a pleasure bringing our ideas on persistence and hinterlands together on a collaborative project at Toms Point more than a decade after we first worked together on an archaeological survey at Tomales Bay State Park.

Several additional experts deserve credit for their knowledge and help interpreting archaeological faunas and archaeobotanical remains, including Anneke Janzen (China Camp and Toms Point), Cristie Boone (Toms Point), Rob Cuthrell (China Camp and Toms Point), Tom Wake (China Camp), GeorgeAnn DeAntoni (Toms Point), Amanda Hill (Toms Point), and Alec Apodaca (Toms Point). Paul Engel and Carola DeRooy (Point Reyes National Seashore), Bryan Much (Northwest Information Center, Sonoma State University), Adam Gillitt and curators (Alameda Museum), Laurie Thompson (Anne T. Kent California Room, Marin County Free Library), Dewey Livingston (Jack Mason Museum of West Marin History), Ginny MacKenzie Magan (Tomales Regional History Center), Madeline Fang and Natasha Johnson (Phoebe A. Hearst Museum of Anthropology), and friendly staff at the Bancroft Library (UC Berkeley) and DeGolyer Library (Southern Methodist University) helped with aspects of my archival and archaeological collections research. Radiocarbon and obsidian hydration dates were provided by Beta Analytic Inc., DirectAMS, and Origer's Obsidian Lab. Scott Byram and Rob Cuthrell lent their expertise to magnetometer, resistivity, and GPR surveys at China Camp State Park and Toms Point. Shellfish seasonality data were analyzed at UC Berkeley's Laboratory for Environmental and Sedimentary Isotope Geochemistry and the Inductively Coupled Plasma Spectroscopy Facility. Brenda Arjona and Magdalena Olvera eagerly volunteered to help catalog the Toms Point glass assemblage. Obsidian from China Camp was analyzed with assistance from Steve Shackley at the Geoarchaeological XRF Lab (formerly at UC Berkeley), and I happily acknowledge Lee Panich, GeorgeAnn DeAntoni, and Peter Banke for their enthusiastic help analyzing the Toms Point obsidian and chert artifacts.

Weaving together two major archaeological undertakings into a single cohesive narrative took some doing and I am grateful for several people who helped with different phases of this book project. Special thanks go to Allyson Carter, Scott De Herrera, Amanda Krause, Archaeology of Indigenous-Colonial Interactions in the Americas series editors, and the University of Arizona Press team for ushering this project along from initial concept to final book. Three peer reviewers shared terrific ideas for improving the manuscript. Barbara Rogoff gave valuable feedback on the book's prospectus, and Liz Soluri, Khal Schneider, Lee Panich, and Kat Hayes generously set aside time to read and comment on an earlier draft of my book.

Since 2015, I am fortunate to have the support of several people at my intellectual home and community of UC Santa Cruz. Special thanks go to faculty and staff in the Department of Anthropology, especially Jon Daehnke, Judith Habicht Mauche, Cameron Monroe, Diane Gifford-Gonzalez, Eréndira Quintana Morales, Richard Baldwin, and Chelsea Blackmore. Within and outside of the Anthropology Department, I also appreciate the encouragement from Mark Anderson, Hillary Angelo, Nancy Chen, John Brown Childs, Guillermo Delgado-P., Rebecca Hernandez, Amy Lonetree, Renya Ramirez, and Barbara Rogoff. And I would not be where I am now without the friendships and votes of confidence from my Pacific Legacy family—especially John Holson and Lori Hager—and Lynn Gamble, my faculty mentor as a University of California President's Postdoctoral Fellow.

My closest and most reliable source of strength and advocacy is my family. For their love and encouragement, for reading *everything* I ever wrote, and for joining me in the field to excavate, map sites, and cook meals for my China Camp field school students I thank my parents, Kathryn and Philip. Thank you to Khal and Irene, the best brother and sister I could ask for and whose unconditional support, humor, and families—Cori, Greta, Bill, Xavier, and

Oscar—have lifted my spirits many times over. At UC Santa Cruz (UCSC), I also appreciated small moments to step away from work and devour burritos at Vivas with my Aunt Paula. Cheering for me beyond California, I also thank Dee, Dave, Ted, and Tom.

Finally, it gives me enormous pleasure to dedicate my book to Kathaeryne Elizabeth Soluri. For every hour spent in the field and lab, throughout grad school and my postdoc, during the first few years of employment at UCSC, and behind every page of this book, Liz has cheered for me selflessly and enthusiastically. In just the last year of intense writing, sheltering in place, coping with wildfires and foul air, and adjusting to online instruction, Liz's love, wisdom, compassion, laughter, diversions, Cabrillo College office (during the scuppering blackouts of fall 2019), research assistance, and her reassuring and restorative sense of perspective have helped me profoundly and give greater heft to the words "thank you."

The Archaeology of Refuge and Recourse

Introduction

IF THEY TIMED IT RIGHT, their tule boat wouldn't be pushed out to sea. Fog, strong tides, and the magnificent winds that characterize the Golden Gate of San Francisco Bay were absent that spring morning in 1783 when a Huimen couple named Julúio (pronounced who-LOO-ee-o) and Olomojoia (pronounced olomo-hoEE-a) paddled across the one-mile-wide strait to the Spanish colony clinging to the windblown headlands of the San Francisco Peninsula (figure 1). There, a military fort and Franciscan mission both named for Saint Francis of Assisi had been established by imperial Spain in 1776. Reports of the newly established community along with new ideas, words, and materials—objects of glass, metal, and ceramic—had undoubtedly reached the villages of Huimen people and still other Indigenous Coast Miwok-speaking hunter-gatherer-fisher peoples on the neighboring Marin Peninsula well before 1783. In fact, upon hearing about the strange new settlement, elders in some Coast Miwok communities may have been prompted to relay stories passed on from their predecessors about similar visitors to their homelands two hundred years earlier. Armed with some knowledge of what they might expect, Julúio and Olomojoia decided that the time had arrived to engage their new neighbors and to make the trip to Mission San Francisco de Asís (hereafter, Mission Dolores [SFD]) from their village of Livanegluá, now buried under present-day Sausalito. Accompanying them was their six-year-old daughter who would soon be baptized at the mission and given the name "Rosenda." She was the first Coast Miwok person recorded in the sacramental annals (i.e., registers of Indigenous baptisms, deaths, and marriages) maintained by Franciscan priests at California missions (Huntington Library 2006; SFD baptism 305). The name given by her parents will never be known.

Rosenda's baby sister would be baptized and given the name "Manuela Antonia" three months later in June 1783. During the following winter, Julúio accompanied his third daughter by a second wife, Matópa, to Mission Dolores. Their child, eleven-year-old Matúpa, was baptized and given the name "Jacinta." Julúio and Olomojoia would also eventually join their daughters at Mission Dolores in May 1784, adding their histories to the emerging fabric of this growing pluralistic social setting (Huntington Library 2006; SFD baptisms 325, 356, 369, and 370). Like most missions in California, Mission Dolores would become a home to Native peoples from diverse cultural and linguistic backgrounds where three, four, or more languages were regularly spoken, often "so distinct that generally not a great deal can be understood of one by the other," padres stationed at Mission Santa Cruz commented in the early 1800s (Geiger and Meighan 1976:21). On the same day that Julúio and Olomojoia were baptized at Mission Dolores and given the Christian names "Leandro" and "Humiliana," the church also sanctified their union and those of seven other Coast Miwok couples along with Indigenous Ramaytush people, Ohlone speakers whose homeland was occupied by the San Francisco colony (Huntington Library 2006; SFD marriage 78).

While their motivations and the conceivable benefits of entering the mission may never be known, Julúio and Olomojoia probably viewed Mission Dolores as an opportunity for their daughters to survive in a changing world. In addition to harboring their greatest hopes, like many parents Julúio and Olomojoia probably also carried with them their worst fears, and each voyage across the Golden Gate—between the colony and their Marin homeland—embodied a mixture of intrigue and apprehension. No sooner had Julúio and Olomojoia entered the mission than Rosenda died in November 1784. Four years later Olomojoia passed away at the age of forty-nine; she was followed by Julúio who died in 1794. He was in his fifties. Unlike their parents who did not grow up in a mission, Manuela and her stepsister, Jacinta, would not live past their twenties. Both unmarried and without children, Jacinta died in 1796, and Manuela passed away along with some 235 others during a measles outbreak in 1806 (Huntington Library 2006; SFD deaths 110, 242, 691, 985, and 2161). This six-week epidemic—"the worst . . . of the Spanish era in California"—killed one quarter of the mission Indian population of the entire San Francisco Bay Area (Milliken 1995:193). The disease also spread north to the Marin Peninsula likely carried by individuals fleeing the horrific loss of life at the mission. Forty-year-old Tolipeliuba (baptized and renamed "Luchesio"), another Huimen man, did just that. After seeing his eight-year-old son, Yuclamele, die at Mission Dolores the previous year and his wife, Luluela, succumb to measles in April 1806, according to mission

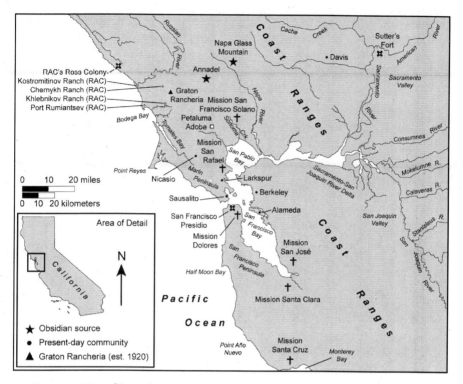

FIGURE I Map of Spanish, Mexican, Russian, and American colonial establishments, key obsidian sources, and other landmarks of the San Francisco Bay region of central California.

records Tolipeliuba "died among the gentiles, where he had fled, frightened perhaps with the death" (Huntington Library 2006; SFD deaths 1879, 2068, and 2280).

The crushing story of Julúio, Olomojoia, and their three daughters is representative of the lives of several thousand Indigenous Californians who were entangled with colonial missions in California between 1769 and the 1830s. By 1832 when missions around San Francisco Bay—the northern limits of New Spain's Alta California province—were transitioning to secularized parish churches, 2,828 Indigenous Coast Miwok people from the Marin Peninsula had entered and received baptism at the San Francisco, San José, San Rafael, and Sonoma missions (Milliken 2009:5). In the space of forty-nine years, over three-quarters of them had perished. Not surprisingly, anthropologists and historians attempting to document California's remaining Indigenous cultures during the early 1900s looked to the missions as one of the most destructive of California's colonial regimes and the primary source of Native cultural loss and assimilation. The tale crafted by anthropologists was thus one of indoctrination and wholesale cultural destruction. Attempting to fathom the experiences of Ramaytush and other Ohlone peoples whose homes became headquarters for evangelizing efforts in the San Francisco Bay region, Alfred Kroeber (1925:464), one of the preeminent anthropologists of the time, determined that they had simply gone "extinct so far as all practical purposes are concerned."

Coast Miwok met a similar fate in the paper trail of American anthropology. Isabel Kelly, one of Kroeber's students at the University of California, conducted ethnographic interviews with two Coast Miwok elders, Maria Copa and Tom Smith, during the early 1930s. In one of the most accessible and widely read accounts of Coast Miwok culture and history, volume eight of the Smithsonian Institution's landmark *Handbook of North American Indians* series, Kelly concluded that a "number of persons today have some Coast Miwok blood but apparently no knowledge of native culture and no interest in it. Effectively people and culture have disappeared" (Kelly 1978:414–15). Viewing this colonial narrative of cultural dissolution from a different perspective, namely my own perspective as a practicing archaeologist and a citizen of the federally recognized and sovereign tribe of Coast Miwok and Southern Pomo, this book focuses on the nearly one quarter of Coast Miwok people who managed to survive the missions. Surreptitiously and sometimes also with tacit support from the very same colonial projects designed to eliminate and extort Indigenous lives, Coast Miwok people and others created outlets within and beyond colonial settlements to resist and endure colonialism.

Returning to the story of Julúio and Olomojoia, between Rosenda's baptism in May 1783, Manuela Antonia's baptism in June 1783, Jacinta's baptism in February 1784, and the baptisms of Julúio and Olomojoia in May 1784, the family made at least seven trips back-and-forth between the Marin Peninsula and Mission Dolores over the course of a single year. Given their decade-long relationship to the mission, this example of Coast Miwok mobility raises additional questions about life beyond mission walls—arbitrary barriers that conventionally define the limits of Indigenous agency and history in the minds of scholars and others researching colonial California. What happened during those trips away from the mission? Did Julúio and Olomojoia leave their daughters at Mission Dolores—perhaps in the care of a Coast Miwok relative, a godparent, or with someone else from another tribal background altogether—before finally acquiescing and taking up residence at the mission? Did they make their trips across the Golden Gate as a family, returning home each time bearing news of their experiences and the new neighbors? How and when was it possible for Native people to come and go from missions and other colonial places assumed to be tightly patrolled? Looking, in other words, beyond the clear tragedy of Julúio, Olomojoia, and their three children devastating loss found at the core of many scholarly accounts of Indigenous experiences in colonial California—their story can also be illustrative of the resilience of Coast Miwok people. Facing death, violence, and the pervading uncertainty of change, Indigenous people of the Marin Peninsula balanced the pull and persistence of place against the unknown possibilities of a dynamic colonial landscape and the adaptability required to survive. History, change, and the future can be read in the story of Coast Miwok people.

Broader Contexts for Colonialism

Between 1769 and the 1830s, Franciscan missionaries directed the construction of twenty-one Catholic missions in Alta California, the name given to stolen Indigenous lands that became a colonial province extending for approximately six hundred miles between the present-day cities of San Diego and Sonoma. Missions represent the starting point, or ground zero, for imperial Spain's colonization of the Pacific Coast and for consecutive phases of colonialism instigated by European nations and the United States that would strike like crashing waves onto the homelands of Native Californians. For the next two centuries, into the 1900s, California tribes endeavored to understand and make do with missions, the short-lived extractive enterprises set up by the Russian-American Company, land grabs by wealthy American and Mexican citizens, and the free-market commerce and genocidal policies of removal associated with the United States. Scholars have deftly examined each of these phases and their assorted impacts on Native American societies. Importantly, however, it is well to keep in mind that each "period" of colonialism is as interconnected as it is accumulating and ongoing, building on the damage wrought by previous colonial activity incrementally up to the present. Similarly, the events, periodization, chronologies, and spatial patterns that archaeologists have come to define so well for California must not outweigh the creative Indigenous responses to colonialism across each phase and over the long term (Lightfoot 1995).

Applying this broader perspective to California, the construction of Franciscan missions represented one facet of a tripartite colonial plan that also included the establishment of pueblos (secular towns) and presidios (forts), which functioned as military and administrative hubs for the province. After a lengthy history, the empire of New Spain was losing money and reforming in the late eighteenth century when Spanish colonizers entered California (Lightfoot 2005:50–51). Instead of urging reluctant citizens to relocate to the remote California frontier two thousand miles north of Mexico City, colonial officials turned to Franciscan missionaries to quickly and economically occupy California before other nations claimed it. As they had done since the sixteenth century in other regions of the Spanish borderlands—including the provinces of Florida, Texas, and New Mexico—California's Franciscan padres instituted a program of *reducción* and *congregación*. This two-pronged approach involved "reducing" (removing) Indigenous people from villages and "congregating" (collecting) them at missions for conversion to the Roman Catholic faith and for lessons in farming and other trades necessary for life as a Christian peasant. Through this program, colonial officials sought to grow a loyal colonial populace out of the preexisting Indigenous one.

Ideally, the padres had also envisioned, Indigenous cultural traditions, languages, and connections to former homes would be easily stripped away once Native people entered the missions. In this sense, it is easy to imagine why anthropologists like Alfred Kroeber viewed missions as the last best place to see Indigenous cultures before acculturation and/or extinction. Several factors—many of them scholarly in origin and others attributed to dramatic changes to the California landscape attributed to humans and forces of nature—support the false spatial logic and narrow temporal focus that underlie Kroeberian essentialism and the formation and reproduction of damaging tropes of Indigenous disappearance. As I explore in the following chapters, however, Coast Miwok and many other Indigenous groups found ways to remain connected to places and cultural practices, and the meeting of colonial and Indigenous worlds was more often grounds for creativity and dynamism, rather than the outright and cataclysmic replacement of the latter by the former. Refuge and recourse—spurred by social memory and the material choices of Coast Miwok people confronting colonialism—reinforced deep-seated ties to place, embodied histories of mobility and engagement with meaningful landscapes, and also nurtured and gave shape to Indigenous cultural legacies that endure and continue to inform Coast Miwok people during and long after their entanglements with short-lived missions.

This book reconsiders the story of California's colonial period and attempts to reorient conventional narratives about Indigenous-colonial encounters in the San Francisco Bay Area to foreground Native American landscapes. To do so requires rethinking the conventional timing and spatial organization of colonial California, adjusting the theoretical scaffolding archaeologists have constructed and applied to be able to evaluate Indigenous-colonial encounters, and reassessing the field and laboratory techniques normally used to detect and study colonial-era places and materials. Just as California missions are probably best understood as Native places constructed, maintained, inhabited and, at times, destroyed by Native peoples, European colonies established throughout the Americas were and continue to be located within the homelands of Indigenous peoples (Panich and Schneider 2014).

These homelands in California, or "Indigenous hinterlands" as I define them (Schneider 2015b), were complex landscapes consisting of a broad meshwork of places and communities of people with unique histories, spiritualties, relationships, agencies, and materialities that framed colonial endeavors. The hinterland, as I apply it, is relational—the product of and setting for dynamic relationships made possible by a constantly evolving cast of Indigenous and colonial agents with unique and emergent interests. The Indigenous hinterland contrasts with the idea of a remote, generic space "peripheral" to a colonial "core"—terms closely associated with world-systems theory and core-periphery models used to trace the spread of capitalism on a global scale and not necessarily the numerous small processes emanating from within colonized populations whose interests frequently shaped colonial policy in novel ways.

As I discuss later (in chapter 2), the Indigenous hinterland concept addresses two important ideas. First, drawing from archaeological theories of resistance, social memory, and place and landscape (Schneider 2015b), the concept puts emphasis on a much-needed accounting of numerous Indigenous places that were contemporaneous with colonial projects and also served as autonomous sites of protection and redirection for Native people grappling with change and colonial assertions of power. Archaeological (e.g., Lightfoot and Martinez 1995) and historical (e.g., Barr 2009; Brooks 2002; Hämäläinen 2008; Zappia 2014) research on borderlands inspires further consideration of hinterlands as important sources of change and as contexts for tracking resilient and novel social groupings, resistance, ambivalence, and situational identities beyond the relatively small frames offered by the study of contact sites alone. Borderlands are "ambiguous and often-unstable realms where boundaries are also crossroads, peripheries are also central places, homelands are also passing-through places, and the end points of empire are also forks in the road" (Hämäläinen and Truett 2011:338). Hinterlands are equally dynamic, socially charged, and cross-cultural landscapes where people from unique cultural backgrounds intermingled and negotiated the conditions and outcomes of their meetings. As I see it, "things"—the material world, including fixed places and portable items—are at the center of these negotiations. Moreover, as settings of social distance and intimacy, hinterlands are places of tension and innovation as well as liminal spaces to disappear or reappear when needed.

Second, the idea of an Indigenous hinterland explicitly acknowledges the necessity to decolonize archaeological discourse, specifically to decenter conventional perspectives on space and time without unconsciously adopting a grammar of colonialism (see Hauser and Armstrong 2012). Terms like "frontier," "borderland," and even "hinterland" derive from Western intellectual traditions that strived to make sense of the anthropological "Other" and reorder seemingly unknown and disorderly spaces. Put simply, we must be aware that one person's frontier may be another person's homeland (Lightfoot and Martinez 1995:473). I place special emphasis on the structuring power of Native places, and I foreground the protracted and protective role of familiar landmarks for Native peoples contending with the maelstrom of colonial violence and structures of domination.

Present-day Nicasio in central Marin County, for example, is the location of the precontact Coast Miwok village named Echa-tamal. During the mission-era, this hinterland community was important "not only for pastoral activities, but for the cultivation of crops by Native Californians who were allowed to live there" (Dietz 1976:17). While former mission livestock, tools, and property were usually taken by prominent Mexican citizens, former military, or naturalized citizens from the United States in the years following the secularization of missions during the 1830s, five Coast Miwok men petitioned for and received the eighty thousand-acre Nicasio land grant in 1835 (Dietz 1976:22). Defrauded of their land in the intervening years, by the 1870s Coast Miwok families living at Nicasio claimed a modest thirty acres (figure 2). They were finally evicted in the 1880s (Dietz 1976:55–63). Born in 1868, Maria Copa recalled her childhood at Echa-tamal during interviews with anthropologist Isabel Kelly. Among other things, Copa recalled the lessons she received from her elders, including Sebastian, one of the original petitioners for the Nicasio land grant in 1835 and a former "cook for the [Franciscan] priests" at Mission San Rafael (Collier and Thalman 1996:320; Dietz 1976:46–47):

> There was an old man called Sebastian, and I used to give him things to eat. I would say, 'papoyis [grandfather], taste this. It is blackberries.' He would take them and say, 'The si'ikatco (si'ika) [supernatural beings] must eat before I do.' Then he would say, 'Ssss,' throwing some outside and some in the fire, and some in the water. It used to make me mad. (Maria Copa in Collier and Thalman 1996:408)

Indigenous hinterlands included spaces for protection. They also included places with enduring histories and sources of knowledge suitable for teaching

FIGURE 2 By the 1870s, the original Rancho Nicasio land grant promised to Coast Miwok families of the former San Rafael mission in 1835 had been reduced from eighty thousand acres to approximately thirty acres. From 1874 until his death in 1875, José Calistro, leader of "certain old and infirm Indians at Nicasio," lived in this cabin, which was bulldozed in the 1960s as an "eyesore" (Dietz 1976:55–63). Courtesy of the Jack Mason Museum of West Marin History.

younger generations. As "reservoirs of accumulated and ongoing history" (Rubertone 2000:436), Echa-tamal and many other places discussed in the following chapters reflect a landscape and bodies of water that were memorialized and value-laden as well as embodied in the practices of the people who dwelled in and moved across them.

Place, Memory, and Mobility in Colonial California

My investigation of Indigenous refuge and recourse in colonial California is framed by theories of place, social memory, and mobility. Place, a concept closely connected to my discussion of Indigenous hinterlands, is a significant factor in how I see Native communities responding to colonialism and persisting in the present-day. Daniel Justice writes:

Perhaps nothing matters more: Indigenous peoples' complex and overlapping sets of relationships, obligations, legacies, loyalties, and languages that deepen as they extend outward in time and space are intimately tied to and dependent on specific places and their meaningful histories. Without these places—on the land or on the water—the rest of that network begins to unravel. For this very reason colonialism in its myriad forms is fundamentally invested in undoing those relationships to place and imposing new, extractive structures in their stead. (Justice 2016:21–22)

In addition to describing the unbreakable bonds that anchor Indigenous communities to their homelands, Justice draws attention to an important distinction between "place" and "space." My use of the term place emphasizes peoples' active and ongoing relationships to important locations and how such places can also be sources of power and direction in people's lives. Space, according to Edward Casey (1996:14), is "a neutral, pre-given medium, a tabula rasa onto which the particularities of culture and history come to be inscribed, with place as the presumed result." The more objectified and passive view of seemingly unoccupied spaces also aligns with the goals of colonialism, particularly efforts to manipulate, redefine, and co-opt Indigenous land as well as conceal Native peoples' constant efforts to assert their place names and histories. While early settlers viewed Californian lands as vacant, William Bauer Jr. (2016:47) writes, "place and place-names undergirded California Indian understandings of their past . . . evoked and argued for a deep historical process whereby they invested particularistic meanings in the land . . . [and] asserted Native sovereignty over the land." Just as we see in the present, an assortment of places informed Indigenous histories and sustained the various strategies Native people deployed to be able to retain and commemorate them.

People's connections to place—their sense of belonging to certain landscapes and histories—are activated by social memory and embodied in daily practice, or routine tasks like fishing, digging for clams, and other pursuits people might follow on a daily basis to navigate and organize the world around them (Bourdieu 1977; Giddens 1979). Maurice Halbwachs (1980:50–52) offers one perspective on social memory, arguing that individuals participate in two forms of memory: "personal memory" and "collective memory." People carry their own personal remembrances, which can be enriched by a collective memory that reflects the remembrances of interest to a larger social group. In this view of social memory, people "encode things with significance" (Appadurai 1986:5), including portable objects and, I would also add, landscapes, places, and immovable features.

Another view of social memory stresses how individuals and groups commemorate place and how places talk back. As Barbara Bender (2001a:4) writes: "We make time and place, just as we are made by them." Landscapes and objects are not simply blank canvases upon which individuals or groups affix their memories. Similarly, memory is not pure recall but a process or dialogue between peoples' understandings of a past and their present conditions (Meskell 2008). Memory (remembering and forgetting) can be manipulated to enhance or conceal particular histories—an especially relevant idea considering current events and the toppling of controversial monuments throughout the United States (e.g., Cohen 2017; Fracassa 2018; Moffitt 2020). In fact, the "'art of memory' is in its tactical and transformative employment," Katherine Hayes (2008:22) writes, and the "application of memory knowledge at the 'right moment' can create sources of power for those who use it with craft, to rupture a stable field of relations." Whether something is understood as remembered or forgotten is a matter of standpoint. Considering colonial California—namely the policies and writings of colonists and settlers, the conclusions of anthropologists, and the destruction of Native American archaeological sites—some aspects of California Indian history have been expunged or forgotten by outsiders. A "humiliated silence," a type of forgetting and ingredient of survival (Connerton 2008:67–68), may have also taken hold in Indigenous communities brutalized by colonialism and hoping to "bury things beyond expression and the reach of memory."

Paul Connerton's (1989:72–73) dual concepts of "incorporating" and "inscribing" memories are instructive for understanding social memory as either routinized bodily practice or intentional and explicit acts of memorialization. Following Connerton (1989), cultural landscapes may also be viewed as generative places of empowerment and venues of social reproduction. Keith Basso (1996) and Julie Cruikshank (2005) offer compelling examples of cultural landscapes as instructive forces in the ontologies and oral traditions of the Native peoples who inhabit them. Cruikshank (2005:11) relates the significance of landforms, such as glaciers and mountains, for Tlingit and Athapaskan peoples in southwest Yukon as repositories of collective wisdom and enduring "points of reference for communicating tacit knowledge" across generations. Oral traditions about key places on the landscape, or local knowledge, as Cruikshank (2005:64) reveals, are interwoven with natural and social histories that connect peoples and places through time and impart practical knowledge and moral content for those traversing landscapes. Among the Western Apache, observable features of the landscape are similarly used as sources of wisdom or instruction by people burdened by despair. Oral narratives with spatial anchors, Basso (1996:91) explains, compel visitors to places to recall stories of events that occurred at those places long ago "as if the ancestors were speaking to you directly . . . [and] bring this knowledge to bear on your own disturbing situation." Like Cruikshank's discussion of tacit knowledge, Basso describes peoples' relationships to places as reciprocal and lived once they become the object of awareness:

> In many instances, awareness of place is brief and unselfconscious. . . . But now and again, and sometimes without apparent cause, awareness is seized—arrested—and the place on which it settles becomes an object of spontaneous reflection and resonating sentiment. It is at times such as these, when individuals step back from the flow of everyday experience and attend self-consciously to places—when, we may say, they pause to actively sense them—that their relationships to geographical space are most richly lived and surely felt. (Basso 1996:106–7)

Neither Cruikshank nor Basso explicitly engage with theories of social memory per se. Their examples, however, demonstrate how some Native peoples might theorize space and marshal oral traditions that implicitly draw on personal and collective memories to affiliate people, story, and place. Oral narratives and, as part of traditions of orality, social memory, are "grounded in the material circumstances of everyday life" (Cruikshank 2005:61; see also Bauer 2016:28–29). Memory's materiality can be seen in the placement of burials, the layout of structures in a village, the scheduling of trips to collect resources, and the accumulation of tools and household waste deposited over thousands of years in a single spot. All of these examples and more leave material traces, and even the physical and habituated act of traveling to important places can transmit cultural traditions, legitimate present social orders but also "keep the past" (Connerton 1989:72). Places mobilize people.

California archaeologists are well-versed in the study of mobility, particularly for evaluating settlement and subsistence patterns, seasonality, and social complexity in hunter-gatherer societies. For many years, however, hunter-gatherer research has tended not to equate regular travel across long and short distances with informed bodily practice but instead as a quantifiable aspect of precontact economic or political organization. The same may be said of historical archaeologists. Mobility and seasonal hunting and gathering are not the typical purview of archaeologists researching colonial encounters (Schneider 2015a). As others have observed (Lightfoot 1995; Scheiber and Mitchell 2010), the distinct research questions, methods, and evidence collected and analyzed by prehistorians versus historical archaeologists caused a rift, or "great divide," in how we understand long-term change in Native

North America. The mission reduction policy described above, for example, was designed to limit and control Native American mobility. Yet, Native people routinely hunted and gathered while residing at missions, and they daily accessed a manifold of ranches, agricultural fields, and orchards where their labor was imperative to the operation of the missions. They moved frequently. Discussed more in chapter 2, fugitivism and furlough represent still other examples of colonial-era mobility—interested actions shaped by longstanding histories of travel that situate Native people beyond the walls of colonial sites. I have found that radiocarbon dating and stable isotope analysis can be fruitfully applied to the study of colonial-era mobility and other resilient traditions just as much as the careful inspection of archival documents and noting the presence of mass-produced metal, glass, and ceramic artifacts.

Reassessments of Native peoples' creative choices during California's colonial period requires reworking fixed definitions of community and mobility (e.g., Bauer 2009:5; Lelièvre 2017:106; Nelson 2020). Widely circulated images of California's bucolic colonial landscapes consisting of walled colonial compounds as well as the maps produced by land surveyors and anthropologists depicting discrete Native American village sites overemphasize stability and boundedness. Points on a map and commonly shared views of rigidly patrolled colonial settings belie protracted traditions of mobility that defined resilient social networks interconnecting people to far-flung places. From the vantage of an Indigenous hinterland where Native people remained or returned throughout different phases of colonial settlement, mobility represents an important yet often neglected practice underlying community-making and senses of place. By viewing travel to and from points on the land as more than a matter of finding food and shelter, a more robust accounting of mobility examines how people moved to evade and engage, to reconnect with friends and kin, and to "attend" to place. A nuanced understanding of mobility further encourages rethinking how Indigenous families negotiated exploitative labor regimes and the various ways people got around by foot and by boat. This reframing of a known and frequently traveled landscape carries important implications for archaeologies of colonialism centered around missions, forts, and trading posts, but perhaps more importantly, it speaks to dynamic communities unmade and remade at different times and for different reasons.

The theoretical framework I employ in this book necessitates rethinking Indigenous-colonial encounters in the San Francisco Bay Area and beyond. In place of powerful colonies and vacant hinterlands, we can begin to imagine the outlines of an expansive, populated, and known landscape extending offshore and deep into the California interior. In lieu of presuming Native people's knee-jerk decisions to accept or violently resist colonial authority, the story of Julúio and Olomojoia reveals how place-based histories and long-term traditions of responding to new people, places, and things—individual and collective memories, in other words—played a role in how Indigenous Coast Miwok rebuffed and acquiesced to colonialism. In a similar fashion, and contrary to destructive scholarly narratives of cultural loss and village abandonment during the colonial era, we can also start to consider how the innumerable and varied trips of Julúio, Olomojoia, and other Coast Miwok people helped reinforce, or define anew, relationships to place and kin. Viewing colonial history and archaeology from the seat of Indigenous places, memories, and mobility, we can begin to see landscapes of resilience. Such landscapes offered places of refuge for those seeking protection from harm as well as recourse—a term I use to describe Native peoples' informed reactions to colonialism that balance cultural traditions, the lived-realities and pragmatic choices of the colonial moment, and anticipated futures.

High-Impact Partnerships, Low-Impact Methods

My approach to the archaeology of colonialism outlined thus far acknowledges harmful anthropological narratives of loss or "little choice" (sensu Milliken 1995)—forms of academic and popular erasure exacerbated by the physical destruction of Native places. With the tendency to focus on individual sites of colonialism (e.g., missions) in California archaeology comes a false spatial logic and thin chronology. By this I mean a narrow temporal window, usually extending from 1769 to the 1830s, that tends to (a) reinforce the notion of a quick collapse of Indigenous cultures from repetitive waves of colonization and (b) disconnect the practices of historical Native Americans from their pasts and their ideas for a future.

In addition to preservation efforts, tourism, romantic views of early California, and a rich "visual vocabulary" of postcards, photographs, paintings, and souvenirs that celebrate and sanitize colonialism (Kryder-Reid 2016:145), archaeological attention to the built landscape (e.g., mission chapels, forts, adobe buildings, and other highly visible features) further reinforces narratives of erasure. The destruction or concealment of Native places attributed to rapid urbanization in the San Francisco Bay Area and other regions of coastal California further amplifies histories of postcontact Indigenous loss. Because many Native places have been destroyed or because they are difficult to see, Indigenous histories are funneled through colonial places resulting in a version of history narrated via the eyes and ears of colonial agents or announced by artifacts collected from within the boundaries of colonial settlements. Here, historians have been particularly skilled at interrogating California's mission archives to spot and elucidate instances of Indigenous agency and self-preservation (e.g., Haas 2014; Newell 2009; Rizzo 2020). Archaeology's focus on sites of colonialism, its construction and deployment of inflexible chronologies, and an overemphasis on site abandonment, cultural loss, or change-as-loss allow relatively little room for discussing Native people's creative responses to colonialism and comparatively fewer examples of research exploring broader landscapes, persistent places, and Indigenous peoples' resilient traditions.

Research on Indigenous hinterlands cannot be done without additional methodological retooling. Hinterlands extended beyond the coast of California to Native communities far inland, but nonetheless were impacted by the circulation of introduced materials, ideas, and infectious diseases (e.g., Arkush 2011; Hull 2009). To conceptualize and study such extensive landscapes of "Native-lived" colonialism (Ferris 2009), I designed an approach detailed in the following chapters that stresses three core themes. First, to research Indigenous hinterlands requires acknowledging the impacts of colonialism, anthropology, and site destruction on the visibility of Native people, places, and histories. Seeing Native people and persistent places on the landscapes around colonial-era installations pushes back against conventional and widely circulated essentialist narratives of cultural loss, acculturation, and village abandonment. Just as Native communities are capable of constructing and wielding their identities for specific goals (Gallivan et al. 2011), so too do Native people maintain and create complex relationships with the world around them. To live at a mission or to intermarry with another tribal member does not mean the forfeiture of former ways.

Second, the kind of archaeology I practice seeks to document the dynamic experiences and resilience of Indigenous communities navigating colonialism. As I discuss above, my view of fluid hinterlands is informed by theories of place and landscape, social memory, and mobility. This perspective also requires new thinking on the variety and forms of evidence that have traditionally defined the archaeology of colonial-era Indigenous communities. The glass beads, metal tools, and pieces of ceramic dishware that archaeologists usually look for and study to help identify "historical" Native American sites can overshadow the innumerable other places where Native people might choose instead to prioritize precontact lithic technology and foodways choices over mass-produced goods and new foods.

Third, I acknowledge and foreground an Indigenous epistemology, or knowledge and understanding of the world that is unique to different Indigenous groups. In particular, I strive to uphold the ethics, values, and ways of knowing within my own community of the Federated Indians of Graton Rancheria, the sovereign and federally recognized tribe of Coast Miwok and Southern Pomo people who are Indigenous to Marin and southern Sonoma Counties and whose ancestors confronted and survived the missions, ranchos, and mercantile enterprises established in their homeland. My thinking and scholarship are informed by my own observations and experiences as a citizen of Graton Rancheria. As a community comprised of families with unique histories and memories, however, I acknowledge that my views and positionality might differ from those of other Graton citizens. My research also articulates with the energetic and transformative field of Indigenous archaeology. In the two decades since a definition for Indigenous archaeology—archaeology that is "done with, for, and by Indigenous peoples" (Nicholas and Andrews 1997:3)—entered scholarly discourse, the field has expanded in new and important ways. From an early focus on consultation in cultural resource management and the repatriation of Native American human remains from museums and other archives (Watkins 2000), Indigenous archaeologists are pioneering new theoretical and methodological approaches to community-based participatory research and heart-centered collaborative practice (Atalay 2006, 2012; Supernant et al. 2020). By prioritizing Indigenous epistemologies, I stress the active role for my community partners in the research process—working together and remaining flexible enough to accommodate a dynamic Native American community of advisors and fellow scholars endeavoring to share and learn more about our collective past and future together.

This cooperative philosophy of community engagement further extends to the sites deemed appropriate for research, the types of field and laboratory methods selected for the research project, and the forms of evidence that can be analyzed. This culturally sensitive approach to the study of Indigenous-colonial encounters pairs well with the tools of historical anthropology. In this approach, which draws from the methods and theories of history and anthropology, the uneventful, or the many "little routines" of daily life (Lightfoot 2005:17), can temper conventional western accounts of colonialism by centering Indigenous people who "act upon circumstances according to their own cultural presuppositions, the socially given categories of persons and things" (Sahlins 1981:67). This approach involves the collection and comparison of multiple forms of evidence, such as archaeological materials, documents, oral narratives, and ethnographic writings and photographs. While I must consider the unique strengths and biases of each source, this holistic approach can help establish a more inclusive and robust understanding of colonial entanglements. Moreover, the integration of other nonarchaeological data sets can ideally reduce the amount of destructive excavation carried out in a project that might otherwise depend on archaeological evidence alone.

My reasons for minimizing excavation are twofold. First, I am part of a Native American community whose citizenry includes elders who observed firsthand the violence associated with destructive archaeological research, such as the kind of work that took place at San Francisco Bay Area shell-mounds throughout the twentieth century (e.g., Schneider 2007b:56–61). As demonstrated by the China Camp State Park (chapter 3) and Toms Point (chapter 4) case studies, the selection and approval of minimally invasive and nondestructive archaeological field and laboratory techniques, like digital mapping, shallow geophysics, targeted excavation of features, X-ray fluorescence (XRF) spectrometry, accelerator mass spectrometry (AMS) radiocarbon dating, and stable isotope analysis, acknowledges the sensitivity and unique privilege of working with Indigenous cultural places and materials. Second, I also make use of previously collected materials that have been stored in museums and other repositories for several decades with little to no interpretation. These and other efforts to reduce my footprint at archaeological sites, to breathe new life into existing collections, and to maximize the amount of information from a variety of evidentiary forms—including evidence based on Indigenous knowledge and values—represent honest efforts at further decolonizing the practice of archaeology.

Book Organization

The Archaeology of Refuge and Recourse is organized into seven chapters, including this introduction outlining the major theoretical and methodological frameworks steering my investigations and interpretations. As I discuss above, the layout of the book is designed to foreground the resilience of Indigenous people and places on the Marin Peninsula of the San Francisco Bay Area and to establish a long-term understanding of their place-based histories and creative responses to missionary, mercantile, and settler colonialism spanning approximately one century (1770s to the 1870s). Chapter 1, "Peopling, Placing, and Erasing Indigenous San Francisco Bay," has two key facets. First, this chapter provides an overview of the Marin Peninsula with an eye toward the geography and environmental setting undergirding Indigenous livelihoods on the Marin Peninsula. I introduce the culture history of Indigenous Coast Miwok-speaking hunter-gatherers, paying close attention to the precontact practices—settlement patterns, subsistence pursuits, technologies, and social organization—that I see persisting throughout the colonial time period. A second aspect of this chapter addresses how Indigenous histories have been systematically erased or obscured from view. In focusing on San Francisco Bay shellmounds, I trace the long history of Indigenous presence in the region and a comparatively shorter but impactful history of cultural and natural disturbances to mounded landscapes. One century of purposeful and inadvertent destruction of mounds and other places—at the hands of both archaeologists and amateurs—conceals histories of place and Indigenous presence while augmenting anthropological "terminal narratives" of Native American disappearance and extinction (see Wilcox 2009). The puncturing and removal of this record, including the topmost deposits of many shellmounds that may contain evidence of postcontact occupations, is particularly troublesome when attempting to understand the continuation of Indigenous communities outside the timeframe and spaces of colonial settlement. A similar archaeological bias addresses the ways archaeologists have either overlooked the possibility of ancient sites as having historical relevance to Native people or disregarded introduced materials as "intrusive."

In chapter 2, "Indigenous Lives, Colonial Time," I examine colonialism in the San Francisco Bay Area, beginning with small-scale, sixteenth-century encounters on the Marin Peninsula. I then focus on colonial settlement in California by representatives of Spain, Russia, Mexico, and the United States from the 1770s to the 1870s. The first part of the chapter discusses missionization, with an eye toward current archaeological research that addresses the broader landscapes of Franciscan missions. I argue that an overemphasis on walled compounds, chapels, and barracks for Native families—the bread and butter of mission preservation efforts and mission archaeology in California— reinforces the idea of static hinterlands with abandoned Native communities. Choosing instead to emphasize the "process" of missions, or constructed and dynamic sites of contestation and confirmation in the past and present, I recast missions not only as settings of control and confinement but also malleable places continually structured by the daily actions and interests of the people who resided at them. As revealed in historical documents, fugitivism, extramural residency, and padre-approved furloughs called paseos are examples of that dynamism, or "building" (Ingold 2012:78). Self-emancipation, creative living arrangements, periodic leaves of absence, and archival and archaeological examples of traditional subsistence and ceremonial practices conducted at and away from missions altogether help raise the profile of hinterlands as constant forces in the lives and decision-making of colonized Indigenous groups. Such continuities, I argue in the second of half of the chapter, speak to an enduring sense of place informed by an unshakeable awareness of the past (and a future) and activated by the very mobility and cultural traditions assumed to have been contained and eliminated by the missions. The resilience of Coast Miwok people can be traced through subsequent periods of colonization by the Russian-American Company (1812 to 1841), Mexico (1821 to 1850), and the United States (1840s to present) represented by the proliferation of private rancho estates, mercantile outposts, and other settlements. Discussion of the Russian mercantile colony of Fort Ross, Mexican Period ranchos, and American sites of commerce like the Toms Point trading post further define an array of colonial franchises folded into the decision-making of post-mission Coast Miwok families who faced violence, disease, dispossession, and exploitative labor regimes while keeping, at all costs, a foothold in familiar lands.

Chapters 3 and 4 present two archaeological case studies investigating Indigenous responses to colonialism during the mission period and afterward. Chapter 3, "Seeking Refuge," focuses on the archaeology of three shellmounds (sites CA-MRN-114, -115, and -328) in Marin County's China Camp State Park that are managed by the California Department of Parks and Recreation. Building from the examples of shellmound destruction in chapter 2 and conventional approaches to California mission archaeology in chapter 3, my study of the three China Camp sites sheds light on the role of some shellmounds as gathering areas for Native people seeking to extract themselves from mission influence. Lithic technology and the remains of plants and animals collected from each site are presented alongside my reanalysis of materials previously excavated from MRN-115 in 1949. Based on the results of AMS radiocarbon dating and XRF analysis of obsidian artifacts, I interpret the chronology and patterns of activity at each site in light of flight and furlough documented in the historical record. Stable carbon and oxygen isotope analysis on archaeological mussel shells offers additional perspective on the seasonal timing of Native people's trips to shellmound refuges. Helping to assess colonial-era Native American mobility practices, shell artifacts can also be interpreted as a type of "escape crop" (Scott 2009:187–207) Native people turned to when mission food rations were in short supply. As I discuss in the conclusion of this case study, the collection and processing of wild foods, producing and using stone tools, and the manufacture and adornment of shell artifacts all leave material traces that can tell us more about the careful and persistent choices of Native people facing crisis—archaeological patterns atypical of most archaeological research on colonialism. The results of my work and examples of research in other areas of California draw attention to the necessity of creatively rethinking the sites, chronologies, and artifacts that have normally segregated prehistoric and historical archaeology and abbreviated long-term Indigenous histories.

Chapter 4, "Finding Recourse," examines the archaeology and ethnohistory of Toms Point, a small peninsula managed by Audubon Canyon Ranch and located on the shore of Tomales Bay in western Marin County. Toms Point is named after a white settler, George Thomas (Tom) Wood, who operated a trading post on that point of land during the mid-nineteenth century. Before George Wood claimed the land for his own, Coast Miwok called the place "Seglogue," and residents of this community occupied a middle ground where the geopolitical interests of two imperial powers (Spain and Russia) converged and precipitated a landscape continually refashioned by an ever-changing cast of people and activity. Before that, the landform was home to Indigenous Coast Miwok for at least three thousand years. The Toms Point trading post, a short-lived hub of free-market enterprise, was staffed at least in part by Indigenous Coast Miwok laborers hailing from Tomales Bay and by other Native people from the surrounding region. At Toms Point, in the wake of the missions, Coast Miwok and other Native people picked up the pieces of their lives and started rebuilding. Historic maps and documents, existing collections, and archaeological materials from three archaeological sites (CA-MRN-201, -202/489, and -363) provide rare windows onto the long-term histories of place and place-making among Coast Miwok resisting and making do with colonialism. Community once again hinged on mobility, social memory, and place. As exploited labor, Native people traveled between Toms Point and other farms and mills established throughout Marin and southern Sonoma Counties. Trips to assorted destinations throughout the region, however, simultaneously retraced attenuated pathways and helped link dispersed friends and family. Mobility—as reflected in historical and archaeological records—reinforced memories of places and Coast Miwok claims to those places. Accordingly, Toms Point and other post-mission sites represent important places of recourse, consensus-building, and commemoration as well as steppingstones archaeologists can look to for connecting an obscured archaeological past to resilient and living Indigenous communities.

There are two main components of chapter 5. First, I compare and discuss the results of archaeological investigations at China Camp State Park and the Toms Point Preserve. Six sites define an occupational history that spans at least six thousand years. As a Native archaeologist studying the history of my own community, I seek to reconcile the evidence for resilient Indigenous people against some of the most brutal and inhuman acts designed to dispossess or entirely eliminate California Indians, erase Native identities and places, and silence Indigenous languages. Research from other regions of California, mission records (e.g., sacramental registers and questionnaires), historical accounts, and my archaeological study of colonial-era Indigenous foodways, technologies, and the seasonal routines of colonized Native American communities reflect a broader and enduring Indigenous landscape that helped buffer many of the impacts of colonial intrusion. The second half of the chapter includes a more concrete example of Indigenous resilience, or resistance and rebuilding efforts carried out by Coast Miwok people since the late 1700s. Focusing on fishing and shellfishing practices among late nineteenth- and early twentieth-century Coast Miwok families, I argue that we need to look differently at the land, at Native-lived histories of colonialism, and at the novel ways Native people held onto the past while finding new ways to make a living.

The conclusion revisits the book's main arguments. For many Indigenous societies of California, the arrival of colonial institutions and associated materials, livestock, and ways of life threatened the unique sovereignties, political organizations, languages, subsistence pursuits, senses of place, and other characteristics that defined these cultures for millennia. Coast Miwok people of the Marin Peninsula, including people like Julúio and Olomojoia, made difficult choices for themselves and their families about whether to interact with colonial sites or to avoid them at all costs. Significantly, and quite unlike the either-or essentialism espoused in the writings of early anthropologists, what often goes overlooked are the numerous ways Native people appear to have navigated the constant reality that they "must change *and* remain the same" (Silliman 2009:226; emphasis in original). As seen in the archaeological record at China Camp and Toms Point, and in the notes and illustrations found in archives, Coast Miwok found recourse amid a constantly evolving field of colonial rules by actively seeking refuge and protection in the hinterland and by continuing to hunt, gather, weave, dance, sing, and conduct still other long-standing cultural practices. Similarly, choosing to enter a mission, rancho, or trading post, to marry people from other tribes, to fashion a tool from a discarded glass bottle, to reside in Western-style houses, or to consume shellfish alongside cuts of pork does not reflect an extinguishment of culture. Through these and other practices Native people creatively reaffirmed their connections to place and cultivated a sense of belonging within homelands increasingly becoming home to others.

Much more than an academic exercise, in viewing Californian colonial encounters from a different non-Western perspective, this book represents my attempt at recentering Native places and, thereby, doing archaeology differently. I invite readers to consider the decision-making that took place in relationship to meaningful Indigenous places far beyond the adobe, wood, and brick walls of colonial programs. This reworking of a colonial-centered history not only foregrounds persistent places and the experiences of postcontact Indigenous communities but also reflects a "very different type of archaeological practice" that puts emphasis on Indigenous concepts of time, space, and knowledge production through the design of scholarship that is relevant to a present-day Native American community (Atalay 2006:295–96). Taking the long view informed by Indigenous and Western (archaeological) epistemologies, the following chapters give shape to an inseparable bundle of Native peoples' memories of how things used to be; the tasks, choices, successes, and shortcomings that make up the rhythms of daily life at different colonial moments; and understandings of a hoped-for future. A collection of past experiences, agency, and imagination underwrite a Coast Miwok sense of belonging. While some Indigenous families, like that of Julúio and Olomojoia, succumbed to colonial violence, many more succeeded in creating and capitalizing on opportunities to remain connected to the people and places that mattered most to them. While under threat, these enduring relationships bound together Indigenous and colonial worlds and ultimately gave rise to broader avenues for persistence and the resilient communities we still see in the present.

I

Peopling, Placing, and Erasing Indigenous San Francisco Bay

> While the history of the shellmounds of this region probably reaches back
> more than a thousand years into the past, it must have extended almost to the
> threshold of modern times.
>
> —MAX UHLE, 1907

EARLY ONE MORNING IN SEPTEMBER 1907, thirty-two-year-old
Nels C. Nelson set out on an ambitious archaeological survey to systemati-
cally record all of the shellmounds ringing the shoreline of San Francisco Bay.
Choosing to begin his survey in Sausalito, Nelson caught a ferry from San
Francisco where he lived and was enrolled as a student in the University of
California's newly established program in anthropology. Compared to urban
San Francisco, which was still rebuilding from the 7.9-magnitude earthquake
and fire that destroyed much of the city in the previous year, the Marin Peninsula must have been welcome relief to Nelson as much as a logical starting
point to begin his survey. Arriving in Sausalito, warm autumn light activated
the spicy aroma of peppernut trees and filtered through the leafless branches
of scraggly buckeye trees populating the forests around the sleepy shoreline
community (figure 3). Heading clockwise from Sausalito around San Francisco Bay, Nelson would eventually walk or ride trains around San Pablo Bay,
travel east around Suisun Bay, and then meander south past Berkeley and
Oakland until finally looping around the lower reaches of San Francisco Bay
and the extensive tidal marshes near the communities of Alviso, Palo Alto,
and San Bruno. "Tramping some 3000 miles of littoral" (Mason 1966:393),
Nelson recorded 425 mounds around San Francisco Bay between 1907 and
1908 (Nelson 1907, 1909a). Before transferring to New York in 1912 to
begin a career as curator of North American Archaeology at the American
Museum of Natural History, Nelson expanded his survey to include over fifty
more shellmounds on the Pacific coast between the Russian River and the
Golden Gate, including Tomales Bay (Nelson 1909b).

FIGURE 3 "New or North Sausalito," circa 1890. Nelson's "Mound No. 3" can be seen already partially demolished. Roy D. Graves Pictorial Collection. Courtesy of the Regents of the University of California, the Bancroft Library, UC Berkeley.

Nelson's methodology was quite unusual for the practice of archaeology at the time. In addition to conducting a pedestrian survey designed to account for similarities and differences between sites across a wider region—the first of its kind for San Francisco Bay and an approach more closely associated with a style of archaeology conducted decades later—Nelson recorded the appearance, composition, and condition of many of the sites he visited. Concerning the composition of shellmounds, as a student Nelson also conducted archaeological excavations at Ellis Landing Shellmound where he worked with paleontologist John C. Merriam. Nelson rubbed elbows with University of California anthropologists such as Alfred L. Kroeber, Frederick W. Putnam, and fellow graduate student Samuel A. Barrett, all of them collectively engaged in a departmental mission to "salvage" information about precontact aboriginal California cultures and languages before they disappeared for all time. In the San Francisco Bay Area, Nelson would pioneer many of the techniques that now define the subfield of archaeology as a historical science, including excavation by stratigraphic layers to track changes in material culture through time.

Traveling between shellmound sites during the early 1900s, Nelson was also acutely aware that he was likely to be the last person to see many of these sites. As predominately coastal sites hugging the thin strand between bay waters and higher elevations, the condition of many of the shellmounds that Nelson and his contemporaries studied had already been impacted by centuries of wave action, erosion, animal burrowing, and other forces of nature that carved holes into the mounds or flattened them entirely. Even more alarming, many mound sites had also been systematically demolished by human hands. Residents of Sausalito hoping to enhance their curio collections with artifacts and their vegetable gardens with midden soil had already torn apart "Mound No. 1," the first shellmound recorded during Nelson's survey. Throughout San Francisco Bay, entire shellmounds or large sections of them had been removed and repurposed as fertilizer for agricultural fields or as road base for the streets of rapidly growing cities. Other sites were simply razed and built over without second thought. At still other places, archaeologists and amateurs joined forces and further contributed to the removal of California's Indigenous past. In the process of consuming Native places and bodies, newcomers recast Indigenous time and place to fit Western conceptions of history and space.

The aim of this chapter is twofold. I first define the precolonial landscapes of the greater San Francisco Bay region. I focus specifically on Coast Miwok and Southern Pomo people, the original inhabitants of the Marin Peninsula and North Bay lands, as well as on shellmounds, a particular type of site characteristic of the ocean and bay shores in this region. After first briefly defining the environmental setting that ungirded Indigenous livelihoods and informed how Indigenous people would ultimately respond to colonialism, I outline previous archaeological work on the Marin Peninsula. I give special attention to pre-contact Indigenous subsistence practices, technologies, social organization, and mobility to help evaluate the modification and continuation of these activities during the colonial era—themes I address in chapters 3 and 4 when discussing Indigenous refuge and recourse. A second component of this chapter highlights shellmounds as places of considerable research interest and information about precolonial Indigenous populations. Simultaneously they are also some of the most abused places in the San Francisco Bay Area, devoured by a litany of destructive natural and human forces. Such dramatic transformations to the landscape challenge residents, visitors, and seasoned researchers to imagine a topography prior to its cultural and historical scouring. I invite readers to see shellmounds as places of relevance to Native people living on both sides of an artificial boundary separating prehistoric and historical time and space.

Peopling a Place

Environment and Geology

San Francisco Bay is the largest tidal estuary on the west coast of North America. This estuary is comprised of several bays, including two larger bays (San Francisco and San Pablo) and four smaller bays adjoining San Pablo Bay (e.g.,

San Rafael and Richardson) and the Sacramento-San Joaquin River Delta (e.g., Grizzly and Suisun). Within the estuary, freshwater from the Sacramento-San Joaquin River Delta—replenished annually by snowmelt from the Sierra Nevada and Cascade ranges—intermingles with saltwater from the Pacific Ocean and in turn supports a robust fishery and resource-rich saltwater and brackish marshes. In a carefully balanced cycle, snowmelt flushes the delta and bay, deposits nutrients into the ecosystem, and entices anadromous fish like salmon (*Oncorhynchus* spp.) and sturgeon (*Acipenser* spp.) to return from the Pacific Ocean and spawn in the Sacramento and San Joaquin Rivers and numerous inland waterways of California's Great Central Valley.

Focusing on one corner of the San Francisco Bay estuary, the diverse natural habitats found on the Marin Peninsula mirror the unique ecological diversity that is typical throughout California. Walking across the peninsula west from Larkspur to the Pacific Ocean—a distance of less than ten miles—the elevation climbs to 2,500 feet at the summit of Mount Tamalpais before returning to sea level. Tule (*Schoenoplectus acutus*) marsh, redwood forest, oak woodland, chaparral, coastal prairie, and riparian zones are all found along that same ten-mile transect. Three types of coastal environments surround Marin County: open sandy coastlines, rocky intertidal coast, and lagoon/estuaries. Within the San Francisco Bay estuary, before widespread environmental degradation associated with Euro-American colonization, extensive tidal marshes and mudflats hosted lush plant communities, countless bird species, shellfish, and other creatures. Bay waters teemed with sturgeon, salmon, shark (e.g., *Triakis semifasciata*), bat ray (*Myliobatus californicus*), and schooling fishes like herring, smelt, and silversides (Clupeiformes, Osmeriformes, Atheriniformes). Cormorant (*Phalacrocorax* spp.), western grebe (*Aechmophorus occidentalis*), and ducks, geese, and swans (family Anatidae) relished the protected and nutrient-rich waters of San Francisco Bay, while California quail (*Callipepla californica*), woodpeckers (family Picidae), hummingbirds (family Trochilidae), birds of prey (e.g., family Falconidae and family Accipitridae), turkey vulture (*Cathartes aura*), California condor (*Gymnogyps californianus*), and other birds filled the forest canopy and sky. The mosaic of Marin habitats also included terrestrial and sea mammals, such as assorted small mammals, bear (*Ursus* spp.), mountain lion (*Puma concolor*), coyote (*Canis latrans*), tule elk (*Cervus canadensis nannodes*), mule deer (*Odocoileus hemionus*), harbor seal (*Phoca vitulina*), sea lion (*Zalophus californianus*), and sea otter (*Enhydra lutris*).

The Pacific Ocean and the rugged cliffs, beaches, and intertidal zones of the Point Reyes Peninsula form the western boundary of Marin County. Sandwiched between Point Reyes and the higher elevations found on the Marin Peninsula, the infamous San Andreas Fault lies below Tomales Bay, an elongated estuary measuring approximately 25.5 kilometers long and one kilometer wide. Lush forests—consisting of redwood (*Sequoia sempervirens*), Douglas fir (*Pseudotsuga menziesii*), Bishop pine (*Pinus muricata*), oak (*Quercus* spp.), California bay (or, peppernut, *Umbellularia californica*), buckeye (*Aesculus californica*), manzanita (*Arctostaphylos* sp.), toyon (*Heteromeles arbutifolia*), and other plants—west of Tomales Bay contrast with the exposed hills found along the bay's eastern shore. Much of western Marin County now hosts private ranches with copious pasture for grazing livestock; yet wildflowers and perennial grasses—including native bunchgrasses—continue to grow in grasslands east of Tomales Bay. At the southern end of Tomales Bay near the community of Olema, creeks and tributary streams feed extensive freshwater marshes and form narrow canyons that in turn become shelter for birds, deer, and small mammals. This tranquil setting contrasts with lands around the mouth of Tomales Bay to the north, which include windswept dune and rocky intertidal habitats bordering the frigid waters of the Pacific Ocean. Eelgrass (*Zostera marina*), waterfowl and shorebirds, sea lion, various invertebrates (e.g., clam, mussel, and oyster), bat ray, shark, and other schooling fishes thrive in the shallow Tomales Bay estuary. Prior to their overhunting by Euro-American settlers, Marin's waters and lands also hosted sea otter nurseries and herds of tule elk.

Geologically, San Francisco Bay "reads like a Russian novel with a very large cast of characters" (Sloan 2006:48). Tectonic activity over the past 140 million years contributes to the geologic tapestry of the San Francisco Bay, as well as the varied terrain and complex blend of ecosystems and microclimates described so far. Formed by the persistent subduction of the North American and Pacific Plates, an assortment of faults and the Franciscan, Great Valley, and Salinian Blocks give rise to the diversity of rocks and minerals found in the region (Sloan 2006:49). For the Marin Peninsula, the San Andreas Fault marks the boundary between the Franciscan and Salinian Blocks and gives shape to the peninsula's unique geology: rocks found east of the fault include basalt, radiolarian chert, graywacke, and serpentinite associated with the Franciscan Block. Rocks found west of the San Andreas Fault are associated with the Salinian Block carried north over the past 110 million years (Sloan 2006:49–62, 68–70). Sedimentary fill and tertiary volcanic rocks also contribute to the unique geologic terrain of the San Francisco Bay region, and to the varied lithic menu available to Indigenous Coast Miwok peoples.

For all of the bodies of water and features of the land, and the plants, animals, insects, rocks, and minerals that dwelled there, Indigenous Coast Miwok and Southern Pomo people maintained a story and a purpose. Sharp cutting tools could be knapped from obsidian and chert, finely tipped awls were shaped from the bones of deer, chunks of basalt could be shaped into sturdy milling equipment, and a flabbergasting list of plants were tended, collected, and transformed into meals, medicine, cordage, construction material, and finely woven baskets. Borrowing from Basso (1996) and Cruikshank (2005), the Marin landscape at contact was alive and enriched by places with power, memory, instruction, and opportunity that also structured human action.

Indigenous Peoples of the Marin Peninsula

Indigenous peoples of precolonial San Francisco Bay thrived in a varied and dynamic landscape shaped by fire, erosion from wind and rain, periodic drought, tectonic activity, and sea level rise. Since time immemorial, the Marin Peninsula has been the ancestral home of Indigenous Coast Miwok people who inhabited numerous small village communities, each with distinct territories and cultural identities. For instance, Indigenous communities around Tomales Bay inhabited lands that included bay tree and redwood forest, grassland, riparian habitat, wetlands, and intertidal zones bordering the sheltered Tomales Bay estuary as well as the rugged Pacific coast. On the other side of the peninsula, Huimen, Tamal Aguasto, and Omiomi peoples maintained homelands with redwood forest, oak savanna, intertidal marsh, and other habitats suited to warmer temperatures along San Pablo Bay.

As custodians intimately familiar with the world around them, Coast Miwok people managed the environments of the Marin Peninsula, which provided food and raw material needed for subsistence, domestic life, ceremonies, and commerce. It is also a storied landscape integral to Coast Miwok identity, oral history, and survival. Each tree, mountain peak, creek, and boulder represents an ongoing story. As Greg Sarris, chairman of the Federated Indians of Graton Rancheria, warns, "if we forget the story, say if we see the old oak tree as just a big thing with a gnarled trunk and hanging branches, if we forget that the tree is a living spirit with a story, we might lose a lesson important to our survival here" (Sarris 2017:231). The land is a source of power for Coast Miwok people who continue to live and interact with it. It was, after all, a Coast Miwok medicine man named Tom Smith who in a contest with Big Jose, another medicine man, caused the 1906 earthquake that laid waste to the city of San Francisco (Sarris 2002). The relationships between people and place can nourish and devastate.

When colonists arrived in California beginning in the late 1500s, several small-scale hunter-gatherer polities populated the Marin Peninsula and spoke a common Coast Miwok language (figure 4). Adding the suffix "-let"

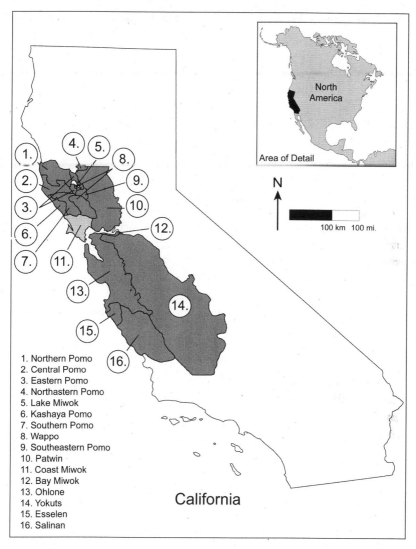

FIGURE 4 Map of California Indian language groups, or "tribes," of coastal central California.

to tribe, "tribelet" is a demeaning anthropological term coined by Alfred Kroeber (1955:307) to account for the extraordinarily high population density and diversity of Indigenous languages, as well as the uniquely small size of Indigenous social and political groupings for most of California. Simply put, the complex social and political landscape of Indigenous California is unlike anywhere else in North America, and Kroeber identified several unique

characteristics that distinguish California's Indigenous sociopolitical groupings from other Native American tribes. These attributes were subsequently
revised (Bean and Blackburn 1976) and, more recently, neatly summarized
by Kent Lightfoot and Otis Parrish (2009:79–80) to account for territory
size, population density, political organization, and the leadership of Indigenous groups. A tribe's leadership, for instance, was generally vested with
certain individuals who possessed strong oratory skills and the authority to
settle disputes and schedule events. For Coast Miwok communities, a *hoipu*
(headman) and *maien* (headwoman) shared leadership. In addition to giving
advice and resolving disputes, the hoipu "harangues . . . [and] tells the people
to be good . . . almost every evening" (Collier and Thalman 1996:344). The
responsibility for scheduling dances, selecting dancers, hosting visitors, and
finding doctors to heal group members was given to the maien. "The hoipu
is a boss . . . [yet] maien bosses everyone, even hoipu," a Coast Miwok elder
named Tom Smith once recalled (Collier and Thalman 1996:343, 347).

An estimated thirteen distinct tribal communities comprised the territory
of Coast Miwok peoples (see Milliken 1995). This territory includes the entire
Marin Peninsula from the Golden Gate north to Tala-lupu (or "Stand-Rock"
near the mouth of the Russian River) and it extends east from the Pacific
Ocean to Sonoma Creek (figure 5). One of these groups, the Tamal Aguasto,
formed communities on the east side of the Marin Peninsula, including
Point San Pedro where China Camp State Park and the three archaeological
sites discussed in chapter 3 are located. Shotomoko-cha (or Cotomko'tca),
Ewu, and Awani-wi are the names of three Coast Miwok villages recorded
in Tamal Aguasto territory (Kelly 1978:415; Milliken 1995:242). Olema,
Echacolom, Segloque, and at least eight other distinct tribal groups inhabited lands around Omóta-húye (big point, or Point Reyes) and Tamal-liwa
(Tomales Bay) in western Marin County (Milliken 1995:254). Segloque (or,
Sakloki) and Xotomcohui (or, Shotomko-wi) are also the names of major villages in Segloque territory, which includes present-day Toms Point and the
archaeological sites examined in chapter 4. To the north of Tomales Bay and
extending from the mouth of the Russian River east to the Santa Rosa Plain,
Kabemali, Konhomtara, and Bitakomtara are the names of Southern Pomo
peoples bordering Coast Miwok lands. Today, the federally recognized and
sovereign tribe of Coast Miwok and Southern Pomo people—the Federated
Indians of Graton Rancheria—recognize the lands, waters, natural resources,
and cultural places of Marin and southern Sonoma Counties as integral components of their ancestral territory.

The linguistic "hyperdiversity" of California's estimated seventy-eight
mutually unintelligible languages is unrivaled on the North American con-

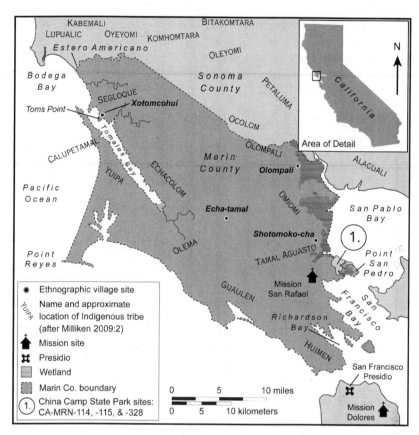

FIGURE 5 Map showing the names and approximate locations of Indigenous Coast Miwok and Southern Pomo tribes after Milliken (2009:2). Approximate location of China Camp State Park study sites (CA-MRN-114, -115, and -328) at right.

tinent (Golla 2011:1). The Coast Miwok language is part of the Penutian language family. Southern Pomo peoples speak an entirely different language—as different as French and German languages—belonging to the Hokan language family. There are seven Pomo languages: Northern, Central, Eastern, Southeast, Southern, and Kashaya (Southwestern) Pomo. The Penutian family of languages includes the other four Miwok (or, Mewan) languages associated with Indigenous Lake Miwok, Bay Miwok, Plains Miwok, and Sierra Miwok peoples of the Sacramento-San Joaquin Delta, Central Valley, and central Sierra Nevada, as well as Ohlone peoples of the Monterey Bay and San Francisco Bay regions. In the northern San Francisco Bay region, Samuel Barrett (1908:303–18; see also Merriam 1907) identified two dialects of the Coast Miwok language: a "western dialect" called Olamentko (or, "Bodega Miwok") centered around Bodega Bay and a "southern dialect" called Hookooeko (or, "Marin Miwok") spoken throughout the rest of Coast Miwok territory (see Callaghan 1970, 2004). As I discuss more below, even a basic understanding of Native California's linguistic complexity deepens one's appreciation for the enormous length of time Native peoples have lived in their homelands to be able to create so many distinct languages and identities. It also reflects the stunning patience and ingenuity exercised by Coast Miwok and Southern Pomo peoples listening to each other and surviving together in the midst of colonial violence and displacement.

Coast Miwok and Southern Pomo tribal territories were "large enough to provide enough habitat diversity to buffer the vagaries of environmental perturbations during most years, but small enough to remain manageable from a few village locations that may have been moved once or twice a year" (Lightfoot and Parrish 2009:80). Thus, the great variety of seasonally abundant plant and animal resources, rocks and minerals, and other natural resources within a tribe's territory encouraged relatively small, tightly packed, and densely populated tribal communities that accessed a diversity of resources within well-defined homelands, even as they moved throughout the year. Coast Miwok elders interviewed by anthropologist Isabel Kelly during the 1930s discuss year-round collecting of crab and deer; salmon and steelhead could be fished during winter runs; rails and other migratory birds were available in the winter along with shellfish; acorns were collected, processed and eaten, or stored in the fall; and an abundance of grasses could be collected for seeds in the spring and summer months and eaten with berries and sundry small fish and game (Kelly 1978:415–16).

In addition to the dietary value of wild plants and animals, many resources have two, three, four, or more uses. The wide assortment of plants growing on the Marin Peninsula, for example, ensured that Coast Miwok and Southern Pomo people had access to food, medicine, and raw materials for ceremonies, tools, and structures. Both Washington clam (*Saxidomus nuttalli*) and red abalone (*Haliotis rufescens*) were eaten. The shells of these animals could then be transformed into clam bead money and lustrous abalone shell ornaments. Every part of a deer—antlers, bones, hide, meat, tendons, intestines, and hoofs—was put to use (Lightfoot et al. 2009:247). From the world around them, Native people fashioned an array of tools, including finely woven baskets, cordage, nets, tule and redwood bark houses, lightweight tule balsas for transporting people and materials around the bay, bone and shell tools, and stone tools made from obsidian, chert, and basalt. To access these and other resources, friends and family members, and significant places within their homelands, Indigenous Coast Miwok and Southern Pomo people cultivated traditions of mobility.

Archaeologists working in the southern North Coast Ranges have defined a seasonal settlement pattern in which Native groups typically moved either by foot or by tule boat between dispersed summer camps established along coastlines and larger inland winter villages (Lightfoot 1992). For the San Francisco Bay Area, Banks and Orlins (1981), Luby et al. (2006), King (1970a), Milliken et al. (2007:105), Parkman (1994), and Slaymaker (1974) have all proposed models for understanding the seasonal mobility and settlement practices of precontact Indigenous groups. The models generally emphasize Native peoples' periodic aggregation around a single larger village site—a larger mounded site, for instance, with two or more satellite encampments—for ceremonies, socializing, decision-making by leaders, and other planning. As center points, larger villages would have been composed of a permanent population and permanent structures, such as sweathouses, conical bark houses, and semi-subterranean ceremonial roundhouses, whereas smaller seasonally occupied satellite villages included temporary structures like open-air ramadas and tule houses (Lightfoot et al. 2009:211). For the Marin Peninsula, Slaymaker (1974:13) argued that the central village—larger mounded village sites like Shotomoko-cha (CA-MRN-138)—would have also represented a "place of identity and importance" for Coast Miwok people returning from distant seasonal camps to participate in dances and other rituals. Discussed more in the next chapter, shellmounds located some distance from missions might still have served as center points for Native people, in which case mobility and trips to these and other important meeting spaces helped reaffirm connections to family, history, and the salient features of home (Schneider 2018).

Archaeological approaches to hunter-gatherer mobility in western North America primarily apply evolutionary theory to evaluate the roles of food-collecting and reproductive fitness in Native peoples' seasonal travels. Despite the implicit sense of activity conveyed in the word mobility, priority was also given to settlement, or staying put, rather than to travel and the routes required to traverse landscapes. This "sedentarist ideology" is at the core of Western concepts of land use or that "benchmarks for occupancy are those practices—such as monumental architecture, large-scale infrastructure, urban development, and agriculture—that permanently alter the land and water" (Lelièvre 2017:74). It is also often the highly visible "fabric heavy" components of a landscape that receive the most attention from archaeologists (Byrne 2003:170–72). For San Francisco Bay, this would include more permanent mission buildings and, as seen in Nels Nelson's regional survey, even prominent Indigenous shellmounds discussed more below.

As part of my efforts to decolonize archaeological concepts of time and space in colonial-era California, I foreground the deep traditions that helped inform how Indigenous peoples responded to colonialism and persisted. I view mobility, how Native people creatively made and unmade their communities (Schneider 2018), as a central part of refuge-seeking and the recourse required to navigate the dual commitments of tradition and remaining flexible enough to accommodate change. Reworking rigid definitions of residence that overemphasize stability and illuminating the ability of Native people to frequently move, band together, and disband to improve their condition necessitates a new understanding of mobility as equal parts movement, emplacement, obstinacy, and reassertion. My perspective is informed by the writing of Michelle Lelièvre (2017:19) who defines "movement" as the "comingling of *lived* practices, *conceived* imaginaries, and *sensual* perceptions," or travel that is socially informed, contingent, and multisensory. From Laura Hammond (2004), who researched emplacement among modern Sudanese refugees, we can also view travel as an emergent process in which even unknown spaces can be transformed into personalized homes. People are "never nowhere," Barbara Bender (2001b:78) reminds us, but always in relationships with place. Mobility and keeping tabs on salient places, seasonally available resources, annual rituals, and family members scattered across a region increasingly usurped and fractured by colonial forces also carries a dose of obstinacy and defiance as Denis Bryne (2003) and Mikah Pawling (2016) demonstrate for Indigenous peoples traversing colonized homelands of Australia and Maine. Fluid and malleable social lives can in fact be quite powerful and trouble efforts to build and maintain empires (e.g., Hämäläinen 2008), as well as contain and police Native bodies.

Mobility also reflects memory and movement that embodies long-standing traditions of travel. Epistemology, or how people come to know and understand the world, is at the very heart of the mobility concept. The physical and multisensory act of retracing the steps and trails cut by your ancestors while listening, seeing, and sensing the world as you move through it reawakens the past. Each heel strike on known land or paddle stroke seated in a tule balsa simultaneously takes stock of present conditions and anticipates a certain future. Remaining mobile throughout the late nineteenth and early twentieth centuries, Native people circulated between home rancherias and the demands of wage labor at farms, trading posts, mills, houses, ranches, and other settler work sites. In doing so, they traced the contours of tradition and, as William Bauer Jr. (2009:5) suggests, etched even newer paths for building and sustaining community. How far back does this pattern go? To help answer this question, the following two sections introduce and critique the archaeology of San Francisco Bay.

San Francisco Bay Archaeology

A Note on Chronology

During the last century, archaeologists in North America—including those working in California—have devised and furiously refined chronological sequences of Indigenous histories using chronometric dates (e.g., radiocarbon dating), relative dating techniques (e.g., obsidian hydration analysis and seriation), and the presence of diagnostic or time-sensitive artifacts (e.g., bead types, projectile point types, material types, etc.) in archaeological sites (e.g., Beardsley 1954; Bennyhoff and Hughes 1987; Groza et al. 2011; Milliken et al. 2007). For much of the twentieth century, however, archaeologists excavated and dated sites without the permission, participation, and authority of Native American communities. As others have observed (e.g., Scheiber and Mitchell 2010), the practice of excluding Native people from the interpretation of their own histories supports—and is informed by—narratives of Indigenous cultural loss built around false divisions between "prehistoric" and "historic" time, places, and objects. The creation of chronological sequences privileges a Western conception of time that foregrounds particular materials as "evidence" for the presence or absence of Indigenous peoples. This evidence is often more representative of the assumptions archaeologists harbor about when and where Native people should be living rather than the often unexpected realities of where Native people actually lived and when and how they used those places. In the following chapters, my employment of chronometric dates in the Western style is tempered with an understanding that Indigenous Coast Miwok and Southern Pomo people have resided in their homelands since time immemorial and that they are still here.

Many of the features of Coast Miwok mobility and social organization discussed above are characteristic of a period of time known as the Late Period of California "prehistory," which extends from the era of colonization to approximately 500 years ago (740–180 BP [years before present], or 1210 to 1770 CE [common era]). To better understand the continuities and transformations taking place among tribes during the colonial era, I also study the Late Period Phase 1 (740–440 BP, or 1210–1510 CE) and Phase 2

(440–180 BP, or 1510–1770 CE) (figure 6). The materials and traditions associated with the Late Period are the result of practices and ideas taking shape during the Middle Period (2160–940 BP, or 210 BCE [before common era] to 1010 CE)—a period of time that represents the transformation of even older traditions and technologies practiced during the Early Period (5350–3150 BP, or 3400–500 BCE). And so forth.

Two transitional phases—the Early/Middle Period Transition (2450–2160 BP, or 500–210 BCE), or "EMT," and the Middle/Late Period Transition (940–740 BP, or 1010–1210 CE), or "MLT"—account for gradual shifts from older to newer ways of doing things as well as the continuation of some cultural expressions beyond arbitrary temporal benchmarks (Groza et al. 2011). Other archaeologists favor a geologic time scale to emphasize the complex relationship between long-term environmental change and the development of Indigenous societies during the Terminal Pleistocene (25,000–11,700 BP), Early Holocene (11,700–8200 BP), Middle Holocene (8200–4200 BP), and Late Holocene (4200 BP to present).

Excellent summaries of San Francisco Bay archaeology are provided by Byrd et al. (2017); Lightfoot (1997) for the Middle Holocene; and Lightfoot and Luby (2002) for the Late Holocene; Moratto (1984); and King (1970a:277) for sites excavated on the Marin Peninsula before 1970. Archaeological sites predating 8200 BP are exceedingly rare due to the small size and high degree of mobility among Pleistocene and Early Holocene human groups and because rising Holocene sea levels inundated older archaeological sites during the formation of San Francisco Bay. At Clear Lake, north of San Francisco Bay, archaeologists excavated Clovis artifacts from the Borax Lake site (CA-LAK-36) making it one of only a few recorded Pleistocene-era sites in central California (Moratto 1984:82–85). Six Early Holocene sites were identified during a recent overview of San Francisco Bay archaeology (Byrd et al. 2017:3.21–3.22). By comparison, more than sixty sites date to the Middle Holocene, including one of the oldest places in Marin County, CA-MRN-17.

Most well-dated deposits date to 2450–1050 BP (500 BCE to 900 CE)—a period of time at the beginning of the Middle Period viewed as the "golden age" of shellmound communities (Lightfoot and Luby 2002:276). After this time, human populations and the number of archaeological sites increase and consolidate. In the East Bay, for example, Lightfoot and Luby (2002:272) document cycles of shellmound occupation and disuse from the Early Period to Late Period Phase 2, as well as a shift from a broadly dispersed collection of nineteen individual mound sites occupied contemporaneously during the Middle Period to a cluster of six mounds and three satellite sites inhabited during the Late Period Phase 2. This clustering pattern suggests that over

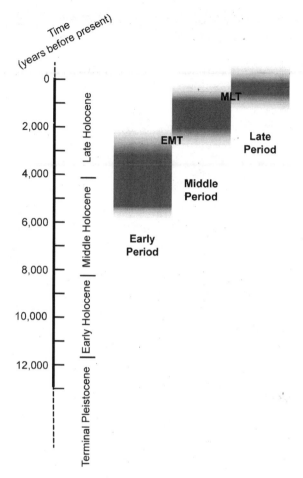

FIGURE 6 Illustration showing conventional archaeological chronology for Central California.

time distinct communities formed around a central hub, or larger shell-mound, similar to the historically documented tribal sociopolitical organization discussed above.

San Francisco Bay Shellmounds

Introduced at the start of this chapter, Nels Nelson's shellmound survey represents the first concerted effort to treat the San Francisco Bay region as a discrete archaeological unit of analysis, distinct from other regions and from other Native American societies. Research priorities within the University of California's Department of Anthropology during the early twentieth century created the intellectual environment influencing Nelson's work, including the places he chose to study and the techniques he applied to understand them. To better assess the "antiquity of man" in California, or the cultural chronology of Indigenous peoples, Nelson applied stratigraphic excavation techniques to discern occupational sequences at some of the larger shellmounds he encountered during the survey. A focus on taller, more conspicuous mounded sites set the tone for the next century of mound research.

Archaeological sites bearing the shells of marine and freshwater mollusks are ubiquitous in river, ocean, lake, and estuary environments around the world, and they have a long history of archaeological study (Trigger 1986). Shell "midden" or "kitchen midden" (*kjökkenmödding*, from the Scandinavian language) are terms often used to describe sites with a high shell content (Stein 1992:6). Yet, the term "midden" is particularly cumbersome because not all shell-bearing sites were used as dumps for the refuse of daily shellfish processing. The idea that California Indian sites are trash dumps is also derogatory. Given that many shellmounds contain human burials—one or two individuals, or large cemeteries of 400 or more people (e.g., Leventhal 1993; Luby and Gruber 1999; Nelson 1910b)—these are places that should instead be viewed as sacred sites symbolic of longstanding relationships between the living and deceased. As spaces to dine, dance, and bury the dead, I also view shellmounds as multifaceted sites, or "full-service villages" (Luby et al. 2006:196–97), where mortuary practices and domestic activities (e.g., food preparation, cooking, and other daily chores) took place.

Shellmounds are typically oval or oblong in form and they range in size, from shallow deposits covering the space of a modern football field and measuring only one to two meters tall to larger sites measuring over thirty feet tall (Lightfoot 1997:31). Nelson (1909a:335) reported a "promiscuous mixture" of organic soil, fire-affected rock, sand, charcoal, ash, and the shells of bivalves and gastropods layered within many shellmounds. Human burials, cooking features, botanical and faunal remains, and bone, stone, and shell artifacts are also frequently reported within excavated mound sites. Shellmounds, shell middens, shell scatters, and other sites reflect the extension of a pattern of Native American mound construction found in most regions of North America. For California, mounded sites are not restricted to the San Francisco Bay Area. Although many have been destroyed by archaeological study, river erosion and channelization, and intensive agricultural development, Native people constructed large earthen mounds along the banks of the Sacramento and San Joaquin Rivers of the Central Valley. One of the largest mounds excavated during the 1930s, the Windmiller Mound (CA-SAC-107), included human burials and diagnostic artifacts that archaeologists used to establish one of California's first chronological sequences (Moratto 1984:178–81).

With roots reaching back to the late nineteenth century, hobbyist artifact collecting for private collections and archaeological study of shellmounds have a deeply tangled history in California (Moratto 1984:226). W. E. Saxe's brief excavations at the Sand Hill Bluff site (CA-SCR-7) in western Santa Cruz County during the early 1870s mark one of the first "scientific" efforts to study a central California shellmound (Moratto 1984:226); yet, as I discuss later, early archaeological efforts are preceded and outnumbered by numerous instances of casual collecting. Beginning with Nelson, Kent Lightfoot and Edward Luby (2002) identify three main pulses of scientific study of San Francisco Bay shellmounds. The first period of shellmound research includes Nelson's survey and excavations in the San Francisco Bay, Sacramento-San Joaquin Delta, Tomales Bay, and at sites found along the Pacific coast up to the Russian River (Nelson 1907, 1909b). During this initial period of mound research, archaeologists closely studied the components of mounded sites to determine the age of each site; work that paved the way for quantitative studies during the next period of shellmound research (Gifford 1916).

During the second period of research between 1940 and 1960, the application of quantitative methods and analyses increased (Cook and Treganza 1947; Gifford 1946; Greengo 1951; Treganza and Cook 1948). For example, column sampling was introduced as a method for extracting marine shells, which could then be quantified to help answer questions about evolutionary change and ecological relationships between hunter-gatherer-fisher peoples and local environments. During the 1950s, archaeologists also increasingly adopted radiocarbon dating to answer questions about the age of shellmounds and further refine regional chronologies (Meighan 1953). Growing numbers of students attending university and enrolling in archaeology courses fueled the "California School of Midden Analysis" as well as the University of California Archaeological Survey (UCAS), which formed in 1948 (Heizer 1949; Mason et al. 1998:304; Waselkov 1987:141). Archaeological studies of shellmounds on the Marin Peninsula were especially common during the mid-twentieth century. Following the excavation of an entire shellmound in Solano County (Treganza and Cook 1948), CA-MRN-20 on Richardson Bay was excavated as a salvage operation and exercise in compositional analysis (McGeein and Mueller 1955). Archaeologists excavated 19 burials and 250 cubic yards of soil at CA-MRN-20 but groaned about a "meager" collection of artifacts (McGeein and Mueller 1955:53). Several Coast Miwok sites at Point Reyes were also excavated intensively for evidence (e.g., Chinese porcelain, iron spikes, and other artifacts) of Francis Drake's visit in 1579 and Sebastian Rodríguez Cermeño's 1595 shipwreck (e.g., Heizer 1941a, 1947; Treganza 1959).

The third and current period of shellmound research is marked by a florescence of field methods, specialized analyses, and theoretical approaches since the 1960s. Continued urbanization of San Francisco Bay and the appearance and growth of cultural resource management (CRM) archaeology resulted in increased study of shellmounds, in many cases remnant shellmounds that had already been bulldozed or excavated (e.g., DeGeorgey 2013). For Marin County, CRM excavations of shellmounds—many of them previously recorded by Nelson—took place before the construction of new roads, parking lots, subdivisions, and other development projects between Sausalito and Novato. The "Drake Quest" continued as archaeologists excavated additional sites around the Point Reyes Peninsula (e.g., Shangraw and Von der Porten 1981). The 1970s also saw the excavation of several large archaeological sites, including a Middle Period cemetery (CA-MRN-27) in Tiburon (King 1970b) and three Late Period and ethnographic Coast Miwok villages: Echa-tamal (CA-MRN-402; Dietz 1976), Olompali (CA-MRN-193; Slaymaker 1972), and Shotomoko-cha (CA-MRN-138; Slaymaker 1977). The Miwok Archaeological Preserve of Marin (MAPOM) was also founded in 1970. This interest group advocates for the preservation and interpretation of Indigenous Coast Miwok places and history. Co-organizers of MAPOM, including Betty Goerke and Sylvia Thalman, met and worked together as volunteers on Charles Slaymaker's excavations at CA-MRN-138. Sylvia Thalman's expert knowledge of Coast Miwok archaeology, ethnography, and mission sacramental registers later guided the genealogical research that helped Coast Miwok and Southern Pomo people regain federal recognition in the year 2000 (Emberson et al. 1999; Shanks 2012).

Archaeology of Mounded Spaces

Shellmounds have been the primary focus of archaeological efforts in the San Francisco Bay Area. Focusing on the complex stratigraphy found within many of the larger mounds, archaeologists quickly learned that they could confidently track changes in artifact types and burial practices to help construct a regional chronology (e.g., Nelson 1910b; Uhle 1907). A few of the most well-known and intensively studied shellmounds are the Emeryville Shellmound (CA-ALA-309) where Nels Nelson and Max Uhle worked, the Ryan Mound (CA-ALA-329), the Patterson Mound (CA-ALA-328), the West Berkeley

Shellmound (CA-ALA-307), the Ellis Landing Shellmound (CA-CCO-295), and the Stege Mounds (CA-CCO-297, -298, and -300).

Of special concern to my analysis, the layering of dietary remains, domestic features, cemeteries, and other attributes suggest a complex, dynamic, and long-term relationship between Indigenous peoples and mounded landscapes. Since the advent of radiocarbon dating, Kent Lightfoot (1997:135) argues that many sites demonstrate a range of purposes and frequent reuse "over extended periods ranging from five to nineteen hundred years." More importantly, shellmounds often have unique histories that cross the arbitrary border between prehistory and modernity—a boundary established and maintained by archaeologists with research interests and methods unique to both sides of the divide (Lightfoot 1995). Many mounds exhibit Late Period components consisting of diagnostic or time-sensitive clamshell beads, corner-notched and serrated projectile points manufactured from Napa Glass Mountain and Annadel obsidian, straight-sided stone mortars, bone awls sharpened for basketry production, steatite pipes, and other materials (Milliken et al. 2007:99). Native diets at this time also reflect the seasonal collection of a wide array of plant and animal species from terrestrial and estuarine habitats. Still other sites such as the Stege Mounds (Von der Porten and DeGeorgey 2015), Ellis Landing Shellmound (Schweikhardt et al. 2011), site CA-CCO-290 on Brooks Island (Finstad et al. 2013), and the Marin County mounds discussed in chapters 3 and 4 demonstrate occupations during the Late Period and colonial era.

A survey of available radiocarbon data from shellmounds on the Marin Peninsula shows Coast Miwok occupations during the Early Period through the Late Period Phase 2 and afterward. A radiocarbon date of 5480 BP (3430 BCE) from De Silva Island (CA-MRN-17) at Richardson Bay is the oldest date for San Francisco Bay and indicates early habitation along the then-formative estuary (Moratto 1984:274). Three thousand five hundred years later, Huimen people living in the same area greeted Juan Manuel de Ayala's ship, the *San Carlos*, as it entered the San Francisco Bay in 1775. Across from De Silva Island on Angel Island, DeGeorgey (2007) documented Early, Middle, and Late Period occupations at CA-MRN-44/H. Among the mounded sites at Point Reyes found to contain sixteenth-century Chinese porcelain—including the Estero site (CA-MRN-232), the Cauley site (CA-MRN-242), the Mendoza site (CA-MRN-275), and others—earlier Middle Period and Late Period components were also documented (Russell 2011:73).

Older Late Period Phase 2 components are also evident at places recorded by Franciscan missionaries, including the Coast Miwok communities of Echa-tamal (Dietz 1976:175–82), Shotomoko-cha (Slaymaker 1977), Olompali (Slaymaker 1972). Excavations at all three sites produced glass beads.

Archaeologists working at Shotomoko-cha (CA-MRN-138) in the 1970s also collected a chipped obsidian cross and a projectile point manufactured from green bottle glass (Slaymaker 1977:164). Both objects show continuity in lithic traditions and experimentation with unconventional raw materials and symbology; they are also poignant examples of the inherent problems with adjectives like "prehistoric," "historic," "Native," and "colonial" when adopted uncritically to classify sites, time periods, and materials. Excavations at CA-MRN-406 on the College of Marin campus, the San Jose Village site (CA-MRN-471), and my investigations of shellmounds at China Camp State Park and Toms Point also demonstrate Late Period and postcontact mound use (Goerke 1994:53; Jackson 1974:86; Schneider 2010:155; and see chapters 4 and 5). To summarize, archaeological sites on the Marin Peninsula provide strong support that many "prehistoric" places remained relevant to Coast Miwok people during historical times. As I explore in the next section, however, a variety of destructive forces has also shielded this interpretation from wider acceptance.

"Obliterating Agencies"

The picture of precolonial San Francisco Bay pieced together by archaeologists over the course of one century is only a partial view. Archaeological interpretations about continuity and change in human societies, economies, and spiritualties are usually based upon samples, or fractions of sites and parts of artifact collections that undergo analysis for developing interpretations about the past. It follows that the long and destructive record of natural and cultural disturbances to archaeological sites in the San Francisco Bay region should then be taken into consideration when developing and evaluating statements about transformations within Indigenous societies. As groundbreaking as Nels Nelson's archaeological survey may have been in the early 1900s, he was also uncomfortably aware that many of the sites he recorded had already been altered by nature and by human hands. In the final report on his 1907–8 shellmound survey, Nelson (1909a:310) comments that the project was "finished probably none too soon, because the obliterating agencies of nature have been strongly reinforced in the last four or five decades by the hands of modern man and the ultimate destruction of every suggestion of former savage life seems not far off." Understanding the various ways shellmounds have been redeposited by natural processes, repurposed by settlers, and researched by amateur and professional archaeologists raises questions about the interpretation of Native American landscapes at the time of European contact and colonization. Discussed more in the following chapter, the incomplete picture of Indigenous places casts light on the production of harmful anthropological narratives of Native American cultural loss and disappearance during the colonial period.

California is a dynamic landscape shaped by tectonic activity, fire, and other forces of nature. Along the Pacific coast and numerous bays, coastal erosion attributed to wave action and sea level rise has been exacerbated and greatly accelerated in recent decades by global climate change—now a regular topic of discussion among tribes, government agencies, researchers, and residents witnessing the steady removal of California coastal habitat and archaeological sites. Farther back in time, eustatic change is closely connected to the formation and expansion of the San Francisco Bay estuary habitat as well as the appearance and development of Indigenous communities and shellmounds around the bay shore (Lightfoot 1997:137–38).

Following a period of global sea level rise associated with the release of water previously trapped within massive Pleistocene ice sheets, by about six thousand years ago the rate of inundation in San Francisco Bay eventually slowed, and tectonic activity and sedimentation encouraged the growth of intertidal marsh (Lightfoot 1997:137–38). From this time to approximately two thousand years ago, brackish water and nutrients entering the bay via spring runoff encouraged the growth of marsh plant communities that in turn provided habitat for oysters and other invertebrates, fishes, and waterfowl—a period of ecological growth associated with the Middle Holocene and a time when Indigenous people deposited the earliest layers of many would-be shellmounds. Through consistent returns and the repetitive deposition of shell, rock, earth, ash, and other material at the same locations over time, Native people "would have raised these coastal places above the nearly flat, extensive, featureless plains of the bay shore marshlands" (Lightfoot 1997:138). This pattern explains why archaeologists often locate the deepest deposits of some shellmounds one to six meters below the current sea level and why early excavators regularly tunneled down to those basal deposits to assess the "antiquity of man" in the region (e.g., Nelson 1910b).

As shellmounds were built up over the past six thousand years, wave action and weathering chipped away at them, often redepositing cultural materials nearby. In 1964, for example, a tsunami triggered by the 9.2-magnitude Alaskan earthquake slammed into CA-MRN-202 on Toms Point, removing part of the site and redepositing materials into Tomales Bay. For "Mound No. 107" located on Point San Pedro, Nelson (1907:182) reported that "much of the shell material has caved down as the bare rocks have been worn away by wave action." Slope wash is another culprit in the reshaping of mounded sites.

Nelson (1907:21) described one mound visited early in his survey as "rough and broken away owing to washing and sliding." CA-MRN-114, one of three sites I examine more closely in chapter 3, is being eroded by a seasonal stream; yet, while runoff is certainly impacting this site, the problem of erosion is exacerbated by the construction of an artificial culvert nearby that seems to have rerouted the stream since the time of Nelson's survey and recording effort.

Additional natural disturbances to shellmounds can be attributed to plants and animals, which thrive in the organic soils of artificial mounds. In many cases, Nelson reports the presence of freshwater springs as well as oak and buckeye trees—potential sources of food for Native peoples—that grew in the vicinity of shellmounds. Of the several buckeye trees and elderberry shrubs Nelson (1907:186) reported growing "on and immediately about" CA-MRN-115, however, one buckeye tree has since toppled over, creating a large hole in the site and displacing archaeological material in the tree's root ball. Beyond "trees, weeds, and shrubbery" (Nelson 1907:64), burrowing gophers (e.g., *Thomomys bottae*) continually churn sediments and materials layered within coastal California archaeological sites. Even more troubling are the assorted invasive plants and animals introduced to California by European and American settlers (Preston 1998); they too have taken their toll on the condition of shellmounds. To water cattle, many dairies established throughout Marin County during the nineteenth century were placed near the same freshwater springs that supported Indigenous communities. While ranchers leveled some shellmounds and constructed buildings on top of them, the roots of fast-growing eucalyptus trees planted by ranchers as windbreaks penetrated mounds, and scores of archaeological sites have been "cut up by cattle trampling" (Nelson 1907:68).

Disturbances attributed to human hands amplified the natural processes already reshaping San Francisco Bay shellmounds. From 1848 to the 1850s, the gold rush attracted upwards of three hundred thousand migrants to California and precipitated the rapid growth of San Francisco Bay towns, as well as the expansion of infrastructure required to support those growing communities. While forces of nature steadily shaped and redeposited the contents of shellmounds, urbanization accelerated the destruction of coastal sites as shell-rich soils were repurposed for an assortment of other needs or studied by amateurs and professionals participating in archaeological "science."

As a construction material, soil with a high shell content was sought after because it compacts and drains well; it can be used as temper to bind clay, mud, and other material into cement, bricks, or masonry; and by burning the shells, it could be transformed into quicklime and used as a hardening agent in plaster, cement, and mortar (Ceci 1984:67–68). Franciscan padres at Mission San Carlos Borromeo (Mission Carmel), for example, instructed Native laborers to dismantle nearby shellmounds and extract abalone shells and human bone needed for the lime used to seal and white-wash adobe buildings (Harrington 1945:70). As early as 1866, roads constructed on the Marin Peninsula used shellmound soil as a key ingredient (see also Byram 2009). During summers in the late 1800s, residents of San Francisco flocked to the sunny resort town of San Rafael to escape the fog. While some tourists arrived directly by boat, others traveled north from Sausalito by wagon on roads newly fashioned from local mound sites. "A new and beautiful shell road has been made across the marsh," boasts one newspaper report, "the shells . . . are taken from the mounds around the old Indian rancherias, which abound in the neighborhood" (*Marin County Journal* [MCJ] 1866:2).

Growing urban communities and bustling commerce of turn-of-the-century Marin County came at the expense of shellmounds and an untold number of Coast Miwok bodies buried within. Pulses of shell road construction continued into the 1890s. In 1897, for instance, a nearly complete Sir Francis Drake Boulevard—one of the longest east-west roads on the Marin Peninsula bisecting the county from San Quentin to Point Reyes—was said to be in "excellent condition, and for a long stretch where the Indian mound or shell dirt had been used the boulevard was perfect" (*Sausalito News* [SN] 1897b:1). New roads connecting mills near Alto to ships anchored at Richardson Bay also relied on "Indian mound dirt" placed atop layers of rock and gravel and then rolled smooth (SN 1896:1). The success of this "first class highway" from Alto encouraged additional mound quarrying. Editors of a local newspaper appealed to its readers and civic leaders: "Would it not be possible to secure more of this material and place it on the roads? [The Marin County Supervisor might make] . . . some sort of arrangement with the owners of the property upon which the dirt is found . . . to use it in improving the roads. It would be to their benefit as well as the community at large to have smooth roads" (SN 1897a:1).

By the late 1800s San Francisco Bay shellmounds had been folded into the Gilded Age economy, assuming new value during an era of rapid economic growth as "arrangements" were made for their demolition and repurpose for a variety of domestic, leisure, and commercial uses. In addition to the creation of shell roads, the tops of some mounds became foundations for new homes. John Thomas Reed, one of the first white settlers on the Marin Peninsula granted Rancho Corte Madera del Presidio by the Mexican government in 1834, constructed his adobe house "on the old Indian shellmound near Millwood" (SN 1928:3), which is likely a reference to shellmound CA-MRN-10 where "it is said that big chief Marin, after whom the county is named, was

born on this spot" (Nelson 1907:40). By the time Nels Nelson arrived at
the mound in 1907, however, much of the site had been removed and was
"daily diminishing" (Nelson 1907:38). In San Rafael, J. O. B. Short offered
unsuccessfully to "donate" a shellmound (probably CA-MRN-626/H) as the
location for the new Marin County courthouse (MCJ 1872b:3) and final resting place for another Marin County pioneer, George Thomas Wood (MCJ
1872a:3). In addition to repurposing entire mounds, shell midden was val-
ued for still other Western hobbies practiced by a growing leisure class. For
example, while excavating a shellmound in San Rafael in 1902 and "carting
off the shell earth to make a tennis court foundation," workers encountered
three Coast Miwok burials and a flint "battle axe" prompting excitement and
speculation about still other "valuable relics" soon-to-be unveiled once the
mound was "torn up" (*San Francisco Call* [SFC] 1902:20).

Some mounds were leveled and repurposed as construction material to
build roads in Marin County. Other mounds were quarried as fertilizer for
the region's burgeoning farms and ranches. Similar to the history of dismantling large earthen mounds in other regions of North America (e.g., Pauketat
2009:2–3), shellmound soils containing the remains of plants, animals, and
human beings—piled up over centuries by the gradual accumulation of
decomposing organic matter—were highly prized by gardeners (Lightfoot
1997). On an industrial scale, shellmound soils fertilized Californian vineyards
and agricultural fields. An 1872 report to the United States Congress from the
commissioner of agriculture provides the following viticulture advice: "if [vol-
canic soils] cannot be had for the vineyard, a shellmound may be accepted as
next best in character, and capable of giving a good wine in great abundance"
(Taylor 1872:114). Before Silicon Valley, many farms and orchards established
in San Francisco's South Bay benefited from their close proximity to shellmounds such as the Castro Mound (CA-SCL-1), which was marketed as "Indian mount top soil" and "California Guano" (Pilling and Fenenga 1950:5).

Many shellmounds in Marin County met a similar fate. Concerning
Mound No. 3 (CA-MRN-3) in Sausalito, in 1903 (four years before Nels Nelson started his survey) one resident ran advertisements in the local newspaper
announcing "dirt for sale from the Indian or shellmound . . . at 25 cents per
load" (SN 1903:3). City roads already cut through the site by the late 1800s
and a laundry business had been constructed on top of the shellmound, but
enough of it remained to entice Nelson back in 1910 to excavate a trench
through the remnant site (Nelson 1910a). Mound No. 1, however, the first
shellmound recorded during Nelson's survey was "practically all carted away"
(Nelson 1907:19). In one of the more ghoulish examples of the erasure of
Indigenous places in Marin County, an article published in 1896 details the

combined impacts of amateur archaeology and quarrying. As proving grounds where new scientific techniques and speculation incrementally replaced Indigenous history with a Western narrative of "lost races" (i.e., California Indians) and "new man" (i.e., white settlers), shellmound destruction and the repurposing of shell midden deepened the chasm between past and present. Chipping away at Mound No. 1 with pick and shovel and loading his wheelbarrow with shell and bone, one "modern Sausalitan" commented: "It makes good chicken feed . . . the stuff makes the hens lay better" (SFC 1896:16).

Shellmound Archaeology and Junk Science

The wanton destruction of San Francisco Bay shellmounds during the late nineteenth and early twentieth centuries flattened many sites and redistributed the dense piles of shell, ash, charcoal, animal bone, artifacts, and human remains along new roads and onto sporty tennis courts, as well as into domestic gardens, commercial farms and orchards, and chicken coops. In this form of colonial violence targeting Indigenous places and histories, Native American skeletal remains and belongings gradually accumulated on the shelves of museums and private curio cabinets—property and commodities of the bustling Gilded Age economy, as well as new symbols of California's distant prehistoric past disconnected from any living Coast Miwok person. Giving definition to these harmful practices, Social Darwinism—the theory, now discredited, that human groups become distinct biologically, or more fit, based on their capacity to utilize technology—and the newly emerging concept of "race" solidified settler colonial claims to supposedly vacant Indigenous lands and resources and also shaped perceptions about Indigenous societies in North America as primordial and doomed to extinction. This dark stew of racism, sexism, settler colonialism, and shellmound demolition defined the parameters of archaeology around San Francisco Bay and compartmentalized Indigenous history as distinct from the history of the modern world.

As the settler population of California continued to climb during the late 1800s and early 1900s, excavations and speculation informed county histories and newspaper stories that provided newcomers with information about the region's Indigenous peoples and their disappearance. J. P. Munro-Fraser's *History of Marin County, California* (1880), a who's who of pioneering white men in the county, describes California Indians as "anything but an easy subject for civilization" and references Paul Schumacher's archaeological work at Santa Barbara Channel shellmounds to help interpret "Indian remains" (shellmounds) in Marin County (Munro-Fraser 1880:24, 102). The "firsting and lasting" narratives within Munro-Fraser's (1880) history employ the "Vanishing Indian" trope to fortify white settler narratives of belonging and ownership (O'Brien 2010). Such histories were widely read and repeated, they permeated public consciousness, and they often presented archaeological finds in support of pioneer histories. That just about anyone who could wield a shovel or pickaxe was encouraged to do archaeology may also explain the pervasiveness of commonly held assumptions about the disappearance of Native people.

Amateur digs took place at many mound sites throughout the region. As "investigators in scientific research," children, women, and men all took part in the excavation of Native American sites and burials (SFCr 1892:12). "Gold fever" and "feminine curiosity" motivated three women to excavate shellmounds on Hunters Point south of San Francisco in 1893. The "Hunters Point Belles" exhumed burials and shell ornaments by hand for display in their homes as curiosities and, although they did not find gold, the article assured readers that "untold wealth might be brought to the gaze of eager eyes—that gold and silver had been probably buried with the Indians" (SFC 1893:3). During the fall of 1892, a reporter for the *San Francisco Call* working on behalf of the California Academy of Sciences excavated a shellmound on Alameda Island near Oakland—one of two "Sather mounds." A second mound was excavated in the early 1900s by amateur archaeologist Captain Clark during the extension of Santa Clara Avenue. The project removed 450 burials and a brass 1768 British medallion found two feet below the surface (Vigness 1952:10).

Alerted by stories of locals who "played football with Indian skulls . . . [,] buried treasures [that] became the playthings of rollicking children" (SFC 1892:8), *Call* reporter J. H. Griffes secured permission to excavate the shellmound from the landowner, Peter Sather, and from Sather's Chinese tenants who discovered human bones in their vegetable garden. Familiar with the techniques used by archaeologists of the time to assess chronology by digging a single, large trench through the center of a site, Griffes excavated Native American graves—removing "a good peck measure" of fragmented bones from one burial—and then speculated that due to the size of the mound it may have once contained the "throbbing heart of a great chief of the Tamals . . . surely, no ordinary, thieving, drinking redskin was buried here" (SFC 1892:8). Observations like this and at least seven subsequent articles reporting on the *Call's* excavations at the Sather mound published that September promoted the widespread practice of casual digging in the San Francisco Bay Area and the new role of archaeology for bolstering scientific racism and commonly held misunderstandings about Native American cultures.

Recreational digging and collecting also took place on the Marin Peninsula. Three boys hunting ducks in a marsh near Larkspur in 1910 discovered
artifacts and the bones of two Native bodies eroding from a shellmound. "No
uncommon occurrence" to find Native American skeletal remains in Marin
County, the newspaper story suggested that the remains were "considerably
more than normal length" (SFC 1910:1)—a commonly shared observation of
the time period. The work of "removing the burying grounds of the old . . .
Indian Rancheria" at Erskine B. McNear's property on Point San Pedro (near
China Camp State Park) resulted in the exhumation of more than twenty
individuals, including supposedly several of immense proportions and one
measuring over seven feet tall (*Marin Journal* 1907:6; see also SN 1904:1).
That Indigenous peoples of the San Francisco Bay Area were imagined by
non-Native settlers as giants further suggests the fabrication of a mythological
past used to justify settler colonial claims to Indigenous lands (Trigger 1980).

Nels Nelson is usually described as the first archaeologist to systematically
survey and excavate sites in the San Francisco Bay Area—the starting point
for shellmound research in the region for the next century and a pioneer of
archaeological techniques that would come to define the subfield of archaeology (Trigger 2006:280). Yet, even at the early date of 1907, Nelson struggled
to stay ahead of the rapid destruction of the Indigenous sites he aimed to
document. For this reason, he was motivated to return to some of the more
intact shellmounds for further study. When Nelson returned to excavate a
trench at "Mound No. 3" (CA-MRN-3) in Sausalito as well as mounds at
Larkspur and San Rafael, newspapers heralded his findings as "invaluable" to
the "scientific world" (SFCr 1910:8). Many other sites were erased, however.
Arriving at "Mound No. 84" in San Rafael, Nels Nelson learned that the
site had already been "culled over . . . and all the relics were shipped to the
museum in London" (Nelson 1907:157). Countless examples like this suggest
that San Francisco Bay archaeology was already greatly compromised by the
start of the twentieth century. Even more critical to the argument presented
in this book, Native people were systematically written out of history and
a broken archaeological record further diminished what could be said about
Native American history and presence.

For some of the larger shellmounds that escaped immediate destruction
and could be studied by an archaeologist, Nelson and cohort maintained an
open mind about site chronology (despite what was being reported in local
papers). Concluding his report on the archaeology of Ellis Landing Shellmound (CA-CCO-295), Nelson (1910b:402) suggested that similarities in
tool types appearing in upper and lower levels of the mound reflected "no
important breaks in the culture . . . and the last occupants of the shellmound

at Ellis Landing were probably Indians similar to those that have lived in Middle California within historic times." Max Uhle, an Andean archaeologist who excavated the Emeryville Shellmound (CA-ALA-309) one summer while visiting the University of California, offered a similar assessment: "While the history of the shellmounds of this region probably reaches back more than a thousand years into the past, it must have extended almost to the threshold of modern times" (Uhle 1907:36). The Ellis Landing and Emeryville Shellmounds as well as the provocative observations of Nelson and Uhle, however, did not stand the test of time. Both mounds were destroyed and archaeologists increasingly focused on plumbing the depths of mounded sites in keeping with new disciplinary priorities (i.e., building regional chronologies).

The continued destruction of shellmounds in Marin County throughout the twentieth century reinforced the temporal boundaries within which self-styled prehistorians operated. Published one year before Congress passed the Termination Act of 1953, ending federal recognition for scores of Native American tribes including eventually Graton Rancheria in 1958, the following example of a salvage effort at CA-MRN-168 in Ignacio (north of San Rafael) carries added significance:

> In the distance could be seen the bulldozer whose gleaming steel blade would in a moment scatter the orderly record of two thousand years of California history. Marin with its wealth of Indian sites, perhaps 500 in all, has become of particular concern to U.C. students due to large scale construction projects in the county which threaten to destroy skeletons and artifacts from time to time. The burials are usually discovered close to the bottom of shellmounds, heaped up from countless Indian feasts which took place 2000 years ago near campsites. Bulldozers leveling sub-divisions, often uncover the mounds as they push a pile of shell. When stopped in time, *the dozers do no damage to the store house of prehistoric Indian history in Marin down deep below.* It is then that owners of property at Ignacio, Greenbrae, Tomales Bay and Pt. Reyes, where mounds have been found, have contributed to posterity by allowing technically trained archaeologists to examine them before the areas are covered with new homes. (*Marin Independent Journal* 1952:M9; emphasis added)

Summary

Long before the first Europeans entered the San Francisco Bay, Coast Miwok people were already well-versed in meeting and overcoming the challenges of a dynamic landscape. Powerful headwomen and headmen made decisions, resolved arguments, and scheduled ceremonies assiduously preserved by previous generations; Coast Miwoks carried sophisticated ecological and geological knowledge about the plants, animals, minerals, and other resources within their homelands; they managed landscapes using fire, pruning, and selective harvesting; flexible and embodied histories of mobility allowed Coast Miwok people to remake their communities throughout the year; and they maintained social networks across land and water to exchange items and ideas as well as to ensure the persistence of group identities, cultural practices, and connections to the places that sustained them.

Shellmounds are among the places that supported Coast Miwok resilience. As sacred sites encapsulating the memories, guarded traditions, and materials of the past, shellmounds are also historical sites that offer valuable insights for navigating the present moment. Ethnographic sources are rife with Coast Miwok place names that carry meaning and power (Collier and Thalman 1996:4–15). Regular movement across the Marin landscape for subsistence, trade, and other reasons reinforced these relationships to place in a recursive act of "reviving and revising" the past (Basso 1996:6). That many cultural practices are recorded in twentieth century ethnographies and practiced by twenty-first-century Coast Miwok descendants speaks to the enduring role mobility plays in connecting people to place. Into this ancient and complex world stepped Euro-American colonists—first during two sixteenth-century visits and then in full force during the late 1700s—bringing another set of challenges to a long record of Indigenous successes and transformations on the Marin Peninsula.

Weather, rising seas, plant life, and tunneling animals moved and removed pieces of San Francisco Bay shellmounds and continually redeposited sediments and artifacts beyond their primary contexts. As European and American colonists entered California between the late eighteenth and twentieth centuries, they instituted new programs and policies to control Indigenous people, and they devised new uses for Indigenous places. Franciscan padres instructed Native laborers to make use of shells buried in some mounds for creating the lime used to whitewash adobe buildings, tan hides, and process corn. By the late nineteenth century, many shellmounds throughout the region had been quarried and repurposed as fill for roads. Other sites were cleaved apart to lay track for railroads. Organic-rich shellmound soil was desired for gardens, chicken feed, and agricultural fields, and mounds provided sturdy foundations for houses and other new construction. Antiquarians, relic hunters, and a growing number of professional archaeologists would also take turns consuming buried and cremated Native American bodies and belongings as curiosities and as evidence for establishing a prehistoric chronology for the region's Indigenous groups.

Reliant on shellmounds to establish a temporal sequence for central California, however, the erasure of Native places also minimized what archaeologists could say about the full histories of Coast Miwok people and other Indigenous populations. Moreover, the descriptions penned by early colonists usually fall short of mentioning the kinds of places where Native people lived (Lightfoot and Luby 2002:277), further narrowing the picture of Indigenous communities on the eve of contact and colonialization during the late 1700s. This funneling effect attributed to site destruction and historical erasures does several things. First, it puts the burden of proof on archaeologists to demonstrate the entire occupational history of a place and not assume its desuetude. Second, it positions missions, other colonial sites, and the associated colonial archive as primary sources of information about Native people during colonial times. In other words, the destruction of Native places—a physical and metaphorical dismantling of Native histories by non-Native hands—erased an untold number of Indigenous stories that may never be told and substituted them with another version of history structured by a Western intellectual tradition.

Third, as I explore more fully in the following chapter, the elimination of Indigenous places amplifies histories of cultural loss and vacant hinterlands in colonial California. The absence of entire sites or the truncated history represented in a shellmound that has been leveled or quarried for over one century must also be considered in light of twentieth-century anthropological narratives of colonialism. An absent or compromised archaeological record underwrites scholarly accounts that emphasize the disappearance of Indigenous peoples and the abandonment of village sites. Fourth, this cropped history sets up spatial and temporal expectations for when and where to find Native American people. For instance, Coast Miwok people are not expected to be visiting shellmounds during the mission period, and few people know about the Coast Miwok families who pioneered the commercial fishing industry at Tomales Bay and Bodega Bay during the mid-1900s. Yet, it is precisely these "secret histories of unexpectedness" that are worth pursuing, Delora (2004:14) writes, "for they can change our sense of the past and lead us quietly, but directly to the present moment." The legacy of mound destruction affects more than just the study of long-term records of Indigenous mobility, memory, and place. It also gives the false impression that colonial power successfully obliterated Native history.

2

Indigenous Lives, Colonial Time

> Never before in history has a people been swept away with such terrible swift-
> ness, or appalled into utter and unwhispering silence forever and forever, as were
> the California Indians.
>
> —STEPHEN POWERS, 1976 (1877)

IN THE LATE AFTERNOON OF October 2, 1816, the *Rurik*, a two-
masted Russian brig weighing 180 tons and carrying an international crew
of soldiers, sailors, a surgeon, a naturalist, and an artist, rounded the Marin
Headlands and cruised effortlessly through the Golden Gate. Sailing past
the Spanish Fort San Joaquin, later renamed Fort Point, garrisoned soldiers
unfamiliar with the Russian flag employed a speaking trumpet to politely
ask to which nation the ship belonged. After the crew identified themselves
as representatives of Russia, the *Rurik* exchanged salutatory cannon fire with
the fort and then proceeded to enter San Francisco Bay where it would remain
at anchor for the next month.

During their stay, the *Rurik*'s captain and lieutenant in the Imperial Russian Navy, Otto Astavitch von Kotzebue, would meet with Luis Antonio
Argüello, commander of the San Francisco presidio—concourse designed to
surreptitiously explore the limits of power each empire attempted to assert
in California. The *Rurik*'s official artist for the four-year around-the-world
expedition, Louis Choris, also rowed ashore to observe the new environs and
prepare finely detailed illustrations of the flora, fauna, and Indigenous peoples
residing in this corner of the world. The paintings, later reproduced and published by Choris in 1822, were likely the first glimpses of California Indians
for many Europeans. In one painting, three men gamble baskets and clamshell
beads next to an adobe structure while an audience of men and a woman with
nursing child anticipate the outcome. Two Yokuts men are depicted hunting
with bow and arrow in another painting. In two more illustrations, mounted
soldiers with lances escort groups of Native men toward the presidio while
the *Rurik* rests at anchor on the horizon, and two Native people paddle a

tule boat on the San Francisco Bay while a third passenger huddles under a striped wool blanket. In still another painting likely sketched when Choris, Kotzebue, and other *Rurik* crew members attended mass at Mission Dolores, California Indian men and women adorned with colorful pigments, flicker feather headdresses, shell ornaments, and feather skirts dance in the mission plaza in front of two Franciscan padres and an audience of countless Indigenous onlookers. As interpreted by Choris, at the conclusion of Sunday mass, "the Indians gather in the cemetery, which is in front of the mission house, and dance. . . . Their music consists of clapping the hands, singing, and the sound made by striking split sticks together which has a charm for their ears; this is finally followed by a horrible yell that greatly resembles the sound of a cough accompanied by a whistling noise" (Mahr 1932:97).

The diverse cultural backgrounds of the mission's Native occupants and their dance regalia, baskets, and other material culture captivated the twenty-one-year-old artist, and Choris would go on to produce additional portraits and close-up illustrations of many of these items. Perhaps one of the most striking messages read in these illustrations and the events that unfolded during the *Rurik*'s month-long stopover in California is the persistence of Indigenous cultures at this Spanish colony. Four decades after Mission Dolores was established in 1776, Native people still practiced and asserted their knowledge about the manufacture, display, and purpose of material culture in a setting designed to erase Indigenous authority and knowledge. Even within the destructive mission setting, Native people danced for themselves, for their loved ones buried in the mission cemetery, and for the future of their communities and traditions. Quite unlike the observation made by Stephen Powers, an early visitor to California and chronicler of late nineteenth-century California Indian tribes whose confidence in the destruction of Native peoples was echoed by scholars and the public for the next century, Native people persisted in still other ways. They continued to make decisions about how and when to visit and engage with still-familiar worlds beyond mission walls. Such material and memory choices are at the core of resilient cultural practices conventionally viewed as being eradicated at the outset of colonization. Indeed, imperial Spain's flimsy grasp of its northern frontier created a context for accommodation and resistance, and the mission and colony of San Francisco can best be described as Native places created, maintained, and largely inhabited by Native people.

The perspective I choose to foreground was not always part of public and academic discourse. Even today some scholars adopt a carceral lens to depict California missions as places of heavily patrolled confinement akin to modern day prisons (see Schneider et al. 2020). Anthropologists and historians harboring essentialized views of Indigenous cultural identities pored over the letters and reports of Franciscan padres, and they quantified sacramental registers—catalogs of the births, deaths, and marriages of Native people at the missions—to conclude that many tribes either vanished at missions or had changed so much that they could only be on the fast track to oblivion. Missionaries supposedly "made a clean sweep" of tradition-bound Coast Miwok communities that could not adjust to new ways of life (Colley 1970:156; see also Kelly 1978). Cultural extinction or diminishment became the narrative strategy for comfortably linking late nineteenth- and early twentieth-century Indigenous communities—the tribes that Stephen Powers and later anthropologists understood as impoverished, acculturated, and vanishing—to missions as the primary instigators of that loss. The convenient invisibility of postcontact Indigenous people continues to embolden the settler state—including individuals, companies, and institutions that all benefit from their occupation of unceded California Indian homelands.

My perspective stresses the various ways Native people remained connected to their homelands and life-sustaining practices during the mission period and afterward. In recent years, a growing number of archaeologists are exploring the broader contexts of colonial enterprises in the Americas. As part of this movement, scholars are increasingly redefining the spatial organization of colonial landscapes and adopting nuanced perspectives on the role of Indigenous power, agency, and extramural spaces in shaping colonial projects in dynamic borderland settings (e.g., Panich and Schneider 2014). In my work (the focus of chapters 3 and 4), I investigate Indigenous refuge, recourse, and the continuing role of persistent places of safe haven and redirection within "Indigenous hinterlands" (Schneider 2015b). This is a concept I developed that builds from theories of resistance, social memory, and place and landscape to address the structuring power of Native places in colonial encounters, rather than the marginality normally attributed to them in distorted public and scholarly views of colonialism in California. Theorizing the continued and purposeful role of homelands and homewaters in the lives of colonized Indigenous peoples encourages deeper consideration of how Native people found protection and redirection within those spaces.

This chapter examines Indigenous-colonial encounters with an emphasis on the establishment and operation of Franciscan missions between 1769 and the 1830s. There are two main goals to this examination. The first is to provide a brief background to Spanish colonization of California. Native recruitment, religious conversion, and labor demands at missions were aimed at building a stable population of Christian peasants loyal to the Spanish Crown. Positioned at the northern edge of New Spain, however, these same processes and Indigenous agency undermined efforts at bringing California Indians entirely under subjection. Second, my focus on "process" foregrounds the dynamism inherent to California missions as more than churches with courtyards and four imposing walls (i.e., a mission *place*). Examples of approved furloughs, extramural living arrangements, and illicit flight from missions reflect the interests and motivations of Native people seeking to stay connected to their relations, places, and resources within homelands that remained relevant and powerful.

The Mission *Place* in Colonial California

Robed Franciscan padres were not the first outsiders Indigenous Coast Miwok people observed trespassing in their homelands. From 1542 to 1603, several relatively short encounters took place along the coast of California between Indigenous communities and the crews of foreign ships (Lightfoot and Simmons 1998). At least two meetings took place at Point Reyes. During the summer of 1579, the English captain Francis Drake is believed to have stopped at Tamal-huya (Drakes Bay) to repair his ship, the *Golden Hind*. A second encounter took place at Point Reyes sixteen years later when the ill-fated Manila galleon, *San Agustín*, piloted by Sebastian Rodríguez Cermeño, wrecked in Tamal-huya while en route from the Philippines to Mexico. Galleons like the *San Agustín* facilitated the Manila Galleon Trade Route, which started in 1565 and connected the Americas to Spain's colony in the Philippines. Philippine markets received silver and other American products in exchange for silk, tea, and other goods such as blue-on-white porcelain, which ships like the *San Agustín* ferried across the Pacific Ocean to Mexico.

Just before the *San Agustín* sank in 1595, at least five Coast Miwok men paddled out to the ship in their tule balsas (reed canoes). They boarded the galleon and were given "pieces of silk and cotton and other trifles" (Wagner 1924:13). Cermeño and his crew also ventured ashore and reported "many Indians—men, women and children—who had their dwellings there" (Wagner 1924:13). Iron spikes and Chinese porcelain collected from archaeological sites at Point Reyes, including examples of porcelain fragments refashioned into tools and disk beads similar to clamshell disk beads (Russell 2011:293–98), shed light on early cross-cultural interactions and present a valuable image of sixteenth-century Native communities long before sustained Euro-American colonialism.

Cermeño's brief report contrasts with the detailed account prepared by Francis Fletcher, a chaplain accompanying the pirate Drake. For thirty-six days, Drake and crew repaired and refitted their ship at Point Reyes. They also interacted with local Coast Miwok people. Among the items carried or worn by Coast Miwok, Fletcher described "knitworke" (cordage or woven) headwear, featherwork, and strings of shell beads. Most likely describing clamshell disk beads, according to Fletcher these "chaines" were made of a "bony substance, euery linke [sic] or part thereof being very little, thinne [sic], most finely burnished, with a hole pierced through the middest [sic]" (Vaux 1854:125). Fletcher also described Coast Miwok conical bark houses, or dwellings formed by leaning long strips of redwood bark against one another to form a conical shelter (Vaux 1854:121). The houses, he added, "being many of them in one place, made seuerall [sic] villages here and there" (Vaux 1854:131). Fletcher's narrative and Cermeño's report paint a picture of a richly cultured, creative, and populous Coast Miwok homeland.

Europeans did not return to Coast Miwok territory for nearly two hundred years after Cermeño's departure from Point Reyes. In 1775, Juan Manuel de Ayala sailed into San Francisco Bay, setting in motion plans for the formal colonization of the region and the eventual establishment of Mission Dolores the following year. Discussed more in chapter 4, in 1775 Juan Francisco de la Bodega y Quadra would also sail into Bodega Bay and explore Tomales Bay in search of a suitable harbor to claim the land and block the empire-building efforts of other countries (Edwards 1964:256). Despite attempts to establish a permanent settlement at Bodega Bay during the 1790s, however, it was only after the Russian-American Company established Fort Ross and a port facility at Bodega Bay in 1812 that Franciscan padres were motivated to construct a mission north of the Golden Gate in 1817. From the 1770s to the 1870s, the Marin Peninsula represented a borderland consisting of a dynamic cast of colonial agents with interests that intersected with those of the deeply rooted communities of Coast Miwok people who, through their agency and ingenuity, sought to maintain their relevance and authority over a diminishing territory.

Established in 1776, the same year a newly formed United States of America declared its independence from Great Britain, imperial Spain's San Francisco Presidio District included the Presidio of San Francisco, Yerba Buena pueblo, and Mission San Francisco de Asís (Mission Dolores). Between 1777 and 1823, civilian pueblos and five more Franciscan missions—including Mission Santa Clara (est. 1777), Mission Santa Cruz (est. 1791), Mission San José (est. 1797), Mission San Rafael (est. 1817), and Mission San Francisco Solano (est. 1823)—were added to the district. Colonial administrators directed the construction of four presidios/districts along the coast of California at San Francisco, Monterey, Santa Barbara, and San Diego. Each district included a single military fort, multiple missions, and a handful of secular towns—a blueprint engineered to rapidly colonize and control New Spain's northern frontier. As military and administrative hubs, presidios watched over missions and pueblos, implemented policy, and safeguarded Spain's tenuous foothold in Alta California against other foreign interests. Colonial towns such as Yerba Buena (San Francisco), San José, and the Villa de Branciforte in Santa Cruz included businesses and residences for settlers. Missionaries of the Franciscan order had been chosen to advance New Spain's imperial design to "neutralize" the heavily populated California coastal region and transform Native people into loyal Christian subjects of the Spanish Crown (Lightfoot 2005:52–53).

To accomplish their goal, Franciscan proselytizers followed a system of religious conversion designed to inexpensively transform Indigenous groups into Christians. Similar programs had been implemented in other areas of the Spanish borderlands, including colonial Florida, Texas, and New Mexico. In theory, reducción and congregacíon "reduced" numerous Native communities orbiting each mission and "congregated," or collected, them at individual mission sites for religious teachings and eventual conversion. Padres then claimed Native lands around the missions and held them in trust for baptized Indians with the intention of later allocating small homesteads to an emerging class of agrarian, Christian Indians. Except in a few rare instances, however, most lands were never returned. Anticlerical policy within the Mexican government culminated in the secularization of missions during the 1830s and the acquisition of mission land and property by Mexican citizens for their private estates, or ranchos. Thus, through dispossession and forced relocation, evangelism, and lessons in farming, carpentry, leatherworking, and other Western trades, New Spain sought to grow a colonial citizenry by supplanting a preexisting Indigenous population. For missions throughout Alta California, small teams of colonists—typically one to four Franciscan padres and garrisons consisting of a few soldiers—were regularly eclipsed by large, culturally diverse, and multilingual, pluralistic communities of Indigenous peoples who contributed to the construction, maintenance, and operation of the mission manifold. They also created spaces for themselves.

The mission, as both *place* and *process* (Lycett 2004), was a constructed and emergent setting of daily routines and sundry tasks meted out to Native residents and performed under the watchful eyes of the padres to ensure the success of each colony. Discussed more in the following section, tensions between colonial and Indigenous interests reflect fundamental disagreements in worldviews; yet tension, accommodation, and resistance are also generative concepts reflecting a mission "process." Considering missions as Native places, "nearly everything" grown or manufactured in the missions, presidios, and pueblos resulted from Native labor, or the work of Indigenous children, women, and men who occupied positions in a variety of craft, agricultural, ranching, and domestic jobs (Hackel 1998:122). Beyond the mission-presidio-pueblo triad, presidio districts typically included assorted aqueducts and roads, ranches, farms, *visita* churches (smaller churches usually placed in Native communities and visited periodically by a priest), and *asistencia* missions (smaller submissions with a chapel, residences, and other infrastructure) that "filled in the landscape around and between mission headquarters" (Schneider and Panich 2014:15) Sustaining this colonial infrastructure, Native people ploughed fields, harvested crops, tended gardens, served as domestic servants, produced crafts, herded livestock, and manufactured tile and adobe bricks. After the mid-1790s Native people were employed as blacksmiths, gunsmiths, masons, leatherworkers, and they were occasionally "loaned" out for sundry jobs (Hackel 1998:123; Lightfoot 2005:67). To manage large herds of cattle and other livestock owned by individual missions, Native people would also gradually learn the skills required to tend and ride horses, and Native vaqueros (cowboys) would play a central role in the economies and recreation of Indigenous communities throughout the nineteenth and twentieth centuries (Panich 2017). For the San Francisco Bay Area, Huicmuse (later known as "Chief Marin") and others translated their knowledge of the tides into new jobs, including piloting mission launches and delivering mail to priests via tule balsa (Goerke 2007:51).

Before the missions, Native people were familiar with the skills necessary for tending the natural world, including managing diverse and seasonally available resources and gathering and processing innumerable plants, animals, and minerals from assorted habitats throughout the year to create food, medicine, building materials, tools, clothing, and regalia. Perhaps more alien to Native bodies and ears was an incessant daily routine divided between prayer and forced communal labor and punctuated by the constant toll of the mission bell signaling the beginning and end of each segment of the day. Within the "bell zone" (Lightfoot and Danis 2018), Franciscan padres claimed control of the daily work and prayer schedules. On a typical morning, the mission bell rang one hour after sunrise, after which Native people assembled for mass, ate breakfast, and then gathered to receive instructions for their daily chores. The mission bell rang again at noon signaling dinner, which was followed by work for approximately three to four hours, evening prayer, and then a third meal (Lightfoot 2005:60).

In light of the rigorous labor programs carried out at missions throughout California, many scholars have sought answers to the question of why Native people joined the missions in the first place (e.g., Milliken 1995).

The underlying goal of missionization was to convert Indians to Christianity, but initial encounters with missions may have been fundamentally experimental—for some, spurred by the desire to "take part in something new and exciting, while others were sent by family elders who had made a calculated decision to ally themselves with the powerful newcomers" (Milliken 1995:221). By law, the conversion of Native peoples was voluntary (Lightfoot 2005:82); yet, Indigenous peoples throughout the Spanish Empire were typically cajoled into entering missions through gifts of glass beads, clothing, food, and other inducements (e.g., Milliken 1995:68). Colonists also turned to corporeal violence, kidnapping, and threats to balance high mortality rates and the constant flight of baptized individuals from the missions (Milliken 1995:95–101; Sandos 2004:102–3).

After baptism, Native people were not permitted to leave missions. As Franciscan historian Francis Guest (1973:204–5) argued, runaways posed a problem for the missions for several reasons. First, baptism reflects membership in the Roman Catholic Church and if someone were to "wander from the mission and return to the wilderness, he might lapse back into paganism." Second, once baptized, Native people were under the jurisdiction of the state and not permitted to renounce their loyalty to the king of Spain. Third, the goal of the mission was to create Christians and participants in civilized society, which could not be done if Native people kept "disappearing, at odd intervals, into the forest." Fourth, baptized Indians were considered legal wards—essentially children or incapacitated adults—of missionary guardians. Fifth, maintaining a steady population of Christian subjects was deemed necessary to meet the goal of fortifying Spain's foothold on the northern frontier.

Others have elaborated on the idea of an all-consuming California mission and the inevitable atrophy of Indigenous homelands—a dominant and inescapable colonial place, in other words, flanked by shrinking and subordinate hinterlands. Milliken (1995) argued, for instance, that many California Indians visited missions because they had "little choice." Drawing from the records of Native baptisms and deaths in San Francisco Bay missions, Milliken (1995:179) continues, by 1803 Coast Miwok villages on the Marin Peninsula had been emptied of people. This fatalistic view of Native-lived colonialism is echoed in the essentialized views of "disappearing" or "extinct" Indigenous cultures and identities espoused by California anthropologists, as well as the false spatial and temporal logics created by archaeological overemphasis on the built landscape. Put simply, all twenty-one Franciscan missions in California have been investigated by archaeologists, and most of them exhibit standing architecture (e.g., walls, chapels, and other constructions). As part of the funneling effect created from the destruction of Native American places around San Francisco Bay (see chapter 1), archaeology inside and around mission buildings—for the purpose of research, restoration and maintenance efforts, and to satisfy nostalgic histories of "early" California—outweighs scholarship exploring hinterlands and skews our understanding of Native history.

With close scrutiny of colonial missions, long-term Indigenous histories yield to Western time keeping with hard beginning and end dates, and Indigenous societies tend to collapse under the weight of four imperial powers over a short span of approximately one hundred years (1770s to 1870s). With little to no archaeology conducted in hinterlands, missions and associated archives continue to represent one-sided and predominant sources of information about how, when, and where Native people of the colonial-era lived. Onerous labor demands, the spread of infectious diseases, malnutrition, high rates of infant mortality, forced confinement, rape, torture, and other forms of physical and psychological abuse at missions devastated Indigenous communities. Compounding the devaluing of Indigenous humanity, the quiet but no less catastrophic impacts of invasive weeds and grazing livestock on hydrology and local plant and animal communities further compromised Indigenous livelihoods. Drought may have further exacerbated hardships, and some missionaries observed clear increases in the number of baptisms during periods of drought (Lightfoot 2005:87; but see Peelo 2009). All of these variables are important for considering the experiences and outcomes of Indigenous-colonial encounters; nevertheless, they address only one part of the story.

In addition to numerous raids conducted by Spanish soldiers and Indigenous auxiliaries to collect baptized people who fled missions for the interior (see Phillips 1993:46), padres administered other concessions to attract Native people to the missions and maintain a stable workforce, preempt revolt, and curb incessant fugitivism. The upshot of tensions emerging from the many and dynamic interests colliding within missions on a daily basis include numerous examples of self-emancipation, cases of extramural residence, and mission-administered furloughs. Discussed next, these examples reflect the mission process as well as unanticipated outcomes that quietly eroded the mission system's own quest for conquest and conversion. They are also important examples of the unwavering relevance and power of Indigenous hinterlands.

The Mission *Process* in Californian Borderlands

There is an irony involved in decentering missions as the places to explore California mission history. What better place for an archaeologist to study the daily routines of Native laborers than the site of a mission workshop, or

an adobe room block for identifying the choices that Native families made
during the evening hours to keep their cultures and communities intact?
Summarizing the enormous amount of archaeological research on California
mission workshops, domestic spaces, and other settings is beyond the scope of
this book. For San Francisco Bay, however, Rebecca Allen (1998), Kent Lightfoot (2005), and Lee Panich (2020) provide important examples of mission
archaeology focused on Indigenous agency and the persistence of Indigenous
identities and cultural practices within settings of control and violence. Missions established both social constraints and opportunities for Native people
and colonists alike, whose daily negotiations and resistances were inspired by
their own histories and cultural protocols.

In addition to building and participating in the mission place, Native
people's agency, or interested action, mediated colonial power and continually
redefined mission settings as more of a *process* or negotiation. Unlike the popular image of a walled "fortress" of spiritual conversion (Bolton 1917:51), Franciscan missions were fundamentally meeting grounds and dynamic settings—
both the product of and a contributor to the borderlands encapsulating them.
Discussed more in chapter 4, the borderland formed on the Marin Peninsula
during the nineteenth century reflected the competing interests of Spanish,
Russian, Mexican, and American colonizers operating within an Indigenous
Coast Miwok homeland. As "powerful diagnostic spaces" (Chang 2011:385),
human bodies, materials, and ideas entered and exited borderlands, and the
conditions for the appearance and departure of people and things were contingent upon ever-changing circumstances, rules, and refusals. Viewed through
the lens of practice and structuration theories, the constant interplay and
productive tensions created from daily negotiations between competing borderland interests contribute to the mission process. Practice theory establishes
that everyday activities are patterned and can reflect the daily "regulated
improvisations" by which people intentionally order and reorder their social
conditions (Bourdieu 1977:78). Structuration theory, moreover, reveals that
human interest and action are constrained and enabled by overarching rules,
or structure, that people draw on to reproduce social systems and uphold their
values (Giddens 1979). These daily negotiations are unpredictable and open-
ended. People have agency and act according to their interests, but they do so
within fields of power that simultaneously restrict and enable.

What does this mean for colonial missions in California? According to
Jackson and Castillo (1995:6), who introduced the idea to scholars that Native Americans could and did resist missions, Franciscan missionaries in
California maintained a "warmed-over version of the sixteenth-century colonial policy of reducción/congregación, modified by two hundred years of

practical experience in missions throughout northern New Spain and the rest of Spanish America." Since the late 1500s, trial and error in the colonization and conversion of Indigenous peoples on the North American continent and constant negotiation resulted in Franciscan padres applying a recruitment and furlough policy in California quite unlike that implemented at other Catholic missions. "Negotiation" took place at times under cover of darkness, "between the houses and behind closed doors" (Lightfoot 2005:113). At other times, negotiations were more brazen, taking on the moniker of "resistance." Resistance to the missions changed over time and took many forms (see Jackson and Castillo 1995:73–80). Resistance included violent and large-scale revolts, such as the 1824 Chumash Revolt, as well as other subtler examples of defiance (e.g., sabotaging equipment, tardiness, work stoppages) that may have escaped the notice of the missionaries, the historian's pen, or even the archaeologist's trowel.

Given the array of reactions and alterations to an intended colonial blueprint, characterizing Native peoples' resistance to missions only in terms of violent reactions to unrelenting colonial authority risks dismissing the wider spectrum of conditions, participants, motivations, forms, and outcomes of dissent (Liebmann and Murphy 2010). Take, for example, Huicmuse, a Coast Miwok man known later by the name "Marino" or "Chief Marin," who was baptized at Mission Dolores along with his spouse, Mottiqui (renamed "Marina") and several other Huimen (Coast Miwok) people in 1801. Approximately one decade later Huicmuse fled Mission Dolores for an unknown reason, but he was soon captured and imprisoned at the San Francisco presidio only to flee again and lead a rebellion against the missions and Spanish military in the 1820s (Goerke 2007). "Resistance" is a term that might best characterize popularized accounts of Marino's attacks on Mission San Rafael and military personnel (figure 7). The resistance concept falls short, however, when trying to account for Marino's role as godparent, alcalde (elected magistrate or overseer), and mayordomo (manager or foreman) in the mission system and his acceptance of penance, extreme unction, and the Eucharist at death (Goerke 2007:152). As seen in the example of Chief Marin, Indigenous agency can ultimately be dulled and reduced to a handful of violent flashpoints that uncritically reaffirm one-dimensional colonial power structures as well as vanishing Indian and noble savage tropes. Moreover, this line of thinking privileges written forms of history that tout colonial authority and frame Native resistance.

Discussed more below, a system of approved furloughs called paseo is an overlooked example of "resistance" that emerged in California and reveals how the accumulated actions and persistent decision-making of Native

FIGURE 7 "Chief Marin of Tamalpais who terrorized the Spanish nearly a century ago." Described as a "fierce overlord of the Golden Gate" (French 1907), the *San Francisco Chronicle* published this dramatized account and illustration of Huicmuse on May 26, 1907.

people could in fact alter the imposed institutionalized constraints of the missions. That is, while the mission "structure" established social constraints, it also simultaneously enabled possibilities for action, and the structure itself was reproduced and transformed—intentionally or not—by Indigenous and non-Native imperatives (Barrett 2001). Furlough, extramural living arrangements, and flight are three mechanisms by which California Indians sought refuge and protection in hinterlands. By continually asserting their interests and remaining connected to people and meaningful places beyond mission walls, they negotiated and transformed the mission process.

Away on Paseo

Paseo was a system that permitted Native people to venture beyond the walls of Spanish colonies. The paseo system first appeared in the Colorado River region of southeastern California and southwestern Arizona. As explained by

Milliken (1995:95), "as more and more people joined the mission from places more than an easy day's walk away, a problem arose concerning the desire of [baptized individuals] to come and go between homeland and mission." Native people carried passes with them during visits to family members, while running errands, or while collecting wild foods. After the 1781 Yuma Revolt, passes were used to monitor traffic to and from colonial outposts and more easily distinguish friend from foe (Milliken 1995). Recruitment of unbaptized Indians and "denaturalization" were two additional motives for paseos. "To convert hunter-gatherer populations the missionary needed not only to congregate them but also to keep them tethered" (Wade 2008:265). Accordingly, missionaries believed that by permitting furloughs mission residents would return to their home villages to profess the benefits of a Christian lifestyle to others and, in doing so, make comparisons between mission life and the supposed hardships of their former life.

The necessity for periodic food collecting trips appears to have been one of the primary motivators for implementing a pass system (Hackel 1998:209; Newell 2009:101); yet, Native people chose to leave missions for still other reasons. As Quincy Newell (2009:70) explains, paseo "translates to something like 'promenade,' hinting at the priests' understanding that an element of recreation was involved as well . . . [yet] these trips seem to have been a time for Indians to relax and visit friends and family, renewing social and familial bonds." In addition to seeking physical and mental nourishment, reports exist of dances hosted secretly in the hinterlands and attended by Indians furloughed from missions and unbaptized communities (e.g., Cook 1960:256; see also Schneider 2021). Some Chumash are known to have departed missions for the Santa Barbara backcountry to prepare ceremonial rock paintings (Johnson 1984:12; see also Robinson et al. 2020). Quincy Newell has also documented some furloughs from San Francisco Bay missions that appear to have been timed to coincide with major life events such as childbirth and death (Newell 2009:161–64). It appears that the structured lifestyle of mission living has been overemphasized, and many more opportunities to depart the missions existed than have been reported. In short, many Native people retained a mobile lifestyle and sustained traditional forms of subsistence and other cultural practices even while ostensibly living at missions. As seen in the administration of temporary passes, it appears that missionaries begrudgingly undermined their own purpose by endorsing a policy that encouraged mobility and helped Native people access and sustain cultural traditions.

As for the duration and frequency of paseos, accounts vary. Paseos seem to have been awarded to some individuals once or twice a year as others have noted (Guest 1979:11; Sandos 2004:94). Foreign travelers visiting Spanish

colonies also share details about the inner workings of missions. While Louis
Choris prepared detailed illustrations of the people and places he encountered
during his visit to San Francisco in 1816, Captain Kotzebue of the *Rurik*
and the ship's botanist, Adelbert von Chamisso, kept journals of their visit.
Chamisso noted that "the fathers allow their Indians, for the most part, twice
a year, a leave of absence for some weeks to visit their friends, and their native
place" (Mahr 1932:81, 83). Kotzebue offers a longer description:

> Twice in the year they receive permission to return to their native homes.
> This short time is the happiest period of their existence; and I myself have
> seen them going home in crowds, with loud rejoicings. The sick, who
> cannot undertake the journey, at least accompany their happy countrymen
> to the shore where they embark and there sit for days together mournfully
> gazing on the distant summits of the mountains which surround their
> homes; they often sit in this situation for several days; without taking any
> food, so much does the sight of their lost home affect these new Chris-
> tians. Every time some of those who have the permission run away, and
> they would probably all do it were they not deterred by their fears of the
> soldiers. (Mahr 1932:63)

The duration of approved furloughs probably also varied depending on
labor demands, the personalities and leniency of some padres, as well as the
distance required to travel to an approved destination. Other unrecorded variables that may have informed when Native people requested leaves of absence
might include ritual cycles, rites of passage such as childbirth and death, and
the seasonal availability of wild foods. As Felipe de Goycoechea, commander
of the Santa Barbara Presidio, observed at nearby Mission Santa Barbara, "it
happens that at the season of the wild fruits they are given permission to pick
them, but for a very limited period of time of two weeks more or less" (Santa
Barbara Mission Archive Library [SBMAL] 1800). In sum, a pass might ex-
pire after a few days or after a duration of one or two weeks.

The administration of passes seems to have depended on the labor needs
of a mission at any given time, the attitudes of the padres, and the behavior
of individuals in the eyes of the padres. As Louis Choris observed during his
visit to Mission Dolores in 1816, passes were given to "those Indians upon
whose return [the padres] believe they can rely to visit their own country,
but it often happens that few of these return; some, on the other hand, bring
with them new recruits to the mission" (Mahr 1932:95). One of the most
detailed descriptions of the administration of approved furloughs comes from
Mission Santa Barbara in a rebuttal to allegations about the mismanagement

of the Alta California missions. Responding to the accusation from Felipe de Goycoechea that Franciscan padres regularly caved to the requests of Native people for time away from the mission, Father Estevan Tapis wrote:

The regular practice at Santa Barbara has always been this: every Sunday after Mass, either at the door of the church or before the room of the father, there is read a list of the fifth part of [baptized Indians] who have permission to go out on an excursion. These names are kept in a notebook so that all can go out on excursions in turn. Those whose homes are in distant *rancherias* are given two weeks of excursion, the rest one week. If during the four weeks they are required to live at the mission anyone gives a reason for leaving the mission, such permission is given him. There are also very many who during the week ask for a free day in order to go fishing, to go to the presidio, or to walk along the beach. This permission is also given them. Only at the time of the gathering of the wheat harvest, which lasts a month more or less, the people do not leave the mission, but after the harvest has been gathered all the Indians leave in two distinct groups, one in each week. Nor is permission given for such excursions if during the week a feast day occurs on which they are obliged to hear Mass. However, in the following week instead of one fifth of the people, two fifths leave the mission.

The wild fruits for which the Christians have the greatest relish and which they seek with the greatest intensity are the acorns and *islay* or *tayiyas*, which is a fruit similar to the cherry and which has within its shell a kind of juice which is very bitter, but which having been mixed with water and heated is edible. The *islay* ripens during the month of September and the acorns after that. We can state positively that in the years when these are plentiful (such years are fewer now), for the period of a month and a half a little more than a kettle of *pozole* is sufficient for all the people who remain at the mission. During all this time the Christians live freely in the open country and on Saturday many come in to Mass [for Sunday] but not all. They do not have the same inclination towards other wild produce, with the exception of the old women. The others who take advantage of the general permission spend the greater part of the fall season hunting for seeds. The same holds true for the fact that many Indians voluntarily abstain from excursions during the weeks immediately following the search for *islay* and acorns, knowing that afterwards they will receive abundant permission to go out as they need to. We do not doubt but that the pagans have more liberty than the Christians, for even to this day they have not subjected themselves to the yoke of the Gospel nor to the precepts of the Church, but this greater liberty denied to the Christians, for the very reason of their being such, is more than compensated for in the clothing and food which the mission gives them whether they are ill or in good health.

All that we have written, to our way of thinking, is the "irrefutable truth." (SBMAL 1800)

Based on this description, Native people who accepted baptism were generally given permission to depart Mission Santa Barbara for a period of time to fish and gather, although "anyone"—baptized or unbaptized—gained permission to leave the mission so that all had their turn at going away. The frequency of departures—every fifth week, according to Father Tapis—suggests an annual furlough of approximately ten weeks for every person capable of making the journey and, while this seems like a generous calculation, Sandos (2004:199) estimates multiple departures throughout the year was normal. Fundamentally, whether designed for the recruitment of additional souls or for supplementing sparse mission diets, paseo was a product of the borderland and a reflection of the mission process. Amid a rigorous daily routine, Native people remained tuned to the seasons, their ritual calendars, and the periodic availability of important foods, medicines, and raw materials despite the efforts of the missionaries to reset the clock.

Extramural Residence

The paseo system raises additional questions about the productive tensions of mission living and, more specifically, the opportunities Native people took to situate their lives and cultural practices beyond the walls of a destructive colonial regime. The permission given to some groups to remain living at their natal communities, "outside the direct daily control of the missionaries" (Lightfoot 2005:65–66), may in fact be one underlying reason for the spatial pattern of federally recognized and unrecognized California tribes at present. Accordingly, missions constructed in arid regions of southern Alta California (south of the Transverse Ranges) may have seen more individuals living "freely in the open country," as Father Tapis described for the Chumash at Mission Santa Barbara, because the warmer desert environment made it more difficult to grow enough food (i.e., domesticated crops) for large mission communities. In more temperate regions of Central California, particularly around Monterey Bay and San Francisco Bay, a policy of reducción/congregación may have been more practical.

This "necessary evil," as Father Fermín Lasuén called the altered residential design (quoted in Kenneally 1965:277), only required baptized individuals to visit the mission once every two weeks to participate in mass, festivals, and other church events (Hackel 2005:259; Lightfoot 2005:65–66). As a result, extramural residence may have afforded more opportunities for individuals to visit their homes and family members, to speak their languages and hold ceremonies forbidden at missions, and to shore up threatened cultural identities by partaking in their cultural traditions. Over the long run, the United States federal recognition process during the twentieth century favored intact communities, or distinct places on a map. I suspect that many more instances of creative living arrangements existed in other regions of California than have been reported, especially when considering the paseo system and the high frequency of flight from missions. These too were important chances to recall familiar landmarks, to remain connected to family members and social networks, and to hunt, gather, and dance. For the United States however, a nation bent on affixing Native Americans to circumscribed reservation and rancheria lands, mobility was a character flaw of "landless Indians," a misleading settler term applied to many formerly missionized tribes in California (K. Schneider 2010), including my own.

Take, for example, Moloccia and Talia Unuttaca. A forty-year-old Coast Miwok man hailing from Bodega Bay, or "Bodega en los Tomales" as Father Juan Amorós noted in Mission San Rafael's (SRM) ledger of baptisms, Moloccia was baptized in the spring of 1826 and given the Christian name "José Talio" (Huntington Library 2006; SRM baptism 1343); also known as "José Talis" or "Chief James Jose Talis" (*Marin Journal* 1922:7). By 1839, following the secularization of Alta California missions, Moloccia is described by Mariano Guadalupe Vallejo as the "Captain of the Tamales [*sic*]" and was allowed permission "to leave [Mission] S. Rafael with those of his tribe, on condition of sending a few men occasionally to hear mass, if any mass should be celebrated" (Bancroft 1886:718). As an elder "Captain" or headman of his Bodega community, Moloccia may have held special status as Toion (or Tóllo), the Siberian term for leader or chief used by the Russians at Fort Ross (Farris 1998:6), or perhaps "Talio" to an undiscerning ear. This case of extramural residence speaks to the realities of life on the Marin borderland where a single Franciscan priest—at the time, Father Jose Lorenzo Quijas who is described as a drunk and overworked due to managing Missions San Rafael and San Francisco Solano (Ashcroft 1992:6)—could not possibly prevent Coast Miwok from returning to their homes.

By 1836, Native people began to "wander away" from Mission San Rafael (Lauff 2016 [1916]:52). Discussed more in chapter 4, some Coast Miwok people returned to Nicasio Valley, the location of the large precontact and mission-era community of Echa-tamal. Others "wandered" even farther but also made sure to return to visit relatives still living at the mission, as well as ancestors buried in nearby shellmounds (Schneider 2015b). Still others reestablished communities at McNear's Point (i.e., Point San Pedro, where China Camp State Park is located) on San Pablo Bay or in their former homelands around Tomales and Bodega Bays (Lauff 2016 [1916]:52). Moloccia's experience seems to fit that of someone who remained connected to their ancestral home in West Marin and also constructed new relationships within and beyond the walls of a mission.

Moloccia's baptism at Mission San Rafael in 1826 was followed eighteen days later by the baptism of his six-year-old daughter, Puqueyac, who was renamed "Rafaela" (Huntington Library 2006; SRM baptism 1344). Puqueyac's mother (Moloccia's wife) was Talia Unuttaca, a Bodega Miwok (Geluatamal) woman. Like Talio, Talia's name may be a misinterpretation of a similar sounding name ending in -éla (i.e., Taléla), the name for "water spirit" derived from the Coast Miwok water moiety (Farris 1998:9). Before marrying Moloccia, Talia Unuttaca was previously married to Andres Aulanoc, a Sugpiaq man from the Kodiak Archipelago working at the Russian mercantile colony of Fort Ross (Arndt 2015; Jackson 1983:240). During this previous relationship noted in detail on Moloccia's baptism record (Huntington Library 2006; SRM baptism 1343), in 1815 Andres and Talia had a daughter at "el Presidio de Ros" (Fort Ross) they named Maja (renamed "Maria Antonia") and shortly thereafter traveled to New Archangel (Sitka, Alaska) to have Talia baptized by the Russian Orthodox church. After Andres died in 1819, Talia and Maja returned to California at which point Talia, or "Josefa" as the padres called her, entered into a relationship with Moloccia; they were married the same day that Moloccia was baptized (Huntington Library 2006; SRM marriage 364).

What remains unclear are the finer details that brought Moloccia and Talia Unuttaca together as well as the paths they and their daughters took in subsequent years. What becomes apparent from this single example are the global and local scales of interaction taking place outside the purview of missions, which come across as minor waypoints in an Indigenous drama spanning the Pacific Coast of North America. "Residence," in this case, includes time spent at Bodega Bay, Mission San Rafael, the Russian outposts at Fort Ross and New Archangel, and countless other places in between. As Robert Jackson (1983:240–41) also notes, this was not a unique case, and Coast Miwok and Kashaya Pomo women regularly formed unions with Russian men and other Native people "with or without the blessings of the church." Moreover, the choices exercised by Native people operated at a local scale.

While Father Quijas tried in vain to hold together the crumbling remains of Mission San Rafael's meager foothold on the Marin Peninsula in 1839, Coast Miwok leaders Captain José Talio—or, quite possibly, Talio or Tóllo Moloccia and Talia Unuttaca—or, perhaps Taéla Unuttaca—did what they could to fortify their home community at Bodega Bay and maintain relevance in the post-mission era.

Fleeing Missions

Turning now to a third example of the mission "process," Native people departed from missions with and without permission. In addition to approved paseos, countless others voted with their feet. I view the agency of California Indians less as a series of violent reactions to a static and inflexible colonial structure and more as informed responses couched in longstanding traditions of mobility and Indigenous epistemologies. Compared to such overt forms of resistance as theft, revolt, and attacks on missions and missionaries, other subtler forms of resistance exhibited at the missions were just as prevalent and transformative. For example, illicit departure from the missions by running away was widespread in the Alta California province but commonly overlooked in a dominance-resistance framework as a simplistic or passive response by those who had no choice but to abscond. This line of thought negatively reinforces the generic idea that missions were inescapable contexts of Indigenous loss negotiated only through violent acts of overt resistance.

Sherburne Cook (1976) distinguished two classes of fugitive: individuals whose escape was temporary and those who escaped long enough to be dropped permanently from the mission rolls. He also added that people fled the missions because of compulsory conversion, homesickness, overpopulation, and enforced confinement as in the case of *monjeríos*, or locked dormitories constructed for unmarried women (Vaughn 2011). Commenting on the imposed gender roles—and possibly the presence of a dormitory for unmarried Coast Miwok women—at Mission San Rafael, for example, Coast Miwok elder Maria Copa stated that "[padres] kept only men at the mission. They kept the women a long way off" (Collier and Thalman 1996:75). The number of people who fled varies by mission and by year, and also hinged on the temperament or managerial inexperience of some padres (Cook 1976:58; Jackson 1994:138; Wade 2013:294). Cook (1976:58) estimated that 4,060 individuals—approximately 12 percent of the total mission population (20,427) for fifteen missions—had escaped between 1769 and 1817. Another estimate suggests 5 to 10 percent of baptized Indians illicitly visited the hinterlands throughout the mission period (Hackel 2005:94–95).

An even smaller percentage of runaways fled and remained away as most aborted their flight or were recaptured. Maria Copa relayed many of the stories of mission life that her relatives once shared, including stories from her grandfather who "used to wash the priest's clothes. Ironed them, too. [And he] used to play the violin for mass" (Collier and Thalman 1996:26). Copa's grandfather also "ran away from the mission. He was afraid to go back. But every time he tried to take a drink of water he heard something hissing. It frightened him so that he went back to the mission" (Collier and Thalman 1996:26). This specific example further alludes to traditional spiritual observances that continued to structure how people traveled and related to the world outside mission quadrangles.

Opportunities were available to leave missions with permission, but padres appear to have been inconsistent in making passes available. During the summer of 1795, 280 Saclan and Huchiun (Ohlone) peoples up and left Mission Dolores for their East Bay homes. An investigation into the event was conducted by José Argüello in 1797, and captured runaways, soldiers, and priests were interviewed to try to understand the underlying motives. Sergeant Pedro Amador, who led an expedition to retrieve the fugitives, and three other mission allies attested that "too much work, too much punishment, and too much hunger" led to the mass exodus (Guest 1973:210). In addition to this climate of punishment, hunger, and labor, one of the two missionaries posted to Mission Dolores, Father Antonio Dantí, is known to have been "a problem, an eccentric, a crank," "fiery and irascible," and "as explosive as gunpowder" (Guest 1973:209, 284), as well as a central figure in the mistreatment of several individuals who later took part in the 1795 flight.

The testimonies from recaptured Saclan and Huchiun runaways are even more revealing (see Milliken 1995:299–303). One of those interviewed, a man named "Tarazon," declared that "he had no motive [to flee]. . . . Having been granted license to go on paseo to his land, he had felt inclined to stay" (Milliken 1995:300)—a clear offense to the padres, according to Francis Guest (1973). Yet, another respondent named "López" explained that "he went one day over to the presidio to look for something to eat. Upon returning to the mission, he went to get his ration, but father Dantí did not want to give it to him, saying that he should not go to the countryside to eat herbs" (Milliken 1995:302). Others in the group reported inhumane treatment and the need to supplement limited mission rations with wild foods. "Homobono" testified that "his brother had died on the other shore, and when he cried for him at the mission, they whipped him. Also, the alcalde Valeriano hit him with a heavy cane for having gone to look for mussels at the beach [even] with . . . permission" (Milliken 1995:301). "Próspero" declared that "he had gone one night to the lagoon to hunt ducks for food. For this Father Antonio

Dantí ordered him stretched out and beaten. Then, the following week he was whipped again for having gone out on paseo. For these reasons he fled" (Milliken 1995:303). Still another captured runaway, "Mílan," declared he was "working all day in the tannery without any food for either himself, his wife, or his child. One afternoon after he left work, he went to look for clams to feed his family. Father Dantí whipped him. The next day he fled to the other shore, where his wife and child died" (Milliken 1995:302).

Flight from missions has often been viewed in simple terms because of its ubiquity in many contexts of colonialism. It was inevitable in settings of domination, some have argued. "Apostasy began as soon as conversion began," Cook (1976:57) noted. Even Father Junípero Serra shrugged his shoulders: "It will happen that one day, because they are punished or reprimanded, another day, because they fear punishment, yet another day because they have friends over there [in the wild], little by little they will flee" (quoted in Tibesar 1955:409). Yet, by dismissing Native flight from California missions as a natural or unavoidable part of the process of colonization, the complex entanglement of fear and optimism that culminated in an act of flight becomes masked. Paseo, examples of extramural residence, and instances of Indigenous apostasy are all forms of mobility, or traditions of bodily movement performed and informed by social memory and knowledge of the wider world, including places to secure seasonally available foods, places for social interchange, and places of refuge and protection.

Whether carried out in secret or with pass in hand, extramural trips afforded opportunities to reactivate Indigenous epistemologies and reengage with the persistent people, practices, and places that informed Indigenous ways of knowing. With some exceptions (e.g., Newell 2009:57), traditional cultural and ecological knowledge did not fully evaporate once a Native person stepped foot inside a mission as several archaeologists have carefully documented (see chapter 3), nor was knowing when and where to go simply the generic result of fear and poor living conditions. Trips away from missions represent informed and deliberate choices as several of the Saclan and Huchiun testimonies introduced above exemplify. Sometimes fleeing to *la otra banda* (the other shore) involved food collecting and respite. At other times, these trips might involve caring for sick family members or conducting mortuary rites for deceased loved ones (Newell 2009:161–64). In one arresting example from Mission Santa Cruz, Franciscan padres enumerated the baptisms and deaths of Native people between the years 1811 and 1814, and of the fifty-two reported deaths in 1813, the padres noted twenty-three individuals who had passed away "on their land where they had fled" (Marquínez and Escudé 1814) (figure 8). All of the examples underscore a fundamental desire among many Native people to distance themselves from violence and

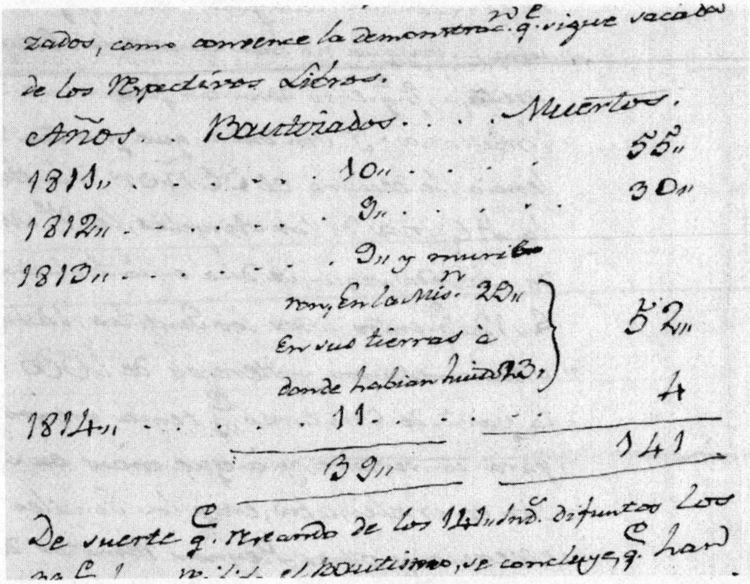

zados, como convence la demonstracion que sigue sacada
de los respectivos Libros.

Años	Bautizados	Muertos
1811	10	55
1812	9	30
1813	9 y murieron en la Mision 29, En sus tierras à donde habian huido 23	52
1814	11	4
	39	141

De suerte que restando de los 141 Ind. difuntos los ... se concluye que han

FIGURE 8 Twenty-three Native people, nearly half of the fifty-two recorded deaths at Mission Santa Cruz in 1813, "died on their land where they had fled," according to Padres Marcelino Marquínez and Jayme Escudé. Courtesy of the Santa Bárbara Mission Archive-Library.

loss of life at California's missions. Examples such as these also speak to the centrality of Indigenous hinterlands, which continued to factor into the decision making of colonized peoples. Such examples also raise the possibility that many "prehistoric" places remained important waypoints throughout the mission period as sites of refuge and ongoing cultural practice.

* * *

We need not don a hard hat and pick up an archaeological trowel to see that California missions were and continue to be dynamic places. Just as Native people incorporated missions and other colonial projects into their routines and decision-making, missions also represent polysemous and multivalent settings in the present. They are, following Elizabeth Kryder-Reid (2016:11), "potent ideological spaces" for understanding the people who lived and worked at them as well as spaces to reevaluate how historical memory can be fabricated, commemorated, and erased. The multiple interpretations and meanings that people give to and take from missions suggest that they are not static monuments, but rather sites of accumulated and ongoing history. Missions are, Timothy Ingold (2012) might say, building.

A building or *the* building—a static noun, in other words—contrasts with the present participle, *building*. Rather than reflecting an activity that has come to an end, buildings are never really complete, and, like most things, they have active lives, or "itineraries" (see Joyce 2012), beyond their immediate or intended use. To give an example, two Catholic dioceses have invited California Indian communities to missions to participate in public apology ceremonies events that share common ground with public apologies to Indigenous peoples and attempts at reconciliation in other postcolonizing settler nations like Australia and Canada. Ceremonies held at Mission San Rafael in 2007 and Mission San Juan Bautista in 2012 were attended by tribal leaders and citizens of the Federated Indians of Graton Rancheria (Mission San Rafael) and the Amah Mutsun Tribal Band (Mission San Juan Bautista), church officials, and the public. Both events culminated in a "mass of reconciliation" and apology by a bishop for past wrongdoings carried out by the missions against California Indians, including forced relocation, religious conversion, and cruel punishments (see Ashley 2007; Taylor 2012).

The two events speak, on the one hand, to the ironic role of missions for reaffirming and broadcasting enduring Indigenous histories despite the trauma of the past and the ongoing violence of untruthful mission narratives. On the other hand, these are uneasy connections to sites that remain deeply controversial. It is the dynamism of missions past and present that reminds me that California missions failed and why, ultimately, discussions that dwell on confinement and devastating colonial sources of power risk minimizing our capacity to see the legacies of resilient Indigenous peoples. One-sided histories of walled, impenetrable missions cast broader landscapes and the activities of Native people as irrelevant and run the risk of limiting deeper questioning about the central role of Indigenous hinterlands. Given my characterization of the place and, most especially, the process of California missions, for those individuals who chose to "put a piece of forest between themselves and the long arm of the invaders" (Axtell 1982:38), where did they go? Case studies presented in the next two chapters provide some answers to this question.

Summary

A column called "Ask Doctor Coyote" once published in *News from Native California* magazine featured letters from readers seeking advice and answers to questions about various topics such as etiquette at tribal events, tips for

applying to college, aspects of ceremonial practices, and other matters. The
following letter encapsulates the central ideas presented in this chapter.

> Dear Doctor Coyote,
> Why do California Indians participate at missions today? I see lots of
> California Indians at mission events and taking part in history days and
> giving tours. Aren't they angry at what happened to them because of the
> missions? I'd think they would stay away from those places.
>   —*Louie from San Luis Obispo*

> Dear Louie,
> Well, who better should be there than the families that built the places?
> Indian folks take pride in the efforts of their ancestors and the Spaniards
> didn't build those missions by themselves. It seems to this old coyote that
> it is a pretty good thing when Indian folk can help to tell their own his-
> tory and keep alive the memories of their grandfolks and what they went
> through by keeping it an Indian spot on the map. After all, they were here
> first. Don't be confused, be happy you now get a chance to hear the rest of
> the story. (Anonymous 2000:14)

The correspondence between "Louie" and "Doctor Coyote" touches on the
relationships, ambiguous outcomes, and historical silences that continue to
frame public perception of colonial history in California, as well as the "process" of missions as multivalent spaces of contestation and confirmation for
California Indians past and present.

False perceptions of space and time contribute to the idea that Franciscan
missions were omnipotent settings of Native confinement and conversion
and that Indigenous senses of place and cultural practices ceased to exist
after 1769 or disappeared shortly thereafter. The gradual destruction of Indigenous sites beginning in the late nineteenth century compound the problems with terminal narratives and vacant hinterlands. Indigenous presence in
California—minimally, thirteen thousand years of accumulated knowledge
and familiarity with the land—gives way to a Western history consisting of
non-Native personalities, major events, and the rapid colonization of Indigenous homeland over a short span of one hundred years. A narrow temporal
focus reinforces the idea of colonial-sponsored Indigenous collapse. It tends
to overlook the interactions taking place in California during the sixteenth
century and the changes already happening within Coast Miwok communities
responding knowledgeably to the influx of new people, materials, and ideas.
It also tends to forget that Franciscan missionaries continued to promote their

faith to California Indian communities, such as the Xabenapo (Big Valley) Pomo at St. Turibius Mission at Clear Lake, into the late 1870s and after (Barrett 1908:191).

Looking beyond a highly visible built landscape associated with each of the twenty-one missions established in colonial Alta California (i.e., the mission place), greater attention to process broadens our awareness of constructed mission settings and dynamic borderlands around them. As seen at the outset of this chapter, for example, the image of missions as walled compounds tends to overlook the porous nature of these frontier institutions, including the ebb and flow of ideas, materials, and people from different nations and ethnic backgrounds, as well as the inherent dynamism of pluralistic social settings (e.g., Lightfoot et al. 1998; Voss 2005). My focus on process further stresses Native peoples' informed responses to colonial imposition, and that resistance did not always entail violent reaction to colonial oppression. As I have argued, examples of self-emancipation, creative living arrangements, and periodic leaves of absence (paseos) reflect the productive tensions of everyday life in a California mission and the idea that the interests and activities of Native people could in fact transform the overarching structures of domination put in place by Spanish colonizers. Moreover, enduring traditions of mobility— purposeful and culturally informed movement grounded in memory and longstanding histories of travel—put California Indians outside the mission walls and on lands routinely viewed as being empty of people. Persistent places drew them back. As to where they went, what they did when they arrived at their destinations, and what this might mean—these are questions I intend to answer in the next three chapters.

3

Seeking Refuge

There are a hundred hiding places.

—ALFRED L. KROEBER, 1925

CUK-CUK-CUK-CUK! THE PIPING CALL of a pileated woodpecker contrasted with the dull rattle of archaeological trowels scraping against the metal hardware mesh of our sifting screens as we worked under the canopy of a large buckeye tree. My small crew was focusing on two archaeological sites in a cluster of three shellmounds tucked away in the forest of China Camp State Park. The buckeye tree provided welcome shade as the mercury steadily crept past one hundred degrees Fahrenheit, but the slow and deliberate work of clearing brush, plucking ticks from our bodies, avoiding poison oak, mapping, augering, and identifying materials collected from each site—and preparing all of the notes, field records, illustrations, and photographs throughout the process—seemed especially tedious in the heat. Marin County's banana belt generally enjoys warmer weather than the foggier corners of San Francisco Bay (one reason why Franciscan padres founded a mission at San Rafael in 1817), but the excessively hot July temperatures necessitated the purchase of a cooler and a pit stop at the local convenience store to buy popsicles for a cool lunchtime snack.

Apart from the clamshell disk bead and obsidian projectile point we found during the previous field season, to most people familiar with colonial period deposits, the two sites probably seemed exceedingly dull at first glance. No colorful glass beads like those found at other colonial-era sites dusted the surface of the shellmounds. Apart from some metal hardware and several bullet cartridge casings attributed to ranchers who constructed fences and ran cattle in the area before the park was established, metal artifacts were scarce. And nine pieces of pottery—including fragments of a porcelain rice bowl and salt-glazed stoneware—most likely reflect the presence of other minoritized ethnic groups, certainly not Indigenous Coast Miwok people fleeing from or "taken to" a Spanish mission, as one archaeologist hypothesized after completing work at the larger of the three shellmound sites in 1949. Without such obvious material cues as glass, metal, and pottery, how would we assemble a story about the experiences of Indigenous people contending with foreign invaders, their institutions and ideas, and the materials, plants, and animals they introduced? Pondering instead the many thousands of fragments of mollusk shell, splinters of animal bone, chunks of charcoal, and flakes of chert filling our archaeological screens, conventional narratives of colonialism and the places that make up that history would need deeper exploration and thought.

Countering master narratives of vacant mission-era hinterlands and the annihilation of San Francisco Bay Indigenous cultures at the hands of colonial invaders, this chapter foregrounds Indigenous homelands as the cardinal priority in the study of Indigenous experiences of colonial power. As chapters 1 and 2 show, archaeologists have tended not to look to shellmounds as sites containing information about the lives of Native people during the late 1700s. Many mounded sites have been destroyed, or anthropologists simply assumed that missions had effectively erased Native communities from the map. Colonialist and essentialist views of culture change have been "pervasively efficacious: natives were extirpated, the impact was fatal, the colonized were dominated and assimilated" (Thomas 1994:15). Diaries penned by early visitors to California sometimes mention Native people and the large communities they encountered during their travels; yet, these same accounts are also imprecise about the role of mounded villages among Native groups, leading some archaeologists to assume that shellmounds fell into disuse during the Late Period Phase 2 (1510–1770 CE) before Mission Dolores opened its doors in 1776 (see also Lightfoot and Luby 2002:275–76). An absence of evidence, or small quantities of materials dismissed as "intrusive," foreclosed entire landscapes as irrelevant for studying Indigenous peoples' responses to colonialism. In this process, Indigenous sites of history and empowerment are reduced to a handful of park names, trail routes, street signs, and other "subliminal imprints" marking the modern urban grid (Nabokov 2006:257). Considering such widespread examples of apostasy and flight from missions, a system of approved furlough, and patterns of extramural residence associated with the California mission process discussed in the previous chapter, where did Native people go? Where did they find refuge, or sites of protection *and* places to defiantly sing, dance, mourn, and prepare meals?

This chapter presents an archaeological case study oriented around these and other questions. The work centers on three unassuming shellmounds tucked away in a forest within a small park neighboring the city and suburbs of San Rafael. My research and writing foreground Indigenous places, history, and epistemology and, by doing so, I draw attention to places of refuge, or familiar and unfamiliar places to which people return to evade and maintain physical separation from persecution (Schneider 2015b:699). This point of view is different from the approach scholars normally adopt for evaluating Indigenous-colonial encounters. I acknowledge the impacts of colonialism, anthropology, and site destruction on the visibility of Indigenous histories. I further address the dynamic and contradictory experiences of Indigenous people who may have crossed the threshold of a mission church but also resisted Catholic doctrine and newly introduced modes of living by remaining mobile and connected to home.

This approach also upholds the ethics, values, and knowledge of my community of Graton Rancheria. In the archaeology I practice, I stress an active role for community partners in the research process—valuing my fellow tribal citizens as advisors, participants, and scholars endeavoring to learn more about their history—and I compare multiple forms of "evidence" to build a more inclusive and robust understanding of the past while also lessening the impacts and shortsightedness that may come from a project drawing on the methods and insights of archaeology alone. The oral narratives of tribal members, archaeological finds, and clues buried in the reports, maps, and photographs stored in assorted archives can help reveal resilient Indigenous people, places, and practices that, as histories of Marin County heretofore would have us believe, never existed.

Evoking an Indigenous Hinterland

Accounts of mission-era California have been steeped in violence perpetrated against Indigenous communities, essentialized views of Native American identities, and the loss of meaningful relationships to ancestral places. It was a "time of little choice" for Indigenous peoples, according to the title of one of the most widely read accounts of San Francisco Bay colonial history (Milliken 1995). This blunt discourse of imminent destruction with few options overemphasizes the quick pace of Indigenous collapse after 1769. By 1803, Milliken (1995:179) estimates, Coast Miwok communities on the southern end of the Marin Peninsula had been emptied of people and, further peeling back Marin's Indigenous landscape, by the 1830s "all tribal lands within forty miles to the north of San Francisco Bay and eighty miles to the east were empty of villages" (Milliken 1995:220).

In addition to the narrow temporal focus, misperceptions about the mission "place" reinforce a false spatial logic that eschews Indigenous concepts of place in favor of a readily identifiable built landscape comprised of permanent mission churches with impenetrable walled compounds. This focus on colonial buildings has been amplified since the late 1800s by tourism and preservation efforts advancing a bucolic vision of colonial California and by rapid urbanization in many areas of coastal California (Kryder-Reid 2016). As discussed previously, the funneling effect created by, on the one hand, the study and protection of mission architecture and, on the other hand, the destruction and underrepresentation of less perceptible hinterland sites of heritage, channels Native histories and experiences of colonialism through missions and their associated archives—a pattern that values mission archives and related points of view (Schneider et al. 2020). Eye-catching events and other information deemed noteworthy form narratives "filtered through the eyes and inkwells of nonnative interlocutors, in which indigenous perspectives were systematically excluded" (Liebmann and Murphy 2011:4).

The letters and reports of Franciscan missionaries would have us believe in their totalizing power. Several historians and archaeologists are exposing a very different picture of California missions as predominately Native places (e.g., Haas 2014; Lightfoot 2005; Newell 2009; Panich 2020; Zappia 2014), and close rereads of the colonial archive offer new perspective on the enduring power of food collecting, dances, craft production, mortuary practices, and other strategies of Indigenous survival (e.g., Brown 2018; Brown et al. 2018; Schneider 2021; Schneider et al. 2018; Panich 2015). By focusing on "process," in other words, we can better account for the dynamism that was inherent to these borderland institutions. Missions were quite unlike the popular image of cloistered settings of Indigenous conversion and domination. Sexual violence, physical and psychological abuse, corporal punishment, malnutrition, and the circulation of deadly diseases hampered Franciscan efforts to create viable colonies of Christian farmers. Native people also resisted the missions. Resistance took many forms, including revolt, attacks on missionaries, and other "hidden transcripts," James Scott's (1990) term for the subtle, but no less powerful, acts of resistance that may have gone unnoticed because they happened frequently and often in secret. Illicit flight, approved furloughs, and taking up residence in one's homeland can also be counted among the forms of resistance to colonial imposition. Shaped by the constant tension between the agency of Indigenous people and colonizers, the mission process created unforeseen spaces for repudiation and resilience.

Archaeology at missions over the years provides strong evidence for the retention and modification of Indigenous cultural practices within public and private spaces (Lightfoot 2005:96). Continuity and change are heralded by dietary remains, including: domesticated plants and animal taxa mixed with the remains of locally available shellfish, fish, plants, and terrestrial game (e.g., Allen 1998); ground stone implements and flaked stone tools manufactured from obsidian and chert as well as tools fashioned from introduced metal, glass, and porcelain (e.g., Panich et al. 2018b); large quantities of traditional clam and *Olivella* shell beads mixed with thousands of colorful glass beads (e.g., Panich 2014); modified bone, including whistles, awls, and other tools (e.g., Deetz 1963; Greenwood 1978:522–23); and evidence of basket weaving coincident with pottery production (e.g., Brown et al. 2018; Peelo 2011). Tobacco seeds, plummet-shaped "charmstones," stone and bone tubes, and rock crystals have all been unearthed from California missions, and these materials hint at the continued role of traditional medicines and curing rituals within mission communities (Cuthrell et al. 2016; Lightfoot 2005:108). Father Lasuén may have expressed disdain that missions' Indigenous residents "are accustomed to their abominable fiestas, and the memory of them is invoked at all hours" (Kenneally 1965:276), but few people now question this reality. Despite growing evidence for the persistence of rituals, foodways, dances, technologies, and other activities carried out privately and in plain view of Franciscan proselytizers, considering the sources of those meals, tools, medicines, and regalia exposes a conceptual blind spot in archaeology: defining the extramural world. The Indigenous hinterland concept is intended to recenter Indigenous home spaces as paramount to understanding responses to colonialism (Schneider 2015b). Researching hinterland landscapes entails three key facets: rereading the colonial archive to identify the agency of Indigenous people; revisiting existing archaeological reports and collections; and asking different questions.

First, as detailed in chapter 2, flight, furlough, and establishing residence outside the walls of missions might more accurately reflect the interested actions of people responding in informed ways to evolving circumstances. Accounts of food-collecting trips, seeking refuge, and adhering to important rites of passage (e.g., childbirth and death) should give us pause to consider the routes, destinations, and mobility required to sustain these practices. Second, researching hinterlands demands rethinking the spatial, temporal, and material categories archaeologists have used to define "prehistoric" and "historic" places, time periods, and artifacts. Third, looking beyond the bounds of California's colonies, archaeologists can rediscover persistent places of power, memory, protection, and recourse for Native people and redefine communities bearing histories that extend across the "great divide" in archaeology (Scheiber and Mitchell 2010)—a necessary change in perspective that will lead to new questioning. Ultimately, the aim is not to reinstate an outmoded colonial-Indigenous dichotomy of marginalized Indigenous spaces and zones of colonial authority—a problematic spatial model dismantled by archaeologists over the past several years. Additionally, "hinterland" might not be the best descriptor for characterizing persistent and powerful Indigenous spaces encroached upon by colonial invaders. Since so few examples of hinterland research exist, however, developing the hinterland concept will ideally bring about greater awareness—and further recentering—of the landscapes and places that helped sustain Indigenous communities and identities.

By the mid-1900s some archaeologists recognized that some areas of the Marin Peninsula had in fact played a role as important safe haven for Native people fleeing or avoiding missions (e.g., Beardsley 1954:19). In Marin County, however, the search for evidence of Francis Drake's 1579 visit and Sebastian Cermeño's 1595 stopover took priority. Indeed, why would someone research the homes and livelihoods of Native people who had survived the missions and rebuilt their communities? Anthropologists had by the early 1900s already erroneously determined that California tribes that interacted with missions failed to maintain their cultures, identities, and senses of place. This logic trickled into archaeological practice, including the idea that Native people could only be studied at certain places, during particular time periods, and through the analysis of specific material types. In one example of this mentality, an archaeological site record produced for a shellmound on "Indian Beach" at Tomales Bay notes "quantities of nineteenth century material: nails, broken bottle glass, crockery, etc . . . [but] no aboriginal artifacts [and] definitely not worth excavating" (Meighan 1952). A simple formula is revealed in this and other similar archaeological assessments: California Indians who interacted with missions did not survive the missions. Nothing could be further from the truth.

Archaeologists were often quick to dismiss the ideas that Native people could evade colonialism and that many had done so by remaining close to home. As a residential site for an unknown number of Native people as late as the twentieth century, the site record for "Indian Beach" and other Marin County archaeological site records and reports produced during the twentieth century can actually be quite revealing and useful for tracking Indigenous presence. While many of the shellmounds that Nels Nelson recorded in the early 1900s had already been destroyed, he also noted "some of the smaller sites *between San Rafael and Petaluma* . . . [were] occupied by the Indians as late as 1870" (Nelson 1909a:347; emphasis added). For a cluster of shellmounds north of Berkeley, Nelson (1907:343–44) learned from local residents that Native people, "were seen in the vicinity camped on the banks of the San

Pablo and Wildcat Creeks, at places which . . . in 1853 they 'dressed in white mans (Spaniards) clothes, lived in brush shelters, and were very big, husky fellows.'" In 1897 outside Stockton, California, a father-and-son team collecting artifacts from an earthen mound met an Indian man "about fifty" who said he was born on the mound (Schenck and Dawson 1929:306–7). In still another example, a property owner living near a shellmound in east Contra Costa County in 1913 provided archaeologist Llewellyn L. Loud with the following history:

> There was a band of 40 or 50 Indians living on the mound in 1850. They worked for [Francisco Galindo and Salvio] Pacheco, two Spaniards who had the land around the mound. The informant C.B. Nottingham who settled [in] Walnut Creek in 1852 says there was an epidemic in 1853 and "I saw about 9 dead there at one time, dying off there all the time, I think most of the band died at that time." He saw these "Mount Diablo" Indians i.e. the survivors off and on for 10 years afterwards and a short time ago saw an old man & woman nearly blind at Clayton. He thinks they live in the hills beyond Clayton, & has a faint recollection that their name is Soto. Most of the band on this mound could speak Spanish . . . the Indians on this mound dug a hole 3 or 4 ft deep in the sloping side of the mound. Willow poles were stuck up around this hole so as to make a house 6 to 12 ft in diameter. The poles were covered with tule mats, or thatched with loose (unwoven) tule or grass, & daubed with mud. Besides a smoke hole at the top there was only one opening, the door on the lower side of the sloping mound. It was high enough to walk into by bending the body at right angles at the hips. (Loud 1913:25)

Why would a "band" of upwards of fifty Spanish-speaking Chupcan and Julpun (Bay Miwok) peoples choose to live on this mound? Wage laborers by day, contracted to Rancho Monte del Diablo (Pacheco's property) and probably other adjacent land grants straddling Carquinez Strait (Bancroft Library 184?a), they probably returned to the mound at night for storytelling, meals, rest, and other aspects of life unseen by foreign eyes to restore connections to kin and place. Requiring very specific bodily performances from its guests, even the mound reasserted its relevance via the memories and movements of those who engaged with the wisdom and history of this place.

The cluster of "Ynigo" mounds in Santa Clara County offers a similar example. Loud (1912:97–98) suspected that most of these shellmounds "were occupied by Indians at the time the Spanish came, although . . . excavation showed no sign of white contact except 4 or 5 sawed bones, the deepest being inches deep. The burial of Ynigo on the 'Smaller Ynigo Mound' might indicate a general custom of burial on the mounds at the time of the Spanish arrival." Loud evokes the name "Lope Inigo," an Ohlone man baptized at Mission Santa Clara. In a rare example of a California Indian who succeeded in securing land from the Mexican government after the secularization of the missions (Bancroft Library 1849), Inigo's Rancho Polsomi was especially dear to him. Among the rolling oak-studded hills and lush tidal marsh contained in Inigo's south San Francisco Bay land grant, several shellmounds held the remains of his ancestors and would eventually be Inigo's chosen resting place after his death in 1864 (Shoup and Milliken 1999).

Despite such compelling historical examples of populated and value-laden Indigenous hinterlands, archaeological evidence of such continuity has either been limited or dismissed. Evidence for postcontact histories of shellmound use include scattered examples of imported metal, glass, and other artifacts often found on top and in the upper layers of some shell-mounds. Examples include the British medallion found at the Sather mound on Alameda Island, a brick "of Spanish make" found on a Sausalito mound, and a Mesoamerican "three-legged metate" from the West Berkeley Shell-mound (Nelson 1909a:347), although most of the time these finds were dismissed as "intrusive" artifacts (Mann 2005). Accordingly, objects that do not gel with archaeologists' preconceptions of Indigenous technology are seen as anachronistic. Chronology is also conflated with ethnicity (Panich and Schneider 2019), as seen in the labeling of glass, metal, and ceramic "Caucasian artifacts" excavated from the precontact and postcontact Coast Miwok village site of Cotomko'tca (CA-MRN-138). Archaeologists labeled these materials as "intrusive" because they were viewed as incompatible with the assumed history of shellmounds. Their continued occupation threatened the very fabric of time.

Archaeologists, newspapers, and everyday citizens denied the coevalness of Indigenous lives and epistemologies through the piecemeal dismantlement of the Indigenous hinterland (Fabian 1983:31–35; see also Thrush 2007:8). Native people could not be contemporaries of settler states, and Indigenous history could not be untethered from prehistory. Yet, the seamless divide between modernity and a remote, prehistoric past guarded by missions becomes unstitched by still other archaeological finds at places like China Camp State Park and Toms Point and from examples of Native people dwelling within the very same landscape assumed to have been wiped clean of Indigeneity. Under the canopy of California bay and buckeye trees at China Camp, in the small piles of shell, earth, ash, and rock filling our archaeological sifting screens lay another rendering of time and place.

An Archaeology of Refuge

Almost three decades have passed since the 1992 Columbian Quincentenary when archaeologists started to look seriously at the diverse peoples and types of places and materials ensnared, transformed, preserved, and created anew in Indigenous-colonial encounters. As Patricia Rubertone (2000:435) advised, however, archaeology at places of contact and sites of colonization tends to overshadow theoretical and methodological approaches for studying "Native presence"—an admonishment that bears repeating. Recentering Indigenous hinterlands in the study of local responses to colonialism can recast formerly "vacant" landscapes as settings with history, memory, and empowerment and brings into focus a much wider array of places where Native people remained living and sought refuge. Archaeological studies of refuge stress the important role of places—entire continents broadly speaking, but also regions and individual sites—for protecting and sustaining threatened cultures and identities (Schneider 2015b; see also Bernard 2008; Bernard and Robinson 2018; Bernard et al. 2014). One obstacle for researching refuge has to do with the logistics of detecting places that were supposed to be undetectable. On this point, a fundamental challenge of locating and researching the hideouts of imperiled human groups is neither unique to California nor is it an insurmountable issue for archaeologists (e.g., Sayers 2014; Weik 1997). As I discuss later in this chapter, perhaps more difficult for an archaeology of refuge is overcoming the mindset, deeply engrained in American archaeology, that only certain places and artifacts can be counted as evidence of Indigenous presence.

China Camp's Layered History

I conducted archaeological field investigations at three shellmounds—CA-MRN-114, -115, and -328—in China Camp State Park, a 1,500-acre state park with a multilayered past. Created in 1977, the park is named for several Chinese shrimp fishing camps that operated on San Pablo Bay primarily between the mid-1860s to 1905. Before China Camp State Park, Point San Pedro was private property and part of the twenty-two thousand-acre Rancho San Pedro, Santa Margarita y las Gallinas land grant awarded to "Don" Timothy (or, Timoteo) Murphy in 1844 (Bancroft Library 184?b). After Murphy's death in 1853, the land grant was subdivided and sold to people like George McNear who leased land to ranchers, including W. H. Thomas, whose name archaeologists attached to the CA-MRN-115 site (i.e., the "Thomas site") in the mid-1900s. Historic ranch features, such as cement cisterns used to water livestock, are still present in the park.

The McNears also collected rent from Chinese families. As "enclaves as well as factories" (Brienes 1983:81–82), Chinese fishing communities on Point San Pedro made a living and found a sense of protection in their physical isolation from the violence and structural racism of Gilded Age California. In addition to contending with hardships associated with the Chinese Exclusion Act in 1882 and other discriminatory ordinances, Chinese communities faced daily threats to their fishing livelihood from boat "patrols" and exorbitant rents (e.g., London 2001 [1905]:1–9; Munro-Fraser 1880:347). Lending support to the view that Point San Pedro may have also provided seclusion and a space of refuge for colonized Indigenous communities, one historian comments that many Chinese camps at Point San Pedro were "relatively inaccessible except by water, and the shallow depth of the bay at low tides made even that route into a sea of muck . . . access to and from the outside world was almost completely dependent upon boats" (Brienes 1983:81).

Before Rancho San Pedro, Santa Margarita y las Gallinas, the land was home to Coast Miwok people. This unceded Indigenous land was appropriated into the private domain of Mission San Rafael with its establishment in 1817. As an asistencia, or sub-mission and hospital, for Mission Dolores, Mission San Rafael was originally populated by an estimated 230 Coast Miwok people transplanted from Missions San José and Dolores (Milliken 2009:31). Mission San Rafael served another purpose: to recruit additional Coast Miwok and Southern Pomo people and, by doing so, lay claim to lands north of the Golden Gate increasingly encroached upon by the Russian Empire.

To the consternation of Spanish officials, Native Alaskan hunting parties originating from the Russian mercantile colony of Ross (established in 1812 less than one hundred miles to the north) frequently entered San Francisco Bay to hunt sea otter (Milliken 1995:201–2). Sandwiched between Colony Ross and New Spain, the Marin Peninsula—supposedly emptied of Coast Miwok people by 1803—transitioned from a blank canvas to a borderland. While two imperial powers vied for influence over this landscape (and both would ultimately fail to keep California), it remained a space continually inhabited, resorted to, and reimagined by Native people as evidenced by the accounts of foreign visitors. In a reversal of the idea of a vacant Indigenous landscape, the region between Mission San Rafael and Colony Ross according to one traveler in 1822 was "entirely uninhabited by Europeans" but home to the tents of "several unhappy fugitives from Mission San Rafael" and still other Indians "sent out . . . to capture [these] fugitives" (Farris 2012:111). Sailing past Point San Pedro in 1811 Father Ramon Abella also observed five communities that were "still heathen" (Cook 1960:261)—a reference either to extant villages or the encampments of refugees.

CA-MRN-115 is the largest of the three shellmounds I investigated at China Camp. It measures approximately 5 meters tall, 30 meters east-west, 45 meters north-south; the mound covers an area of approximately 1,060 square meters. Two smaller shellmounds—CA-MRN-114 and -328—are situated a few meters north and south of CA-MRN-115 on two natural hillslopes, and all together these three sites form a conspicuous shellmound cluster (see chapter 1). CA-MRN-114 covers an area of approximately 490 square meters, and CA-MRN-328 reaches approximately 824 square meters. This cluster of three mounds is adjacent to a freshwater spring—a permanent water source— less than 50 meters from saltwater marsh.

The history of archaeological study of the three shellmounds is brief. Before I arrived, in fact, the only archaeological research conducted since the park's establishment focused on extant buildings and processing features associated with the Chinese fishing community (Schulz 1988; Schulz and Lortie 1985). CA-MRN-328 was first identified when China Camp State Park was established in the 1970s and, until my research, it had never been studied. In the early 1900s before the park existed, Nels Nelson (1907) recorded "Shellmound No. 115" and "Shellmound No. 114" during his archaeological survey of San Francisco Bay shellmounds. He mapped both sites and described their dimensions, states of preservation, and associated features, including "indications of pits on the top" of CA-MRN-115. Under the auspices of the University of California Archaeological Survey (UCAS), Clement Meighan directed archaeological excavations at CA-MRN-115 in April and May 1949. A student of Robert Heizer at UC Berkeley, Meighan (1953) and a small crew excavated twelve five-by-five-foot units at the south end of the mound; five auger units placed systematically at five-foot intervals running south from the mound; and one pit feature on top of the mound, which was found to be the remains of a semi-subterranean conical bark house (figure 9).

Five-by-five-foot units—considered oversized by today's standards—or the excavation of a single trench through the center of other shellmounds was common practice, since UCAS and most archaeology in California at the time was largely geared toward amassing archaeological data that could then be used to construct distinct regional chronologies. Larger mounds with deeply stratified deposits and Native American burials, which often contained diagnostic (time-sensitive) materials like beads and projectile points, were frequently targeted. Much of this work was also conducted expeditiously and, at the time, screens and shovels were used, but not with regularity. Shovel broadcasting, in which sediment is shoveled and then strewn across the ground surface to expose larger artifacts, was widely practiced. Screens

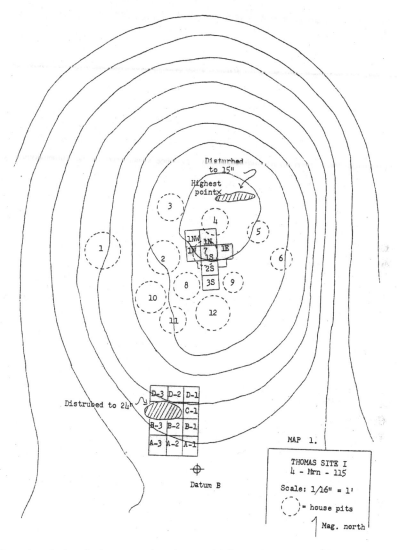

FIGURE 9 Archaeologists mapped twelve circular depressions on top of CA-MRN-115 in 1949, including one (labeled "No. 7") confirmed through excavation as the remains of a conical bark structure. Reproduced from Meighan (1953:15) with permission from the Archaeological Research Facility, University of California, Berkeley.

were used "as a check only," since they were considered "a [poor] reflection on one's archaeological ability" (Meighan 1950:15). Given this context, on the one hand it's not surprising to learn that only fifty-four objects (about 10 percent of the five hundred items collected from CA-MRN-115 in 1949) have X, Y, Z provenience information. On the other hand, Meighan also prepared meticulous notes and field drawings, collected soil samples, and remarkably sampled charcoal from CA-MRN-115 for radiocarbon dating—the first archaeological site in California to produce radiometric dates (Libby 1955). It was cutting-edge research in an era of destructive archaeological practice.

Bone tools, ground stone implements, and flaked obsidian and chert artifacts collected by Meighan are commonly found in San Francisco Bay shellmounds. Other materials collected from CA-MRN-115, however, are quite uncommon when compared to artifact assemblages from other shellmounds. Unique to CA-MRN-115 are burned wood house planks, grass thatching, the charred remains of four baskets, and a five-sided abalone ornament and a corner-notched obsidian projectile point that are diagnostic of the Late Period Phase 2 and after (Meighan 1953). Diagnostic artifacts, stratigraphic observations, and radiocarbon dates led Meighan (1953:6) to conclude that CA-MRN-115 was abandoned by about 1800, and that "it is possible that the occupants of this village were taken to one of the Spanish missions." Revisiting this hypothesis sixty years later, my project entailed two core components. First, to reduce the amount of destructive archaeological excavation at three culturally sensitive and exceedingly rare and well-preserved shellmound sites, I reanalyzed the 1949 artifact assemblage from CA-MRN-115 housed at UC Berkeley's Phoebe A. Hearst Museum of Anthropology (or, the Hearst Museum). This collection consists of over five hundred artifacts (stone tools, animal bone, antler and bone tools, and charred plant remains) and several soil samples, which I did not study. Second, I chose to augment my collections-based research with minimally invasive archaeological investigations at CA-MRN-114, -115, and -328 to further explore when Indigenous Coast Miwok occupied these places. How recently, in other words, did Coast Miwok people live at the shellmounds and what did they do there? These may be deceptively simple questions, but they are questions that have never been asked of a California shellmound.

China Camp Archaeological Project

Archaeological field investigations at China Camp in 2007 and 2008 involved a phased approach in which different stages of field research—survey, mapping, surface collection, and excavation—occurred only after sharing the results of the previous stage and receiving input on the proposed work from the Federated Indians of Graton Rancheria, my primary community partner (Schneider 2010). In addition to soliciting input on a research design and field methods, collaboration involved periodic meetings with Graton Rancheria's Sacred Sites Protection Committee (SSPC)—the volunteer committee of tribal citizens, at the time, primarily responsible for making decisions about the protection and study of cultural resources in our ancestral territory encompassing Marin and southern Sonoma County. At SSPC meetings, we discussed findings and interpretations and created a treatment plan for the inadvertent discovery of human remains. Explicit avoidance of human remains required a carefully orchestrated research strategy involving geophysical survey and the thoughtful placement of excavation units altogether aimed at maximizing the amount of information that could be gathered from each site while minimizing my destructive archaeological footprint.

With permission and support from Graton Rancheria's SSPC, archaeological fieldwork involved digital mapping to produce a high-definition surface model of all three shellmounds (figure 10), especially the numerous depressions—house pits and unfilled excavation units from 1949—covering the surface of CA-MRN-115 (Schneider and Panich 2008). With digital map in hand, the next stage of fieldwork involved the collection of surface artifacts from the three sites to help define activity areas based on concentrations of different material classes (e.g., flaked stone debitage, thermally altered rocks, etc.) and to pinpoint potential areas for further study. At this point, my community partners and I decided to focus attention on CA-MRN-114 and -328.

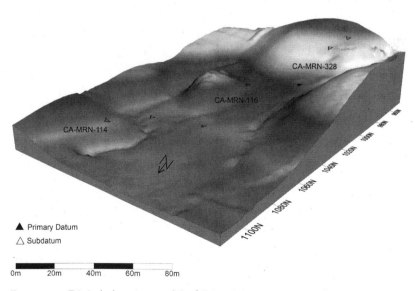

FIGURE 10 Digital elevation model of CA-MRN-114, -115, and -328. Sites CA-MRN-114 and -328 are on top of two natural hillslopes. The CA-MRN-115 mound is constructed by human hands.

CA-MRN-115 would be researched using the surface artifact collection and the 1949 assemblage stored at the Hearst Museum.

The third stage of field research involved geophysical survey at CA-MRN-114 using a magnetometer and an electrical resistivity/conductivity instrument designed to target near-surface archaeological features for further testing or, in the case of human burials, avoidance. With assistance from Dr. Rob Cuthrell, four hundred square meters of CA-MRN-114 was first surveyed with a Geometrics 858 "MagMapper" cesium gradiometer/magnetometer. This instrument is used to identify areas of magnetic susceptibility and other features such as burials, buried architecture, hearths, and artifacts (e.g., ferrous metal, fired clay, and some lithics). Visualizing the magnetometer data using a mapping software package revealed at least eight magnetic features, which I interpreted to be discrete clusters of iron-rich rock piled together by Native people to create earth ovens or hearths. In the following field season, we surveyed an even smaller fifty-four-square-meter area of CA-MRN-114 using an Advanced Geophysics Inc. "Mini Sting" Earth Resistivity/Induced Polarization Meter. This instrument transmits electrical signals into the ground and measures the rate of their return as a proxy for identifying the depth of subsurface archaeological sediments and features (electrical currents travel slower through porous, or "resistive," sediments and faster through moisture-laden, or "conductive," sediments). The resulting electrical resistivity/conductivity map provided an even more precise sense for the sizes and locations of underground archaeological features, including the interface between the overlaying shellmound and underlying bedrock at approximately 1.5 meters below the ground surface.

Using the results of the surface collections, mapping, and geophysical surveys, the fourth stage of fieldwork involved excavations of two one-by-one-meter units at CA-MRN-114 (unit 1080N-1056E and unit 1078N-1056E) and a total of fifty-five auger units at CA-MRN-114 and -328. Of the two excavation units excavated at CA-MRN-114, the electrical resistivity/conductivity data proved especially promising after placing an excavation unit (1078N-1056E) on top of one feature detected during the survey. Excavation in this unit revealed not one but two buried features: a semicircular (i.e., U-shaped in profile) rock-lined hearth ("Feature 1") comprised of thermally altered rock, ash, charcoal, and shell at approximately twenty to forty-five centimeters below the ground surface and an associated ash rake-out ("Feature 2") at approximately twenty to thirty-five centimeters below the ground surface. Both features were collected whole for flotation and paleoethnobotanical analyses.

Auger excavations helped determine the vertical and horizontal extents of both sites and track general changes in soil types and archaeological constituents (e.g., shellfish species, types and quantities of lithic debitage, etc.) over time and across space. Auger units—totaling twenty-nine at CA-MRN-114 and twenty-six at CA-MRN-328—measured four-inches in diameter and were drilled in twenty-centimeter levels until reaching bedrock (anywhere from 20 to 150 centimeters deep, unless a large root or rock impeded excavation). Six auger units at CA-MRN-114 and five units at CA-MRN-328 were not screened. Instead, sediments from these six units were bagged in twenty-centimeter increments and then archived as soil samples.

Artifacts collected from the three shellmounds were cleaned, identified, measured, and cataloged in the lab. Basic artifact classes represented in the China Camp assemblage include botanical, faunal, lithic, and mass-produced items (Schneider 2010:87–138). Within each material class, subcategories further distinguish material types, artifact types, and classes for animal bone and shell (i.e., mammal, bird, fish, invertebrate, amphibian, and reptile). Looking over the bits of shell, rock, flecks of charcoal, and chert debitage, however, I did not immediately recognize anything that matched the types of materials often collected from colonial period sites. Mass-produced items collected from the three shellmounds—objects of metal, glass, and pottery introduced to California with Euro-American colonization—included several pieces of green and brown bottle glass, ferrous metal (five iron cut nails, an iron tack, and a sanitary can), and thirty-one spent bullet cartridge casings of various calibers. Even the two porcelain fragments collected from CA-MRN-115 by Clement Meighan—a small fragment with a floral decal and the base of a Japanese rice bowl, transfer printed in the style referred to as "dashed line"—and the six pieces of salt-glazed stoneware (often used for storage containers) I collected from CA-MRN-114 are most likely associated with late nineteenth-century Chinese families who lived and worked in the vicinity (Costello and Maniery 1987; Felton et al. 1984). There were no *tejas* or *ladrillos* (roof and floor tiles common to Spanish colonial architecture). No majolica (colorful lead-glazed earthenware). No religious medallions. No glass beads. No massive cow bones and no metal tools used to cleave the carcasses of mission livestock.

However, the lithic, shell, botanical, and faunal materials I collected are common in archaeological assemblages from Spanish colonies in California, and they are also described in colonial records (e.g., Allen 1998; Arkush 2011; Cuthrell et al. 2016; Geiger and Meighan 1976; Hull and Voss 2016; Panich 2014, 2015; Popper 2016; Reddy 2015; Schneider 2021; Schneider et al. 2018; Voss 2008). Still other items caught my attention: a sea otter bone that had been purposefully scored and snapped, clamshell disk beads, the pentagonal abalone ornament, and obsidian projectile points diagnostic of the Late Period Phase 2 (1510–1770 CE). These calling cards, in other words, reflected Indigenous peoples who visited the shellmounds at least during the last two hundred years before missionization commenced and, as I discuss below, for some period of time afterward. A surprising story of continuity and change central to Indigenous peoples' responses to colonialism—and fundamental to characterizing the hinterlands and places where they visited—was initially concealed by a noticeable absence of evidence (in this case, common colonial-era artifact types), or an analytical framework in archaeology that uncritically segregates "prehistoric" and "historic" time periods, artifacts, and sites. To capture these ideas, the three China Camp assemblages would require a deeper level of analysis.

China Camp Artifact Assemblages

Archaeological assemblages from CA-MRN-114, -115, and -328 provide a rare glimpse of life in a colonial-era hinterland and, more specifically, the long-term role that some shellmounds and material traditions may have played for Indigenous peoples seeking familiar ground in a time of uncertainty. Analysis of botanical remains, faunal bone and shell, and lithic artifacts showcase the continuities and adjustments taking place within Indigenous communities and across the Marin Peninsula.

Archaeobotanical Remains

Archaeobotanists identified several plant species Coast Miwok people used as sources of food, medicine, and raw material. Among the 196 macrobotanical elements (nutshell, seeds, fruits, and other remains) identified in the hearth feature (Feature 1) at CA-MRN-114 and -385, macrobotanical elements identified in the adjacent ashy feature (Feature 2) are the remains of oak (*Quercus* sp.), manzanita (*Arctostaphylos* sp.), and California bay (*Umbellularia californica*)—trees that produce nuts or berries savored by Indigenous Coast Miwok people before and after colonization (e.g., Collier and Thalman 1996:119–24). Peppernuts (from California bay), for example, were parched, pounded, and made into cakes or simply roasted, a technique that produced an aroma Coast Miwok elder Maria Copa likened to the smell of toasted cocoa (Collier and Thalman 1996:146). Many plant and animal taxa would have also served multiple purposes and, while some plants were frequently sought after for nuts, berries, seeds, bulbs, corms, and leafy greens, they might also be collected and processed for construction material and medicines (see Lightfoot and Parrish 2009).

Several plants have multiple uses. Many grasses, for example, produce edible seeds as well as raw material for creating baskets and medicines (e.g., Amaranthaceae, *Atriplex* sp., *Chenopodium* spp., Poaceae, and *Trifolium* sp.). Lieutenant Ayala and crew, after piloting the *San Carlos* through the Golden Gate in 1775, anchored at Angel Island and interacted with Coast Miwok ambassadors bearing gifts of fish, shellfish, and pinole (Milliken 1995:42). Goosefoot (*Chenopodium* spp.) seeds may represent food remains, but the seeds of some species were also transformed into poultices (Silliman 2004:17). *Trifolium* sp. (clover) seeds were a highly regarded part of the Coast Miwok diet (Collier and Thalman 1996:120–21) and although the plant was introduced to California, a native species, *Trifolium amoenum* (Showy Indian clover), was rediscovered in northern Marin County in 1996 and has been the focus of replanting efforts coordinated with Graton Rancheria. Some grasses, such as Cyperaceae (sedges) and Poaceae represented at CA-MRN-114, would have also been collected to create floor mats, thatched objects, and baskets (Collier and Thalman 1996:190; Lightfoot et al. 2009:219)—all items astonishingly preserved and collected from CA-MRN-115.

Charred plant remains from CA-MRN-115 include several pieces of burned wood planks, fragments of charred basketry, and "grass thatching" all collected from Meighan's pit feature ("House Pit 7"). Meighan (1953:3) counted twenty-four pieces of either redwood (*Sequoia sempervirens*) or oak (*Quercus* spp.) and estimated that these fragments were the remains of planks used to construct conical bark homes. Unfortunately, sixty years of museum storage further splintered the wood fragments and transformed the grass thatching collected from CA-MRN-115 into a mass of charcoal dust. Although no analysis was conducted on the thatched remains, tule and rushes are likely candidates since these plant taxa could be woven into openwork baskets, clothing, bedding, and door coverings (Collier and Thalman 1996:178). Indeed, evidence for plant use also comes indirectly from several fired clay chunks collected from CA-MRN-115. These unassuming objects have plant impressions from when wet clay was applied to the interior of bark homes as "plaster" to waterproof them—a technique, Tom Smith recalled, that also made bark houses last longer than grass-covered homes (Collier and Thalman 1996:178).

Excavations in House Pit 7 also yielded the remains of four plain and diagonal twined baskets (figure 11d). Only rarely and under exceptional preservation conditions do organic remains endure in the San Francisco Bay Area archaeological record. Burned and crushed under collapsed wood planks and then buried in alkaline shell midden soils, the four nested baskets were removed from the house floor at a depth of fourteen inches below the ground surface. The wood planks, Meighan (1953:2) also noted, were collected from a depth of twelve to eighteen inches, slightly below and above the baskets suggesting they may have been neatly stored, perhaps hanging, inside the house. Basket expert Ralph Shanks (2006:86–88) believes the charred remains contain split sedge "roots," a common medium for many California Indian basket weavers to this day, and that all forty-four fragments are plain and diagonal twined with evidence of designs. Coast Miwok people used a wide assortment of baskets including acorn baskets, cooking baskets, seed baskets, sifters, hoppers, storage baskets, and cradles for a variety of tasks. To weave baskets like those found at CA-MRN-115, Coast Miwok people cultivated encyclopedic knowledge about the uses and seasonal lifecycles of plants. They also maintained plant beds and other resource collecting grounds using fire and other management strategies; they crafted other tools such as fine-pointed bone awls; and weavers honored important collecting protocols and processing techniques to be able to construct baskets as functional tools, works of art, and perhaps most of all symbols of their precious connection to the physical and metaphysical worlds around them (Collier and Thalman 1996:155; Lightfoot and Parrish 2009; Shanks 2006:87–88).

Archaeological Faunas

Turning to the faunal assemblages from CA-MRN-114, -115, and -328, zooarchaeologists identified the remains of terrestrial mammal, sea mammal, bird, fish, reptile, amphibian, and invertebrate (bivalve, gastropod, and crustacean) species. Faunal bone and shell are an important reflection of past human diets and peoples' relationships to varied redwood forest, oak woodland, grassland, tidal marsh, and bay habitats. Yet, in the counting and weighing of the many thousands of fragments of mussel, oyster, and clam shells, barnacle fragments, and crab claws; pondering the eerie dental plates of California bat ray and the vertebrae from numerous fishes, including salmon, sturgeon, and shark (broadnose sevengill, Pacific angelshark, and leopard sharks); carefully handling the delicate bones of ducks, geese, cormorants, and smaller shorebirds; and touching the bones of both terrestrial mammals—including, deer, pronghorn, coyote, rabbit, and other small game—and sea mammals (sea otter and harbor seal), one reflects on the ingenuity of Native peoples. Consider the technology necessary to hunt, fish, trap, and collect terrestrial, marine, and avian creatures; the skill required to process a catch and prepare it in a palatable way; and the genius—equally fundamental to gathering, tending,

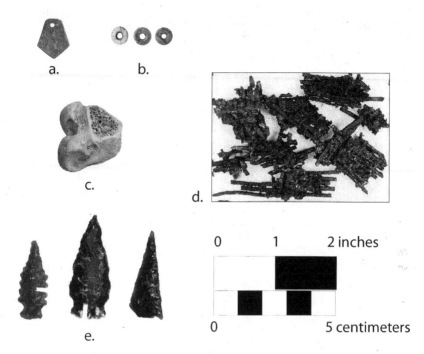

FIGURE 11 Materials collected from the three China Camp shellmounds, include: (a.) a five-sided abalone ornament from CA-MRN-115; (b.) clamshell disk beads from CA-MRN-114 (left) and CA-MRN-328 (center and right); (c.) a sea otter bone with cut marks and (d.) charred basketry from CA-MRN-115; and (e.) obsidian projectile points from CA-MRN-115 ("Rattlesnake" type at right) and CA-MRN-328 ("Stockton" series points at left and center). Note: both projectile points from CA-MRN-328 show cuts from obsidian hydration analysis.

and transforming plants to create food, medicine, tools, and construction material—of knowing when and where to acquire those species. As Franciscan padres at Mission Dolores admitted:

> [Native people] know spring by the appearance of flowers; they know summer because the grasses dry and seeds mature; they know fall because the wild geese and ducks appear and the acorns ripen. Winter they recognize because of the rainfall. . . . They eat whatever they wish if there is anything at hand. In their pagan state they did no other work than to look for food and this they did when the best opportunity was at hand. They look for roots and seeds during the day but they prefer to go hunting for ducks and to go fishing at night because the sea is quieter and the ducks

are congregated in greater number in the lagoons and estuaries. They rest after they have obtained what they want or when they believe nothing further is to be had. (Geiger and Meighan 1976:84)

An example of Indigenous skill and adaptability comes from a single modified bone—a femoral condyle—from a sea otter (*Enhydra lutris*) that was collected from CA-MRN-115 in 1949. Although sea otters in San Francisco Bay were hunted for meat, fur, and bone tools for at least one thousand years before Euro-American contact and colonization (Hildebrandt and Jones 1992:382; Simons 1992:74–75, 87), the bone artifact from CA-MRN-115 dates to a different period of time. Razor-straight cut marks around the femur suggest that the animal carcass was processed using a specific technique for removing the pelt (figure 11c). "Scored and snapped" much like the sea otter bones excavated from the Native Alaskan village site at Colony Ross (Wake 1997:273–74), the modified sea otter bone elicits reflection on Indigenous peoples' colonial-era adaptations of traditional ecological knowledge.

Hunting associated with the North American maritime fur trade fueled the overexploitation and eventual extirpation of sea otters from northern California waters (San Francisco Bay north to Trinidad Bay) by 1820, and market demand encouraged radically altered hunting practices of Indigenous laborers increasingly dependent on the fur trade for an assortment of manufactured goods (Lightfoot et al. 2013:108–11). As early as 1803 and before the establishment of Colony Ross in 1812, Native Alaskan hunters contracted to the Russian-American Company or American Merchants and settlers like Don Timoteo Murphy (see Potter 1942) hunted in San Francisco Bay, usually after portaging across the Marin Peninsula from camps at Tomales and Bodega Bays (Milliken 1995:201–2). Seeing an opportunity to acquire sorely needed resources, Franciscan missionaries also enlisted California Indian sea otter hunters and sold pelts to be able to purchase supplies for missions (Hackel 2005:277–79; see also Mathes 2008:40). A single bone can speak volumes. In this case, it speaks of a landscape populated by Indigenous people with persistent and adaptable knowledge of the natural world.

Similar to plants, many animals had multiple uses. A haul of clam and abalone provides a tasty meal. Their shells could also be transformed into beads and ornaments. A chunk of red abalone (*Haliotis rufescens*) shell collected from the surface of CA-MRN-328 and a five-sided abalone ornament collected from House Pit 7 (CA-MRN-115) more strongly reflect the nondietary uses of this animal, especially because abalone does not live in the San Francisco Bay and would have been brought to the shellmounds from the Pacific coast. For millennia, Native peoples of California transformed lustrous abalone shell into ornaments of various shapes, beads, and, in some places, fishhooks (Gifford 1947). The pentagonal ornament found on the floor of the excavated house pit may have once adorned a necklace, basket, or another item. The unique "keystone" shape first appears archaeologically during the Late Period Phase 2 (figure 11a). Among an entourage of international guests touring Mission San José in 1806, Georg Heinrich von Langsdorff also illustrated five-sided abalone ornaments among the possessions of Indigenous residents, and the ornament type can be seen adorning baskets and dance regalia documented by anthropologists in the early 1900s (Gifford 1947:123; Heizer 1941b:110–11).

Two clamshell disk beads were also collected from the surface of CA-MRN-328, and one clam bead was later found in the small CA-MRN-114 collection at the Hearst Museum (figure 11b). The three clam beads were made from another nonlocal species, Washington clam (*Saxidomus nuttalli*). Clam beads are unique to the Late Period Phase 2, when the production of disk beads rapidly accelerated (Milliken et al. 2007:117), and afterward, when Coast Miwok communities continued to produce and use clam beads as ornaments and money during the nineteenth and twentieth century. Described as "our money" by Coast Miwok ethnographic informant Tom Smith at Bodega Bay in the early 1900s (Collier and Thalman 1996:196), clam beads maintained a prominent role in the lives of Coast Miwok people well after the missions ceased operating (see also Gamble and Zepeda 2002). Though glass beads filtered into Indigenous shell bead economies and ritual practices (Panich and Schneider 2015), many people continued to make, exchange, and wear only shell beads.

Lithics

Casting more light on the technological and ceremonial practices at this shell-mound group, the lithic assemblage of over 2,800 artifacts includes thermally altered rock, ground stone tools, and flaked stone tools and debitage. Over 90 percent of the lithic artifacts are thermally altered rocks or the angular remnants of heated rocks. Blackened by charcoal and ash and shattered by countless fires, such as the fires once contained within Feature 1 at CA-MRN-114, thermally altered rocks are ubiquitous in shellmounds. Many of the ground stone tools—mostly fragments of once-heftier pestles, bowl mortars, hand stones, and other equipment—were collected from CA-MRN-115 in 1949. These unassuming tools are, on the one hand, additional reminders of the countless domestic tasks that took place at shellmounds, the "kitchens" so to speak that helped sustain the community. On the other hand, items like a steatite pipe bowl collected from CA-MRN-328 might best reflect normally unseen (to archaeologists) recreational and/or ritual activities conducted at this place. Steatite pipes appear in greater frequency during the Late Period, and a reed mouthpiece for inhaling smoke would have been attached to the stone bowl. Tom Smith vividly recalled smoking this way: "The first time I smoked with other boys. We went in the sweathouse . . . one man there had a pipe. All the boys tried it. I got drunk, couldn't walk straight" (Collier and Thalman 1996:152). Smith's memory adds texture to the idea of shellmounds as "full-service" mounded villages and not simply refuse heaps (Luby et al. 2006:196–97).

Rounding out the lithic analysis, still other items help narrate the history of CA-MRN-114, -115, and -328 during an era of change. Native people in California created flaked stone tools from obsidian, chert, and other tool stones through flintknapping, a highly skilled "reduction" technique involving percussion and pressure flaking to create projectile points, knives, and other cutting implements. Typological (stage of reduction) and attribute (metrics and morphology) analyses of over two hundred flaked stone artifacts—including debitage (angular shatter and bifacial thinning flakes), cores, core tools, flake tools, and bifacial tools—indicate that lithic reduction techniques transformed over the course of the site's occupation. Specifically, the preparation of cores and the relative ease of access to regional obsidian sources earlier in time (i.e., Middle Period) seems to shift toward the production of expedient chert tools and the use of bipolar reduction on small obsidian nodules later in time (i.e., Late Period and after). While direct access to Napa obsidian had declined long before 1776 (see Schneider et al. 2014), a second explanation for the decline in obsidian tool stone and upswing of chert tool production, explored more below, may have to do with the alteration of regional obsidian exchange networks during the late 1700s (Farris 1989:492). At this time, reduced access to obsidian may have forced Coast Miwok flintknappers to make do with local raw material (i.e., chert) and possibly even rework stone tools cached within shellmounds, a pattern Kathleen Hull and Barbara Voss (2016) document at the Spanish-colonial Presidio of San Francisco. Strategies for maximizing limited resources—such as bipolar percussion on fewer and smaller obsidian nodules and the process of heating chert to make it more workable—may have become more widely practiced among several individuals with an increasingly wide range of flintknapping experience.

Bifacial tools add to this picture. Eleven of the twelve bifacially worked lithic artifacts collected from the three shellmounds are obsidian and, of them, nine were collected from CA-MRN-115, and two obsidian tools (both projectile points) were collected from CA-MRN-328. Six large, bipointed and lanceolate (or, leaf-shaped) obsidian bifaces from CA-MRN-115 could have been manufactured during the Early Period or Middle Period or anytime from approximately 4450 to 1450 BP (Justice 2002:266, 271). This lengthy precontact production history should not overlook the importance of these objects more recently in time, as evidenced by a lanceolate obsidian biface accompanying the doctoring kit of a Coast Miwok elder (Kelly 1978:420). Of the three projectile points (a specific type of bifacial tool) Meighan collected from CA-MRN-115, two are unprovenienced, and one "tanged" point was found during the house pit excavation. This "Rattlesnake" point—a triangular, corner-notched projectile point style used for arrows—could have been manufactured during the Late Period or colonial era when Coast Miwok people still manufactured corner-notched points from obsidian and discarded bottle glass (Justice 2002:403; King and Upson 1970:166; Slaymaker 1977). Two additional projectile points were collected from the surface and upper twenty centimeters of CA-MRN-328. These two "Stockton" series points also date to the Late Period and colonial-era (Justice 2002:353–59), an observation explored more below using elemental analysis (figure 11e).

Weaving a Landscape of Continuity and Change

Accelerator mass spectrometry (AMS) radiocarbon dating, X-ray fluorescence (XRF) analysis and obsidian hydration dating of obsidian artifacts, and a seasonality study of archaeological marine shells add further details about the tempo and nature of shellmound visits by Indigenous peoples before, during, and after contact and colonization. For several reasons, the analytical methods I selected are unusual choices for researching postcontact Indigenous history. For one, although radiocarbon dating has been around since the 1950s, instrumentation advances since then have improved the accuracy of radiocarbon dating and, even now, archaeologists are continuing to improve chronometric dating through advancements in high-precision AMS dating with enhanced statistical modeling (e.g., Holland-Lulewicz et al. 2020). Kent Lightfoot (1995) identified another meddlesome issue for North American archaeology years ago: prehistorians and historical archaeologists tend to operate on either side of an arbitrary disciplinary divide that inhibits the integration of methods and analyses associated with each domain that might otherwise help interpret long-term Indigenous histories before, during, and after contact with Euro-American colonizers. Still another troubling issue reinforcing that scholarly divide: taking evidence at face value. Relying strictly on the letters and records of Franciscan missionaries and their claims to authority, one might assume that Native people were not living at remote shellmound refuges. Scanning artifact assemblages for specific material types, archaeologists have also systematically ruled out many sites as possible postcontact Indigenous places based solely on the absence of introduced metal, glass, and pottery (Panich and Schneider 2019). Reading against the grain, applying a diverse set of research methods, and comparing multiple forms of evidence help weave a landscape of continuity and change.

Clement Meighan and Robert Heizer submitted two charcoal samples for radiocarbon dating—a first for California archaeology in the early 1950s. Characteristic of radiocarbon dating at the time, the charcoal fragments were collected from the deepest and presumably oldest layers of CA-MRN-115. Larger sample size requirements meant extracting charcoal from two different depths (108 and 114–32 inches), which produced two dates (i.e., 633 ± 200 BP and 911 ± 80 BP; Libby 1955:112). These dates were then averaged to produce a mean radiocarbon age of 720 ± 130 BP, or 1035–1432 cal CE (two-sigma, or 95 percent probability) (Meighan 1953:5), suggesting occupation of CA-MRN-115 at least during the Middle/Late Period Transition (ca. 940–740 BP).

Augmenting Meighan's findings, I analyzed eight additional AMS radiocarbon samples from the three shellmounds (Schneider 2010). I collected two samples from the bottom of CA-MRN-114's Feature 1. These samples produced conventional radiocarbon ages of 380 ± 40 BP and 640 ± 40 BP, or two-sigma calibrated calendar ages of 1440–1640 and 1480–1680 cal CE respectively. Additional samples from levels above and below this feature produced conventional radiocarbon dates of 870 ± 40 BP, or 1650–1880 cal CE (above Feature 1), and 1870 ± 40 BP, or 700–940 cal CE (below Feature 1). Radiocarbon samples from CA-MRN-328 produced conventional ages of 940 ± 40 BP (1540–1720, 1740–1750, and 1790–1800 cal CE) and 870 ± 40 BP (1650–1880 cal CE).

I received permission from Graton Rancheria and the Hearst Museum to also gather radiocarbon samples from charred basketry and wood plank fragments collected from the excavated house pit at CA-MRN-115 in 1949. A carefully snipped 251-milligram fragment of basketry returned a conventional radiocarbon age of 280 ± 40 BP (1490–1670 and 1780–1790 cal CE). A 226-milligram sample removed from a wood plank fragment produced a conventional age of 260 ± 40 BP (1520–1590, 1620–1670, 1770–1800, and 1940–1950 cal CE). Importantly, the baskets and wood planks were not collected from the top of CA-MRN-115, as Meighan carefully noted. Archaeologists excavating down to the house floor measured at least twelve inches of refuse and an undisturbed shell lens above the floor, "that cannot all be attributed to fill from the raised margins of the [house] pit" and may, in fact, reflect reuse of the house later in time (Meighan 1953:4). Meighan's observation reflects a pattern documented in other regions of North America where the nearly imperceptible signatures of mobile Indigenous peoples—their continued presence within colonized landscapes assumed to be empty of Native people—are either missed entirely or concealed in the process of calibrating radiocarbon dates with wide margins of error (e.g., Seymour 2010:172–73, 2017). Together with three obsidian hydration dates discussed next, the six AMS determinations suggest occupation of the three shellmounds during the Late Period Phase 2 and mission period (table 1).

With permission from Graton Rancheria's SSPC, I also collected obsidian hydration dates and conducted a source provenance study. For northern California, obsidian hydration is a proven, albeit destructive, technique for obtaining relative calendar dates from obsidian artifacts by measuring the water absorption rate of volcanic glass. After removing a small section of the outer edge of an artifact, the microscopic hydration band, or the outer "rind" that is formed after freshly knapped obsidian begins absorbing atmospheric moisture, is measured in microns and then calibrated to produce a calendar date (Origer 1982). Of the eight items submitted for analysis (table 2), three

Table 1 Summary of AMS radiocarbon assays from China Camp State Park (CA-MRN-114, -115, and -328).

Site (MRN-)	Sample No.[a]	Material	Depth (cm)	ΔR	14C Age (BP)	2σ Cal Age Ranges (CE)	2σ Cal Median Age (CE)[b]
114	Beta-254226	charcoal	20–45	. . .	380 ± 40	1440–1640	1512
114	Beta-254227	shell	20–45	300 ± 35	1020 ± 40	1480–1680	1584
114	Beta-254228	shell	20–40	300 ± 35	870 ± 40	1650–1880	1754
114	Beta-254229	Shell	80–100	300 ± 35	1870 ± 40	700–940	820
115	Beta-250547	basketry[c]	35.6	. . .	280 ± 40	1490–1670, 1780–1790	1580
115	Beta-250548	charcoal[c]	30–45	. . .	260 ± 40	1520–1590, 1620–1670, 1770–1800, 1940–1950	1641
328	Beta-254230	shell	20–40	300 ± 35	940 ± 40	1540–1720, 1740–1750, 1790–1800	1662
328	Beta-254231	shell	120–140	300 ± 35	870 ± 40	1650–1880	1754

[a] Beta Analytic Inc. (Beta) radiocarbon dates funded by a William Self Associates Fellowship.

[b] Median probability ages calculated using Calib 7.1 online radiocarbon calibration program (Stuiver et al. 2020).

[c] Material excavated from CA-MRN-115 in 1949 (Meighan 1953).

Table 2 Summary of obsidian hydration dates from China Camp State Park (CA-MRN-114, -115, and -328).

Site (MRN-)	Sample No.	Obsidian Type	Depth (cm)	Hydration Mean (microns)	Age (BP)	Calendar Age (CE)
114	1	Annadel	surface	...	...	...
114	2	Napa	surface	1.2	221	1788
114	3	Annadel	0–20	1.4	503	1506
114	4	Annadel	30–40	...	...	...
115	5	Napa	surface	...	...	...
328	6	Annadel	0–20	...	...	...
328	7	Annadel	surface	...	...	...
328	8	Napa	20–40	0.9	124	1885

obsidian samples—including two artifacts collected from the surface of CA-MRN-114 and zero to twenty centimeters, and one artifact from twenty to forty centimeters at CA-MRN-328—produced measurable hydration bands of 1.2, 1.4, and 0.9 microns, which calibrate to 221 BP (1788 CE), 503 BP (1506 CE), and 124 BP (1885 CE) for the specimen from CA-MRN-328. A measurement of 1.4 microns corresponds to the Late Period Phase 2; hydration bands of ≤ 1.2 microns fall within San Francisco Bay's colonial era (see Panich et al. 2018a).

XRF is another analytical technique I applied to obsidian artifacts from China Camp. In this nondestructive technique, samples are irradiated with high-energy X-rays, which excite electrons and cause them to eject from atoms within the obsidian. The fluorescent energy created as other electrons fill in the "holes" created by the ejected electrons can be measured and is characteristic of particular elements, which in different concentrations can be unique to specific obsidian sources (Shackley 2005). Analysis and source characterization of twenty-two artifacts helped discriminate obsidian from two key sources: Napa Glass Mountain (n=15; 68 percent) and Annadel (n=7; 32 percent) obsidian flows. Both quarries have long and complex histories of production in Central California and, for the Marin Peninsula, the appearance of obsidian from these two sources is not unexpected given Point San Pedro's close proximity (Jackson 1986). Quite unique, however, is the spatial patterning of obsidian artifacts across the mound group. There are greater quantities of Napa obsidian (n=11; 92 percent) at CA-MRN-115 (and only one Annadel flake tool) and slightly more Annadel obsidian than Napa obsidian (n=3; 60 percent Annadel vs. n=2; 40 percent Napa) in both assemblages from CA-MRN-114 and -328. The only model for obsidian production on the Marin Peninsula suggests that Napa obsidian should be more prevalent at sites closer to San Francisco Bay and that Annadel obsidian should be more prevalent at sites closer to the Pacific coast—a spatial pattern attributed to animosity between ethnographic Coast Miwok communities on both sides of the peninsula (Jackson 1986).

Despite a small sample size, one explanation for this patterning may have to do with the postcontact history of the shellmound group. As places of refuge within an increasingly strained colonial borderland between imperial Russia and imperial Spain, Coast Miwok people may have resorted to these and other hinterland sites for protection, resource collecting, and other activities during the early 1800s. Attempting to ward off Russian advances south from Colony Ross, Franciscan padres directed the construction of a new mission at San Rafael in 1817 and began recruiting Coast Miwok people from communities at Tomales and Bodega Bays to the west (Schneider and Panich 2019). In this increasingly congested landscape, maintaining access to traditional economic flows of obsidian from Napa Valley probably shifted with the establishment of Mission San Rafael in 1817, Colony Ross in 1812, as well as Mission San Francisco Solano in 1823. Access to obsidian was *not* eliminated, as recent studies from Mission San José and the Metini Village and North Wall community at Colony Ross demonstrate (Lightfoot and Gonzalez 2018:55–56; Panich et al. 2018a). As pluralistic social settings, ethnic and linguistic mixing documented at the missions and Colony Ross reflect a time when colonization "moved peoples speaking different languages into territories where they were not the original inhabitants" and probably mirror the kinds of communities formed at hinterland refuges (Johnson 2006:196). When people hailing from Tomales Bay (Tamal-liwa) and Bodega Bay (Yóle-tamal and Koyo-liwa-puluk) started to arrive at Mission San Rafael, they may have still used Annadel obsidian tools or retained economic and social ties to other Coast Miwok traders and perhaps Kashaya Pomo residing at Colony Ross (Lightfoot and Gonzalez 2018:55–56). On paseo or fleeing colonial establishments, Native people could have either visited the shellmounds with their tools or found new ways to tap into the social and economic networks that kept them connected to their favorite resources.

One additional line of evidence comes from the analysis of archaeological marine shells. Similar to studies conducted at other San Francisco Bay shellmounds (Finstad et al. 2013; Schweikhardt et al. 2011), radiometric and stable isotope analyses of archaeological mussel (*Mytilus* spp.) shells from CA-MRN-114 helped identify the seasonal patterning of shellfish harvests by Native people alive during the mission period (Schneider 2015a). By directly radiocarbon dating mussel shells, archaeologists can approximate when people visited shellmounds. For a more fine-grained estimate of the seasons when Indigenous people may have repaired to the coast to harvest and consume mussels, archaeologists can also study local paleoenvironmental conditions—information recorded in the yearly growth rings of bivalves. Carefully and systemically scraping the narrow growth rings on mussel shells produces powdered calcium carbonate samples that can be tested for specific elements such as magnesium and calcium. Magnesium and calcium ratios are a function of water temperature (warm to cool, depending on the time of year) and $\delta^{18}O$ composition will vary in response to water temperature and salinity (wet to dry, depending on precipitation and freshwater runoff). When these data are gathered, normalized, and then plotted, the resulting "seasonal map" provides an indication of site seasonality (see Schweikhardt et al 2011:2306). Comparing the radiocarbon and geochemical data sets, it appears that Coast Miwok people returned to CA-MRN-114 during the Late Period Phase 2 for late spring, summer, and fall mussel harvests, and they likely continued this pattern during mission times.

Foreign guests visiting Bay Area missions confirm this interpretation, as do the Franciscan padres whose records log the time of year when Native people traveled to missions for baptism, food, resources, and to visit relatives. In aggregate, of the 2,828 Coast Miwok baptisms recorded at Missions Dolores, San Rafael, and San Francisco Solano between 1783 and 1832, a gradual reduction in baptisms occurs from April to December (or late spring, summer, and fall) whereas baptisms peak between January and March (winter). Comparing the pattern of seasonal mission visits indirectly recorded in sacramental registers to the pattern of seasonal mussel harvests recorded in the shells from CA-MRN-114 suggests a continuation of seasonal foraging trips to mussel beds and adjacent shellmounds located in the Indigenous hinterland. As Louis Choris observed at Mission Dolores in 1816, "In winter, bands of Indians come from the mountains to be admitted to the mission, but the greater part of them leave in the spring" (Mahr 1932:95). Perhaps not unlike the story of Julúio and Olomojoia introduced earlier in this book, when Native people traveled between their homes and new colonies they struck a balance between the possibilities and resources available in both places, and they created, as best as possible, stability in a sea of change. Much more than a prosaic task, shellfish gathering was a resilient structuring mechanism in the lives of postcontact Indigenous peoples (Hunter et al. 2014; Meehan 1982:40)—a concept I revisit in chapter 5. As "escape crops," a concept I adapt from James Scott's (2009:23) discussion of covert forms of shifting cultivation practiced by refugees in shatter zones "designed to thwart state appropriation," the steady rhythm of seasonal shellfish collecting may have circumvented padres' efforts to bring Native peoples entirely under subjection. Of staggered maturity, requiring little preparation, and well-adapted to an environmental niche that was "difficult to map and control," (Scott 2009:199), hinterland shellfish beds may have provided important sustenance for state-evading peoples as well as spaces to reactivate place-based memories and reawaken traditional cultural and ecological knowledge.

Summary

In probably one of the more widely known examples of an anthropological terminal narrative, anthropologist Alfred Kroeber described the rugged landscape that protected a small group of Yana speakers—including the "last" Yahi, a man given the name "Ishi"—from the white bounty hunters bent on annihilating California Indians during the dark era of government-sponsored genocide. For Ishi and kin inhabiting the rugged terrain of the central Sierra Nevada foothills during the late nineteenth century, Kroeber (1925:342) writes, there were "endless long ridges and cliff-walled canyons [with] patches in which the brush is almost impenetrable, and the faces of the hills are full of caves." "There are a hundred hiding places," he continued, and the region formed "a retreat from which they could conveniently raid" the nearby farms and ranches of white settlers (Kroeber 1925:342). While many people will be familiar with the story of Ishi as the "last" of his people, it is worth pointing out that Kroeberian essentialism falls flat when considering possibilities for persistence in hinterland settings. The presence of imported glass and metal at Yahi village sites, Ishi's proficiency in flintknapping long, thin projectile points from discarded glass bottles, and even Ishi's Spanish vocabulary punch holes in this terminal narrative (Shackley 2001; Starn 2003). Evaluating the history of California Native Americans who evaded colonial invasion can instead help us focus on the sheer complexities of dynamic hinterland communities where a constant ebb and flow of people, materials, and ideas was standard.

Apostasy figures prominently in many historical accounts of San Francisco Bay missions, and hunting and gathering were evidently encouraged at times through the administration of paseos. Franciscan padres did not precisely record where Native people went during their furloughs or after they escaped the missions, but padres' mention of hunting trips, plant collecting, dances, and other ritual practices provides indirect support for a frequented and relevant hinterland (e.g., Geiger and Meighan 1976). Here, the protracted histories of three shellmounds come into focus. As residential spaces occupied for at least one thousand years, Coast Miwok would return to each mound for a variety of purposes—to celebrate life and death, construct homes, weave baskets, smoke tobacco, create sharp cutting tools, and to collect and process many hundreds of varieties of plants and shellfish, fish, waterfowl, and deer for food, medicine, and sundry other necessities. As missions began operating in the region, the elemental fingerprints of archaeological obsidian and mussel shell geochemistry suggest that access to traditional resources shifted to accommodate new social and economic connections. It did not end.

As places of refuge and center points, some shellmounds may have afforded protection to Coast Miwok by anchoring contingent social networks and cultural identities during the colonial era. Peeking through the urban grid featured on a map of 1870s San Rafael, still another shellmound managed to evade destruction (for the time being) and persisted in the minds of Coast Miwok survivors as a multifaceted hub for seasonal feasts, residency, dancing, and mortuary rites. On this "small knoll" in the 1840s, according to one observer, Coast Miwok families with ties to Nicasio and Tomales Bay "pitched their wigwams . . . hauled their clams and held their pow wows during the autumn and Indian summer" (Lauff 2016 [1916]:14). Discussed more in the next chapter, shellmounds and still other places visited and remembered by Coast Miwok people in the decades after the missions were also settings of recourse and places to chart new social trajectories. While no obvious sprinklings of glass beads mark the trail to Point San Pedro, my analysis and comparison of multiple forms of evidence—archaeological, ethnographic, and archival—help give shape to a broader landscape that was continually inhabited, memorialized, and rendered meaningful. I see the persistence of time and place in the dusty layers of three unassuming shellmounds.

4

Finding Recourse

These lands have pertained to our forefathers.

—TEODORICO QUILAQUEQUI, SEBASTIAN, JUAN EVANGELISTO,
LUIS GONZAGA, AND LUIS ANTOLIN, 1839

IT IS SEPTEMBER 1852. As the first rays of morning sun spill over
Bolinas Ridge and reach Tomales Bay, thick fog still stubbornly clings to
the moss-covered bay trees and hovers eerily above the glassy water. Unlike
Point San Pedro and other parts of Marin County where blue sky and sunshine
usually greet early risers, here the sunlight struggles to penetrate the fog and
succeeds only in turning the cool, dark night into a damp, gray morning. The
steady swish of flapping wings echoes off the still water as a flock of cormorants flies north above the narrow estuary toward the Pacific Ocean. As the
sun climbs higher, a light breeze prompts the fog to shift, release its grip, and
then gradually lift to reveal an unusual scene. Working feverishly at low tide,
a team of Coast Miwok people wielding hammers and saws clamber between
the exposed beams and wreckage of the *Oxford*, a three-masted bark that ran
aground in Tomales Bay in the afternoon of July 12, 1852. As the group of
Coast Miwok people paddle and wade back to shore with the incoming tide,
wisps of fog flit among the carcass of the *Oxford*'s now-exposed wood frame,
toying with its quarry (figure 12).

Bound for the bustling gold rush port of San Francisco, fog tricked Captain
McLane who confused the mouth of Tomales Bay for San Francisco's Golden
Gate and unwittingly sailed the 750-ton ship into shallow Tomales waters
where it immediately ran aground north of Toms Point. News of the wreck
quickly reached San Francisco, where readers of *Daily Alta California*'s "Shipping Intelligence" learned of the deaths of two *Oxford* passengers, who had
succumbed to scurvy during the perilous journey to California. Captivated
readers also learned about the ship's precious cargo of ice and ninety barrels of
whiskey worth an estimated value of $250,000 (*Daily Alta California* [DAC]

FIGURE 12 Artistic rendering of the *Oxford* wreck and its dismantling at Toms Point. Illustration by GeorgeAnn M. DeAntoni.

1852a:2, 1852b:2). In response, San Francisco merchants rapidly dispatched teams to dislodge the boat from the muddy sand and, when that failed, they removed pieces of the ship to rescue the cargo within. The ship could not be saved. Stranded in Tomales Bay, however, sheets of copper from the *Oxford*'s copper-fastened hull, metal spikes, brass fixtures, a mast, the entire cabin, and other salvageable material found new use and value among residents of Toms Point. The ship was yet another gift from the sea.

Between 1849 and 1940, over fifty ships found watery graves between Tomales Bay and the Point Reyes Peninsula—many of these wrecks can be chalked up to a dangerous brew of thick fog, foul weather, and West Marin's notoriously rugged coast. Even before California's gold rush, the *San Agustín*, a Manila galleon piloted by Sebastian Rodríguez Cermeño, wrecked at Point Reyes in 1595 while en route to Mexico, laden with luxurious cargo from China. The contents of the *San Agustín*, including colorful blue-on-white porcelain, spilled into the ocean but would eventually wash ashore, where Indigenous Coast Miwok people would make use of it by incorporating the decorative pottery as beads, ornaments, and tools into their world (see Russell 2011).

The story of the *Oxford* shipwreck and its creative repurposing by Coast Miwok people provides a novel window into a time period usually viewed as lacking Indigenous people, particularly ones capable of making decisions about their livelihoods and futures. The individuals carrying pieces of the *Oxford* and its cargo onshore in 1852 were connected to a small trading post established on Toms Point during the mid-nineteenth century. Coast Miwok people sought refuge at this place—their homeland—and it was one community among many others scattered across Marin County in the decades following mission secularization. During the 1830s and afterwards, Native peoples' manual labor sustained trading posts, farms, ranches, mills, and other settler enterprises multiplying across Marin and Sonoma Counties. This work was exploitative and oppressive for those who experienced it; yet, as others have argued (e.g., Bauer 2009, 2016; Silliman 2001b), labor might also be productive, particularly when refracted through the theoretical lenses of memory, mobility, and place.

Taking a more additive perspective, archaeological and archival evidence suggest that Coast Miwok at Tomales Bay also found the recourse necessary to survive incoming waves of Euro-American colonization. I use the term "recourse" to account for Native peoples' informed responses to colonial imposition, specifically their capacity to resist and continue practicing cultural traditions balanced against the lived realities of colonialism and survival. Recourse also conveys the ability to enact change with a desired future in mind. A colonial place created for the benefit of one man at the expense of his Indigenous hosts, the Toms Point trading post was in actuality constructed on an ancient and persistent place that may have helped Coast Miwok forge community during an era of crisis.

Borderland Lives

If we consider late eighteenth- and early nineteenth-century Marin Peninsula to be a colonial borderland, then the coastal strip inclusive of Omóta-húye (Point Reyes), Tamal-liwa (Tomales Bay), Koyo-liwa-puluk (Bodega Bay), and Yóle-tamal (Bodega Harbor) represents the front line of colonial expansion. Borderlands have been conceptualized as "no-man's land," or bordered spaces with blurry edges formed by the grinding friction and empire-building efforts of two powerful colonizing forces (Adelman and Aron 1999). My

understanding of Indigenous hinterlands acknowledges instead the condi-
tioning effects of borderlands and the important outcomes of Native peoples'
strategic interventions, accommodations, antagonisms, and other "border-
crossing itineraries" within intimately familiar landscapes (Hämäläinen and
Truett 2011:340). "Indians knew the regions within which they were safe
or vulnerable," Juliana Barr (2011:9) writes. Culturally situated knowledge
helped California Indians craft spaces of resilience even while others sought
to usurp and control their homelands.

Early Spanish and English Explorations

Introduced in chapter 2, two brief encounters between Coast Miwok people
and English and Spanish explorers took place at the Point Reyes Peninsula
in the late sixteenth century. Approximately 180 years later, Coast Miwok
people faced new and sustained threats to their communities and livelihoods.
In 1775, the same year that Juan Manuel de Ayala sailed into San Francisco
Bay, Juan Francisco de la Bodega y Quadra sailed his ship, *Sonora*, into Coast
Miwok waters. Tasked with monitoring English and Russian activity north
of Monterey Bay, Bodega y Quadra anchored his ship near the entrance of
Tomales Bay (mistakenly identified as the mouth of a large river and given
the name "Bodega Bay") and he recommended that a permanent outpost be
established in the region (Edwards 1964:256). Hearing reports of English
ships resupplying in the bay, Bodega y Quadra further recommended that
any Spanish settlers create alliances with the locals through "gifts of cloth
and beads" (Tovell 2008:312).

Between 1791 and 1795, Captain George Vancouver commanded three
ships—the *HMS Discovery*, *Chatham*, and *Daedalus*—and a team of English
sailors and scientists (cartographers, botanists, and others) in an exploration
of the Pacific world and search for the Northwest Passage. Stopping at San
Francisco in the autumn of 1792, Vancouver dined with Franciscan missionaries and Spanish military officials, and he commented on the Indigenous
inhabitants: "a race of the most miserable beings" with homes "abominably
infested with every kind of filth and nastiness" (Wilbur 1953:26–27). Vancouver also caught wind of tenuously held lands north of the Golden Gate:

I understood that the opposite side of the port had been visited by some
soldiers on horseback, who obtained but little information; some con-
verted Indians were found living amongst the natives of the northern and
western parts of the port, who were esteemed by the Spaniards to be a

docile, and in general a well-disposed people; though little communication took place between them and the inhabitants on this side. The missionaries found no difficultly in subjecting these people to their authority. (Wilbur 1953:30–31)

In the following year when the English expedition reentered Californian waters, Vancouver assigned Lieutenant Peter Puget to inspect New Spain's northern frontier and formally survey Bodega Bay. Puget encountered approximately thirty Coast Miwok men, women, and children. Some, Puget writes, carried "bows and arrows, which they disposed of to our party for beads and trinkets; the language they spoke was a mixture of Spanish and their own provincial dialect, and from this we may infer, that they were either subordinate to the Spaniards, or that they had a constant connection with the settlement at San Francisco" (Wilbur 1953:114–15). Spanish authorities ratcheted up their presence at Bodega Bay after Vancouver's brief visit in San Francisco. "According to Indian reports," Spanish military learned of Englishmen (probably Vancouver on his way to San Francisco in 1792) who stopped at Bodega Bay for wood and water and "asked the natives to get cattle for them" (Bancroft 1884:516). In response, according to Puget's 1793 report, Spain erected a "pole having a stave lashed across its upper end" on a bluff overlooking the entrance to Bodega Harbor (Wilbur 1953:115). This hastily constructed cross formed from a log, spare rope, and a cask stave was likely planted by Juan Bautista Matute just before Puget arrived, and it represented Spain's claim to lands south of Bodega Bay. Yet, as Puget stood on Bodega Head, in reality emissaries of the Spanish Empire struggled to navigate the lands it claimed to possess.

Following Bodega y Quadra's recommendations, Spanish officials selected Juan Bautista Matute to colonize the Bodega Bay region. Two additional ships—including the *Mexicana*, piloted by Juan Martinez y Zayas—were also dispatched with instructions to report on foreign activity on the Northwest Coast and also map Bodega Bay in case Matute failed (Edwards 1964:264). During the summer of 1793, Matute mistakenly (or correctly) sailed his ship, *Sutil*, into Bodega Harbor north of Tomales Bay, not the mouth of Tomales Bay where the *Sonora* had stopped over in 1775. Not surprisingly, Matute found the shallow Bodega Harbor "not capacious enough" for large ships and also lacking in wood required for a permanent colony. Apparently, many trees closest to shore had already been "sawed off," possibly by "Englishmen . . . who took refuge there during a storm" (Wagner 1931:331). Following orders, however, Matute waited for instructions to arrive from San Francisco. During his wait, Matute mapped the bay, constructed a temporary "house," and interacted with "numerous" Indigenous Coast Miwok people (Wagner 1931:331).

Matute's orders were carried by Lieutenant Felipe de Goycoechea who set out from the San Francisco presidio in August 1793 to rendezvous with Matute at Bodega Harbor. After paddling a launch from San Francisco to Bolinas Bay, Goycoechea's party traveled overland to the southern end of Tomales Bay. Near present-day Olema, Goycoechea reported that the occupants of one village fled after seeing the expedition and its thirty horses but were later "pacified" and convinced to assemble at their village, "although they did not all do so" (Wagner 1931:342). Those who did return were given strings of glass beads and food and, by doing so, Goycoechea was able to count approximately 150 people "in the surroundings, in little groups" (Wagner 1931:342). Through gift giving, Goycoechea sought to control the nature and direction of his expedition in foreign land. He was in fact beholden to Indigenous authority since it was Coast Miwok people who instructed the young captain to travel north to Bodega Bay along the western shore of Tomales Bay—a dead end by foot. Along this route, Goycoechea observed a "wonderment of various settlements" (Wagner 1931:343), or at least nine separate Indigenous communities where friendly relations were predicated on gift exchange. Warned by their guides that these communities "were prepared to give us battle," Goycoechea and company wisely traded glass beads and food for "pinole and some little fruits from the beach" at each stop (Wagner 1931:343).

After arriving at Kalupí-tamal (Tomales Point), the far northern end of the Point Reyes Peninsula, Goycoechea realized the "deceit practiced on [him] by the natives" (Wagner 1931:343). He hired a Coast Miwok person to carry a letter via tule balsa to Matute at Bodega Bay notifying him that the overland expedition had to turn around; the letter carrier received a blanket and some glass beads as compensation (Wagner 1931:343). Reaching Bodega Bay after doubling-back and around Tomales Bay, Goycoechea discovered that the *Sutil*—Goycoechea's ride back to San Francisco—had already departed; however, Matute had thought to leave behind "some chickens and pigs" for Goycoechea's hungry entourage (Wagner 1931:344). The expedition failed. That night, as Goycoechea and company prepared to return to San Francisco by foot, Native people from six settlements arrived to see the horses and convince Goycoechea to stay longer. These Indigenous hosts brought water "and some of what the ship had left," and they gave to their colonial guests two bunches of feathers and clamshell disk beads,[1] again, in exchange for glass beads and food (Wagner 1931:344).

Neither a Spanish settlement nor an English fort ever materialized. In 1812, the Russian-American Company (RAC) selected Bodega Harbor as a port to service their mercantile colony of Ross. Throughout the time of Spanish and English exploration and afterward—when Franciscan proselytizers and Russian merchants hatched new plans for the region they viewed as vacant land—Coast Miwok people remained living in and returned to their homeland. When pieced together, the brief but invaluable glimpses of Indigenous people featured in the accounts produced by Spanish, English, and Russian visitors define a well-populated Indigenous hinterland. In addition to the numerous exchanges of food, materials, and information in these early colonial encounters, we can also see Indigenous agency and selective engagements with colonial people, materials, and agendas—a pattern that resurfaces in still other documents produced later in time. One of the more startling revelations is that even at an early date of 1793—one decade after the first Coast Miwok individuals traveled to Mission Dolores—Coast Miwok people spoke Spanish. The people Lieutenant Puget encountered at Bodega Bay, in other words, had visited a mission or, minimally, already possessed tools necessary to navigate a fluid social terrain.

Between the Cross and the Double-Headed Eagle

With the founding of Mission Dolores in 1776, Franciscan padres sought to recruit and convert Indigenous Coast Miwok peoples to Catholicism. Indigenous Tomales Bay and Bodega Bay polities, however, do not appear in mission sacramental records until 1808. In that year, padres baptized 139 Coast Miwok people—including 5 individuals from "coast" communities along Tomales Bay—at Mission Dolores, thereby surpassing the Ohlone majority at this mission up until that point (Milliken 2009:23). Between 1809 and 1817, Franciscan padres at Mission Dolores would record the names of an additional 184 Coast Miwoks from Tomales Bay and 2 individuals hailing from Bodega Bay. With the establishment of Mission San Rafael in 1817, baptisms of Indigenous Coast Miwok accelerated, particularly in response to the presence of Russian-American Company (RAC) agents beginning in the early 1800s (Lightfoot 2005:118–19; Milliken 1995:202). A total of 339 people from Tomales Bay and 95 people from Bodega Bay communities received baptism between 1817 and 1832 (Milliken 2009).

Looking at the numbers of baptisms alone might support the idea that Native peoples of Marin and southern Sonoma County slowly vanished, as anthropologists mistakenly concluded in the 1970s. A closer inspection of the mission archive and sacramental records instead reveals a complex and dynamic social landscape comprised of politically active and savvy

Geluatamal, Segloque, Calupetamal, Xotomcohui, Echacolom, Yuipa polities minimally controlled by the yoke of colonial authority, as seen in the
examples of Tomales people evading baptism—or deciding the terms of
spiritual conversion—between 1819 and 1821 (see Schneider and Panich
2019:28–33). Coast Miwok people traveled frequently to dodge and engage
colonial representatives. They maintained and remade alliances to immediate
and extended family across a broader region, and their familiarity with the
land—the ability to depart upon seeing a Franciscan padre wandering up the
trail, to remain hidden, and to reappear when needed—complicated colonial
assertions of power and authority in western Marin.

The idea that Spain poorly understood and only nominally controlled
lands north of San Francisco Bay is further demonstrated by the RAC's brazen placement of a port facility and warehouses at Bodega Bay (called Port
Rumianstev) in 1812 and the construction of three ranches—Kostromitinov,
Khlebnikov, and Chernykh Ranches—between the Russian River and Estero
Americano. Port Rumianstev and the ranches serviced Colony Ross, a mercantile operation that sought to profit from the maritime fur trade (Lightfoot
2005). The company coerced Native Alaskans to hunt sea otter, sea lion, and
other sea mammals for their highly profitable pelts. The Ross colony was also
home to Indigenous Kashaya Pomo and Coast Miwok people who remained
autonomous in their dealings with RAC administrators by maintaining spatially segregated communities as well as connections to relatives residing
farther inland (Lightfoot 2005:133–36; Lightfoot and Gonzalez 2018).

In the borderland formed between Russia and Spain, Native people found
spaces for protection and recourse. The region was frequented by runaways
from San Francisco Bay missions, as witnessed by Baron Ferdinand Petrovich
von Wrangell who traveled from Bodega Bay to Colony Ross in 1833. Near
the Russian River, north of Bodega Bay, Wrangell

came upon an old woman, who was gathering seeds in a basket woven
of fine root fibers. She was scared stiff. We learned from her, not without
difficulty, that several Indian families were living beyond the next thicket,
who without doubt had already noticed us and had hidden, fearing to fall
into the hands of Spaniards who quite often go out to hunt Indians in
order to convert their prey to Christianity. (Wrangell 1974:2)

As a place of refuge, the interspace between Colony Ross and San Francisco
Bay also offered Coast Miwok, Southern Pomo, and other Native peoples
room to make decisions about which, if any, institutions they should engage.
Just as Indigenous people comprised the majority of the workforce at Colony

Ross and filled many of the skilled jobs and sundry duties associated with the mercantile operation, California Indians performed much of the manual labor outside of the fort at outlying orchards, agricultural fields, and its three ranches (Lightfoot 2005:136–40). The RAC established three ranches south of Colony Ross and inland from the foggy coast where warmer temperatures favored grain and other crops intended to supply Ross and other company outposts (Schneider 2007a). These "colonial" ranches were likely staffed by Coast Miwok and Pomo peoples, "who generally or by force [were] taken from their rancherías for their labor" (Mathes 2008:219).

In addition to threshing floors, a warehouse, kitchen, corral, and boat used at Kostromitinov Ranch near the Russian River, a probate inventory produced before Colony Ross was sold in 1841 lists "a house for Indians" (Essig et al. 1933:70). As RAC administrators (and the Spanish, Mexicans, and Americans) realized, without the "help of the natives living around the Ross settlement, it would have been impossible to harvest the crops because of a shortage of labor" (Tikhmenev 1978 [1862]:232). Accessing the "help" necessary to keep Colony Ross functioning, RAC administrators capitalized on New Spain's geographic blind spot and, especially after the 1830s, the diminishing influence of Franciscan missions. As Father Vásquez del Mercado of Mission San Rafael complained in 1833:

> The Russians of the establishment at Ross gravely harm the mission because they protect the Indians that flee it, then when [Father Vásquez del Mercado] claims them [the Russians] advise them to hide, that the commandant of Ross has reached such a level of daring that he sends Kodiaks to the ranchería of Tamales [sic] to seduce [baptized Indians] to take them, that from this grave damage to morality results, thus the married Indians abandon their families, that in addition there is a very notable theft of livestock because the Russians buy the cattle stolen from the mission and they also steal them and they have many cattle with the brand of the mission, that all of these facts are sufficient to take measures to prevent the fatal consequences that may follow in time. (Mathes 2008:214)

From whom did the Russians purchase mission livestock? As some California Indians were preyed upon by colonizers, still others appear to have been acutely aware of the potential opportunities available to them in their colonized homeland. An exploitative and abusive enterprise (Lightfoot 2005:139), Colony Ross may have also represented an alternative for Native peoples seeking food, supplies, and some semblance of autonomy, instead of becoming "*peones* under a mayordomo" (Weber 1982:66).

"Los brasos del Pais": *Mexican and American Motivations*

In the power vacuum created in the aftermath of mission secularization, upper class Mexican citizens (*gente de razón*) including wealthy families, military officers, and naturalized Mexican citizens worked quickly to acquire mission property (buildings, equipment, livestock, etc.) and land intended to be returned to baptized California Indians. While virulent diseases such as smallpox periodically ravaged Native communities in early nineteenth-century San Francisco Bay Area (Silliman 2004:60–61), many families also struggled to imagine a future for their children during these "dark years" (Lightfoot 2005:214). Some made decisions to retreat into forests and remote locales for protection in their former homelands. Others may have found anonymity in growing towns like San José, San Francisco, and Sonoma. Still others took jobs as domestic servants in private households, or they applied skills in horseback riding, blacksmithing, carpentry, and other mission-acquired trades at new job sites (Lightfoot 2005:211–13). For those who remained living at missions, their labor would fall under the jurisdiction of often-unscrupulous managers (mayordomos) who supervised the operation of the newly formed parishes (former missions) and treated California Indians as a private labor pool. Former mission lands were swiftly consumed by private interests as many hundreds of rancho estates proliferated across California during the 1830s and 1840s. As Weber (1982:123) documents, Mexican California—formerly the remote frontier of New Spain—would also become "rapidly entangled" in the burgeoning American economy, quite literally as American men frequently married into prominent Mexican families to gain access to power and land.

One of the major engines driving the new wave of colonialism in California before the gold rush was the hide and tallow trade, or the sale of animal skins (usually cow hides, but also elk) and rendered animal fat used for soap, candles, and other goods. The seeds of this enterprise were planted during the waning years of the mission period when Franciscan leadership contracted with a British company in 1822 to gather cow hides and tallow in exchange for scarce supplies (Weber 1982:138). American merchants would eventually enter the scene and saturate the market by the 1840s; yet, between 1826 and 1848 Americans alone collected an estimated seven thousand tons of tallow and over six million hides (Weber 1982:138–39). Indigenous labor, or "los brasos del pais" (the arms of the country) as one politician called them (DAC 1849:2), fueled this economy.

California Indians "understood work, and did it, forming, thereby the all-important spoke of the economic wheel," recalled Stephen Richardson, the son of Captain William A. Richardson whose father-in-law, Ygnacio Martínez, was a commandant at the San Francisco presidio (Wilkins 1918:30). In the post-mission era, Native people might work voluntarily as carpenters and blacksmiths, or as vaqueros in service at many missions and ranchos throughout California (Panich 2017). Thwarting the ranchos, in fact, Yokuts riding horseback from the San Joaquin Valley stole upwards of one hundred thousand horses from coastal corrals over a twenty-year period in the early 1800s—a practice widespread throughout California and linked to a captive-and-livestock raiding economy that extended to New Mexico (Zappia 2014). Yet, as Stephen Richardson also remembered, in Marin County Native people who "stayed by the herds while they lasted [were] constant prey of smooth-of-speech men, some of whom became rich by swapping gaudy colored glass beads for cattle. Their knowledge of many useful occupations went for nothing" (Wilkins 1918:31–32).

Kidnapping and forced labor of California Indians were another reality of the time. Lieutenant Joseph Warren Revere participated in—and benefited from—a kidnapping in 1849 hosted by Rafael Garcia (owner of a rancho at Tomales Bay) and accompanied by five mayordomos and twenty-five to fifty Indian vaqueros (Revere 1872:171). After the assault on a camp of suspected horse thieves north of Bodega Bay:

> The prisoners thus pressed into our service were divided equally among our party, submitting resignedly and even joyfully to their fate: they selected those of their squaws and children whom they wished to accompany them; and we all left for home, after rewarding our Indian allies. Arriving at our respective ranchos, our captives were soon domiciled, and supplied with full rations of beef; and, having finished their task of making adobes (sun-dried bricks) for building purposes, they were permitted to depart, laden with good shirts and blankets. Two of the 'bucks' remained with me, preferring good living and kind treatment to their precarious, half-starved condition in their native wilds; and, from savage and graceless "Gentiles," were converted into decent and respectable "Christianos." (Revere 1872:176–77)

Many California Indians were kidnapped and coerced into joining ranchos—a "colonial strategy" also documented at Mariano Vallejo's Rancho Petaluma and at countless other ranchos, farms, mills, trading posts, mercantile projects, and households throughout California (e.g., Reséndez 2016:257–58; Silliman 2004). Structural racism and restrictive laws further pushed Native people into jails and forced labor (Phillips 2016:199). The passage of "An

Act for the Government and Protection of the Indians" in 1850 legalized servitude by criminalizing unemployment and permitting the forced labor of Native American orphans, loiterers, and prisoners.

Driven by profit, the relationships many rancheros had with their work-force were infused with coercion and ambivalence, leading to the conclusion that Indigenous people participated in the ranchos purely out of necessity (Silliman 2004:27). As discussed earlier with reference to Franciscan missions, this perspective may have been true in some cases; yet, perspectives that em-phasize colonial authority also tend to minimize the important ways Native people chose to engage ranchos and other budding enterprises on their own terms, or chose not to engage them at all. Panich (2017) documents how some Indigenous laborers adapted horseback riding, cowboy gear, attire, and other materials introduced at ranchos into their own preexisting and newly emerg-ing cultural repertoires and identities. At some ranchos, California Indians found protection by claiming the last name of the rancho owner. A Coast Miwok woman named Tsupu (Maria Cheka), for example, fled Vallejo's Ran-cho Petaluma for Fort Ross and later became the mistress to Captain Stephen Smith and the mother of three at Rancho Bodega (Sarris 2001). Intermarriage could redefine status as well as familial relationships. On the Marin Peninsula, William Richardson "maintained an Indian refuge at [Rancho] Sausalito as long as he lived. The remnant so protected was large enough to have formed the nucleus for a rehabilitated race" (Wilkins 1918:33).

After secularization, some California Indians would also claim—and receive—land from the Mexican Government, although most of these grants were eventually lost either because of "smooth-of-speech" squatters and law-yers or because US courts rejected these claims after 1851. Mariano Vallejo helped a Coast Miwok man named Camillo Ynitia gain possession of Rancho Olompali in 1843 in acknowledgment of Ynitia's cooperation and "extraordi-nary ability to manage his own affairs" (Carlson and Parkman 1986:244). Five Coast Miwok men (Teodorico Quilaquequi, Sebastian, Juan Evangelisto, Luis Gonzaga, and Luis Antolin) who self-identified as "Christianized Indians" also received the eighty thousand-acre Rancho Nicasio grant in 1835 (Dietz 1976:19). Located approximately halfway between Mission San Rafael and Tomales Bay, Rancho Nicasio included a large precontact village named Echa-tamal (CA-MRN-402), and the area was continuously inhabited throughout the mission period when Coast Miwok people raised livestock and harvested grain for the mission.

Similar to Rancho Olompali and Rancho Polsomi in Santa Clara County (see chapter 3), acquiring Rancho Nicasio was purposeful and empowering in that it was also a significant site of history, resilience, and a place to create a future as a community. "These lands have pertained to our forefathers," the five Coast Miwok men wrote in an appeal to Mexican authorities in 1839, "we are poor and have large families" (Dietz 1976:22). Although their property rights were quickly undermined by a duplicitous Vallejo and other settlers during a string of events in the 1840s, Coast Miwok families continued to reside at Echa-tamal, where they hunted with bow and arrow, farmed, and hosted traditional dances (Collier and Thalman 1996:232). They also worked as domestic servants, as day laborers at farms and local dairies, and as "fishermen" and "clam diggers" at Tomales Bay into the 1880s, when they were finally evicted from their land (Avery 2009:111–17; Dietz 1976:24). Another view of the rise and fall of Echa-tamal puts less power in the hands of land-hungry settlers and more into the Indigenous authority active within Coast Miwok homelands. Maria Copa's grandmother argued that supernatural were-bears were "one reason so few people are left [at Nicasio]. Four times there was a big rancheria at Nicasio, and we were the only ones who were left. All the others were killed: but mostly poisoned" (Collier and Thalman 1996:75). Powerful bear shamans—individuals who frequently dressed in actual bear skins—played an important role in many California Indian societies as executioners and a source of authority for group leaders. As a form of social control, bear shamanism enforced civility purely through the sheer terror of potentially encountering or being killed by a bear doctor (Hollimon 2004). In this case, the wrongdoing(s) that resulted in the poisonings of Echa-tamal residents are unknown.

Seasonal comings and goings of California Indian labor reported at Rancho Petaluma further exemplify novel evocations of precontact traditions of mobility and trip scheduling for resource gathering and social calls. I hypothesize that in their homeland during the nineteenth century, memory, mobility, and a sense of place helped Indigenous Coast Miwok people seeking refuge and the recourse necessary to survive and remain relevant. As George Phillips (2010:323) suggests for Native labor at Los Angeles area ranchos, "acquiring new skills did not necessarily result in the loss of old ones." Discussed more below, just as the spate of newcomers to California found economic opportunity by leveraging and exploiting a built-in pool of potential Native American laborers, the varied and flexible relationships Coast Miwok people kept to ancestral villages, hunting grounds, resource gathering areas, sacred sites, and colonial establishments informed how they moved across, dwelled upon, and persisted on land that was being taken from under their feet.

Written sources of historical information often obscure the agency of Native people who confronted and survived colonial power. By reading between the lines, one sees Native people seeking refuge and finding recourse by learning new languages to share and gather information and resources, by evading the proselytizing efforts of roaming Franciscan padres, or sometimes by participating willingly and unwillingly in Russian, Mexican, and American colonial enterprises. The Toms Point trading post is a case in point.

The Toms Point Trading Post

George Thomas Wood was a New Yorker who ran away from home and made a living at sea. He died in 1879 (in his early fifties) in San Rafael (Schneider and Panich 2019:41). Accounts differ as to when and how Wood arrived in California (see Schneider and Panich 2019), but most will agree that he was living permanently at Tomales Bay by 1849. In this year, Wood established a small trading post at Tomales Bay on a promontory that still carries his name, Toms Point (named for George Thomas Wood, or "Tom" Wood), and he began cultivating the pioneering alter ego that captured the attention of Marin County historians (Munro-Fraser 1880).

Written accounts of George Wood's life in California (e.g., Lauff 2016 [1916]; Munro-Fraser 1880) adopt a vanishing Indian trope in their portrayal of Indigenous Coast Miwok families as central to the establishment of the Toms Point trading post and yet otherwise encumbered by drunkenness, in-fighting, and unavoidable destitution. At Tomales Bay, for instance, Wood "took up his residence at [Toms Point] with a tribe of Tomales Indians . . . [and] took as a spouse a winsome *mohala* of that tribe" (Munro-Fraser 1880:123). The trading post profited initially from the sale of hides and tallow, which were exchanged for a wide assortment of goods unloaded from passing ships. The cargoes might have included items similar to those observed by Richard Henry Dana (1937:77) at Los Angeles in 1835, including: spirits, tea, coffee, sugars, spices, raisins, molasses, tobacco, hardware, crockery, tinware, cutlery, clothing, boots and shoes, necklaces, jewelry, combs, furniture, and more. Wood also enlisted Coast Miwok to collect abalone. The shells were sold to French traders and could be transformed into buttons and other decorative embellishments featuring the lustrous mother-of-pearl. As mission herds and the hide and tallow trade diminished by the 1840s, Wood explored other ways to make a living, including an attempt to purchase a sawmill and by loaning Native labor to neighboring farms, ranches, and mills (Schneider and Panich 2019:40). George Wood may have been able to circumvent many of the challenges of supplying and operating a trading post in remote western Marin County because of the sizeable pool of California Indian laborers still living in the area.

"Tom was the real business manager of the Indian tribes of Marin, Sonoma and Solano counties, and his cabin at [Toms] Point on Tomales Bay was the shipping and trading point for all the Spanish, Russian, French and English trading coasters," recalled Charles Lauff (2016 [1916]:54), a contemporary of George Wood. As seen in Revere's 1849 kidnapping account, Native American vaqueros and kidnapped Indians worked at ranchos throughout the region (see also Silliman 2004). North of Toms Point at the Estero Americano, ranchos owned by Edward McIntosh, James Dawson, and James Black relied on Native labor to tend livestock, grow and harvest crops, and operate mills. Beginning in the 1830s, Mariano Vallejo strategically awarded land grants to McIntosh, Dawson, and Black to block Russian expansion south of Bodega Bay, specifically to "encroach upon [Russian] territory and usurp their possessions" (Munro-Fraser 1880:284). *Diseños* (rancho maps) prepared for the three ranchos collectively include *viñas* (vineyards), *molinos* (mills), a *molino de agua* (water-powered gristmill), a corral, and agricultural fields (Bancroft Library 1858a, 1858b, 1858c), as well as the encroaching "ranchos de los Rusos," or RAC ranches.

All of these settler enterprises hinged on seasonal labor. Yet, while Marin County "pioneers" like George Wood, Timothy Murphy (see chapter 3), William Richardson, and others fashioned themselves as charismatic "business managers" and learned Indigenous languages to be able to manipulate them (Lauff [1916] 2016:54; Schneider 2010:174; Wilkins 1918:24–25), so too did Native people learn the languages of colonists and adapt a language of capitalism to their own movements between far-flung jobs (Sunseri 2017:484–87). Coast Miwok laborers at Toms Point applied skilled trades that they practiced at former missions and ranchos. Among them, Lauff ([1916] 2016:55) observed skilled "carpenters, cobblers, cooks and blacksmiths." Colonized Indigenous communities of California frequently made do with oppressive living and working conditions. Looking closer, seasonal labor and periodic trips to different job sites also appear to have reinforced attenuated social bonds stretched thinly across increasingly fractured homelands. Mobility still mattered to Coast Miwok people and, explored more below and in the next chapter, persistent knowledge of the land helped rearticulate their sovereign claim to it (Bauer 2016:29).

Toms Point Archaeology

Three archaeological sites at Toms Point—CA-MRN-201, -202, and -363— provide important details on the experiences and decision making of resilient

Coast Miwok people who remained living in their homelands before, during, and after five decades of missionary colonialism. Extending into the northeast corner of Tomales Bay, the Toms Point landform is one of three exposed headlands dating to the Pleistocene Epoch (Grove and Niemi 1999), and the Tomales Bay estuary was formed in the last six thousand years as rising sea levels gradually flooded the formerly narrow valley. Discussed more below, Coast Miwok people occupied Toms Point since before the formation of Tomales Bay (figure 13).

Ethnographic records identify several Coast Miwok villages around Tomales Bay, including two in the vicinity of Toms Point—Segloque (also, Sak'-lo'-ke, Seklo'ke, and Sakloki) and Xotomcohui (also, Coto'mkowi, Shotomko-wi, and Sholomko-wi)—although the exact location of both villages remains largely uncertain. Merriam (1907:356) indicated that the village of "Sak'-lo'-ke" was, "on the long point on [the] east side of [the] entrance to Tamales bay." Barrett (1908:308–9) placed both villages at Toms Point, or "on the eastern shore of Tomales Bay at a point a short distance south of the town of Tomales at the entrance to the bay." Kroeber (1925:274) mapped the

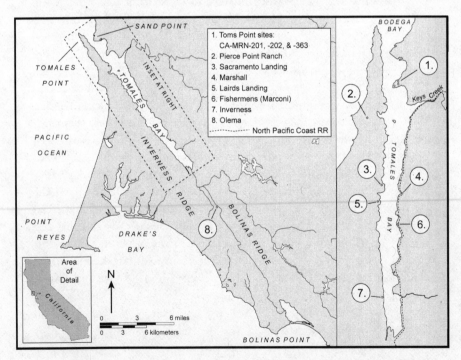

FIGURE 13 Map showing the names and approximate locations of communities and Toms Point study sites (CA-MRN-201, -202, and -363) in the Tomales Bay region.

village of "Sakloki" on Sand Point to the north of Toms Point; the villages of "Shotomko-wi" and "Utumia" are south and north of the town of Tomales, respectively. John P. Harrington's interviews with two Coast Miwok elders—Julia Elgin and Marion (Mariáno) Miránda—in 1939 also include information about Tomales Bay and Bodega Bay villages. Marion identified "Seklo'ke" as "un pedazo de tierra" (a piece of earth), but he did not have any memory of a village in that location (Harrington 1942:16). Others have placed "Shotomko-wi" and "Sakloki" on Toms Point (Collier and Thalman 1996:7) or have equated the village of Xotomcohui on Toms Point with the village of "Campo Verdi" mapped by Bodega y Quadra in 1775 (Dickinson 1957:15). Given these multiple place names and locations, the same name of a village site might also be applied to a constellation of affiliated villages and camps in a larger territory or region (Slaymaker 1982:333–40).

Early archaeological efforts at Tomales Bay include pedestrian surveys and excavations, though never with the explicit goal of studying postcontact Indigenous communities (Gerkin 1967; Nelson 1909b; Peter 1921). Nels Nelson (1909b) recorded approximately one hundred coastal shellmounds between the mouth of the Russian River and Bolinas Bay (south of Point Reyes) as a continuation to his San Francisco Bay shellmound survey (see chapter 1). At Toms Point, Nelson recorded "shell-heap no. 26" (CA-MRN-202) and "shell-heap no. 27" (CA-MRN-201). He described site 27 as a campsite and "very small and insignificant" (Nelson 1909b:12). For site 26, Nelson (1909b:11) reported that "residents of the vicinity spoke of the site as 'an old Indian burying ground' so that presumably skeleton material could be obtained here." The names of Nelson's informants are not provided, but it is possible that Coast Miwok caretakers shared this information as a deterrent to any would-be visitors. Discussed more in chapter 5, Nelson describes resident Coast Miwok people still living near or on top of older shellmounds at many stops along Tomales Bay. Not fully realized by Nelson, however, these "insignificant" sites were in fact places laden with history and value for Coast Miwok people still living in the area. Foreshadowing the next several decades of archaeology in California, the first stop on Nelson's west coast survey, "No. 1, Indian cemetery," is described as a "place still used for burial by Indians living in the vicinity, but may doubtless be excavated with profit in the near future" (Nelson 1909b:2). Cemeteries, shellmounds, and other places remained central to the place-based histories and cultures of Indigenous communities on California's central coast. Unfortunately, many archaeologists ignored or did not recognize this relationship.

Another archaeologist, Jesse Peter, worked at Toms Point for four days in 1921 to collect artifacts and excavate Native American burials to help construct the archaeological chronology for Central California (Beardsley 1948). Unnamed members of the University of California Archaeological Survey excavated five test pits at CA-MRN-202 in 1940 noting only "shell-dirt [and] sandy lower levels" and no human remains (Anonymous 1940). The most extensive collecting at CA-MRN-202 took place in 1964 by Agnes Gerkin (1967), an amateur archaeologist who collaborated with clam diggers to amass "five apple cartons" of obsidian projectile points, ground stone tools, glass beads, dishware fragments, rolled copper beads, bottle glass, and other items from the intertidal zone around Toms Point (currently designated as a separate site, CA-MRN-489). Gerkin collected the 780 items in the aftermath of the Great Alaskan earthquake of 1964, when a tidal wave entered Tomales Bay, smashed into Toms Point, and redeposited a portion of CA-MRN-202 into the bay (Gerkin 1967:3). Neither Gerkin nor anyone else elaborated on the brass door keys, spikes, porcelain fragments, flaked bottle glass, and other "Caucasian goods" (Gerkin 1967:10). The Drake Quest was already in full swing by this time (see chapter 1), and the Coast Miwok were already "virtually extinct" in the minds of anthropologists (Beardsley 1954:16). Only recently have archaeological overviews for the Point Reyes region provided context—and room for studying—post-mission era Coast Miwok history (e.g., Compass 1998; Stewart and Praetzellis 2003).

In 2015 and 2016, I embarked on a collaborative archaeological research project aimed at relocating George T. Woods's coastal trading post. This research was codirected with Dr. Lee Panich (Santa Clara University) and carried out with the permission and support of the Federated Indians of Graton Rancheria (FIGR)—including FIGR's Tribal Council and then newly established Tribal Heritage Preservation Office (THPO)—and Audubon Canyon Ranch (ACR), who currently own and manage Toms Point as a wildlife preserve. Adopting a phased approach similar to my work at China Camp State Park, the first phase of research involved a literature review, specifically a review of relevant historical documents and historic maps created by the United States Coast Survey (USCS) (see Panich et al. 2018d; Schneider and Panich 2019).

This preliminary research was conducted to become acquainted with the region and time period and to minimize the amount of destructive excavation by identifying key features of the landscape for additional study. The location of the trading post, for example, appears on at least two maps created by USCS surveyors (Byram 2013:37–38). In 1856, USCS surveyors placed a benchmark on top of Toms Point and made sure to note other obvious landmarks to help relocate the survey marker. In this case, the benchmark was placed "immediately above, and to the Southward of Tom Vaquero's house" (Byram

2013:38). An accompanying sketch map uses a single black square to denote the structure. It is not clear if members of the survey team interacted with residents of the house.

A second and more detailed USCS map was prepared in 1862 (Kerr 1862). As the American Civil War was being waged, USCS surveyors visited extant Coast Miwok villages ("rancherias") along Tomales Bay and carefully mapped the novel mixture of Western-style and Indigenous architectural choices, including boxy frame houses (squares) and conical bark houses (triangles) probably not unlike the conical redwood bark homes constructed atop CA-MRN-115. A different L-shaped symbol was used on the 1862 map to depict the trading post freshly embellished with materials salvaged from the *Oxford* shipwreck, which is also depicted on the map in the water west of Toms Point. Three triangles—Indigenous conical bark houses—are shown next to the trading post, and all of the structures are surrounded by a dashed line I interpret to be a contour line denoting mounded space (the cartographers used a dot-dash line for fences appearing on the same map).

To further narrow the search area, the second phase of my research involved a ground penetrating radar (GPR) survey at CA-MRN-202 and—based on the result of the GPR survey—digital mapping, surface artifact collection (n=32 units), and the excavation of five one-by-one-meter units at CA-MRN-202 in 2015. With assistance from Dr. R. Scott Byram, approximately seventy-five square meters of the CA-MRN-202 deposit was surveyed using a GSSI SIR-3000 GPR instrument to help define near surface archaeological features and, if possible, the footprints of buildings associated with the former trading post. Based on the results of the surface collection and GPR survey, some features were selected for excavation. None of the five excavation units encountered recognizable structural remains, hard-packed floors, postholes, or other architectural features; however, the assemblage of metal, glass, ceramic, lithic, and faunal artifacts indicate a late eighteenth- and nineteenth-century occupation—an observation confirmed later by multiple AMS radiocarbon assays (see below).

To better situate the Toms Point trading post within the longer arc of Indigenous history, the third research phase in 2016 involved additional digital mapping, surface collection at CA-MRN-201 (n=44 units) and -363 (n=30 units), the excavation of one one-by-one-meter test unit at CA-MRN-363 (the largest of the three sites with an area of approximately 5,100 square meters), and additional excavation at CA-MRN-202 with a focus on evaluating the site's earliest occupations. This work was carried out by an expanded field crew of UC Santa Cruz and Santa Clara University students. Careful inspection of the surface components of CA-MRN-201 resulted in the identification of three loci totaling 1,757 square meters, including one locus ("Locus A") featuring a mix of locally purveyed and imported materials similar to those collected from CA-MRN-202. In 2016, six more one-by-one-meter units and one profile cut were excavated at CA-MRN-202, and eleven auger units were excavated to the north (n=7) and south (n=4) of CA-MRN-202 to assess the horizontal and vertical extent of the remaining site deposit, which currently measures approximately one thousand square meters and three meters deep in some areas. Discussed more below, our expanded field investigations produced still other materials that predate the nineteenth-century trading post by thousands of years.

To this day, in fact, Tomales Bay remains deeply engrained in the culture and identities of many citizens of FIGR. Among FIGR's citizenry are individuals who can trace their family's history back to one of the many communities that stubbornly clung to the shores of Tomales Bay, fished from its waters, collected clams, dove for abalone at nearby Point Reyes, and otherwise persisted. Conducting an archaeology project in such historical and sacred lands required not only seeking permission and developing a thoughtful research design but also ensuring that the work and interpretations remain relevant. To me, this meant maintaining open communication with FIGR and ACR throughout the project, sharing updates and seeking feedback, and keeping the goals, interests, and history of an active community in mind when studying and interpreting the past (see also the Introduction). Applying this philosophy, I also co-organized two events at Toms Point with FIGR's Tribal Historic Preservation Office and Temporary Assistance to Needy Families (TANF) program. For the TANF event, FIGR youth were invited to a picnic, hike, and presentation on Native history at Toms Point. The second event supplemented an archaeological monitoring training program for FIGR adults already in progress through Graton's THPO. The workshop included a presentation and interpretive hike, picnic lunch, artifact identification workshop, and a practice monitoring scenario in which participants tested their knowledge of cultural materials by "monitoring" surface finds in different sections of CA-MRN-363. The events marked the first time in 150 years that so many Coast Miwok people had gathered at Toms Point.

Toms Point Assemblages

Materials collected from CA-MRN-201, -202, and -363 include faunal bone and shell, flaked stone tools and debitage, and ground stone fragments. While these items are not unusual for most archaeological sites in California, the spatial patterning of these finds across Toms Point is particularly intriguing. Bearing in mind differences in sampling methods at each site, we can generally say that introduced materials (e.g., glass beads, window and bottle glass, metal, and ceramic fragments) are restricted to the upper one-half meter of sediment at CA-MRN-202 (the location of the trading post) and one area ("Locus A") of CA-MRN-201. Artifacts collected from Locus A at CA-MRN-201 include flaked bottle glass, glass beads, ferrous and nonferrous metal, and chert and obsidian debitage. In stark contrast, surface-collected materials from the opposite end of CA-MRN-201 ("Locus B") include obsidian and chert debitage and marine shell fragments. The visibly "older" assemblage of materials from Locus B of CA-MRN-201 is similar to those collected from CA-MRN-363: faunal bone, marine shell, lithic tools and debitage, and no mass-produced materials. Discussed more below, the image of Toms Point that emerges is that of a persistent place consisting of ancient sites that may have ultimately factored into decisions about how space could be used during the colonial era.

Archaeobotanical Remains

Nine soil samples were collected from CA-MRN-202 in 2015 (n=4) and 2016 (n=5) for flotation and archaeobotanical analyses. A total of 9,662 specimens were identified to the taxonomic level of family or genus (see Schneider et al. 2018:61–66). The majority of macrobotanical remains are herbaceous grassland taxa such as *Galium* sp. (bedstraw), *Malva* sp. (mallow), and Poaceae (grass family). Despite the prevalence of bedstraw, totaling nearly six thousand specimens, the possible cultural preferences for this plant are unclear and might reflect medicinal use or use as bedding, as the common name implies. Similarly, mallows and plants in the Poaceae taxon may have been collected by Native peoples in mission and rancho settings for food, medicine, and raw material (Silliman 2004:170–71). Low densities of macrobotanical remains belonging to taxa that would have been sought after for food include nutshell from oak (e.g., *Notholithocarpus* sp.), hazelnut (*Corylus cornuta* ssp. *californica*), and California bay (*Umbellularia californica*). None of these species grow on Toms Point presently but could have been accessed at other places around Tomales Bay. A single specimen is identified as wild cucumber (*Marah* sp.), or man-root, which was used for medicinal purposes by some Native people in California (Schneider et al. 2018:62). Other undomesticated plants include Asteraceae (daisy family), *Trifolium* sp. (clover), and *Rumex* sp. (an herb), all of which could have been used for food except that the seed densities are too low to discount other nonhuman explanations for the presence of these taxa. Similarly, a single grain of wheat (*Triticum* sp.) and a seed head from an "Old World domesticated grain" may either represent a past meal or feed for live-stock quartered at the trading post.

Perhaps because people prepared foods differently (e.g., using stoves in-stead of open hearths or earth ovens), the persistence of wild plant foods at Toms Point is not immediately evident based on the low quantities of iden-tifiable remains. However, the presence of domesticated and wild plant taxa suggests change and continuity in the ways Native people interacted with the natural world. Taking this observation one step further, some charred macrobotanical remains (seeds and wood charcoal) might be indicative of traditional plant stewardship techniques, including the continued use of fire to manage plant communities, since wildfires around Tomales Bay are rare (Schneider et al. 2018:68). The strong representation of exotic ruderals in the botanical assemblage—including mallows and pink family (Caryophyllaceae) and mustard family (Brassicaceae) taxa—reflect landscape disturbances, in-cluding perhaps the implementation of prescribed burns or any number of other activities (e.g., corralling livestock, processing hides and tallow, and foot traffic) taking place at this busy coastal hub.

Archaeological Faunas

Turning to the faunal assemblages from CA-MRN-201, -202, and -363, zooarchaeologists identified the remains of terrestrial and marine mammals, birds, fishes, and invertebrate (bivalve, gastropod, and crustacean) animals (see Schneider et al. 2018:57–61). For CA-MRN-201, where only the surface of the site was studied, zooarchaeological analysis focused on shellfish remains for radiocarbon dating. Marine mammals, terrestrial carnivores, ungulates, and small mammals are represented in the mammalian remains from CA-MRN-202. Ubiquitous to coastal California, the remains of small burrowing animals (e.g., gopher, mouse, and mole) were collected from CA-MRN-202 and -363, and they may be more suggestive of postdepositional rodent tun-neling rather than human dietary choices. Sea mammals include sea otter (*En-hydra lutris*) and harbor seal (*Phoca vitulina*). Both animals are represented at CA-MRN-202 by a single bone. Silliman (2004:164) hypothesized that small counts of sea otter and pinniped elements discovered at Petaluma Adobe, approximately forty kilometers (twenty-five miles) away, might reflect trade with coastal communities or hunting and fishing trips to places like Tomales Bay. One sea otter mandible was also collected from CA-MRN-363, further suggesting that capture of this animal from Tomales Bay waters predates the colonial-era fur trade and may represent a longstanding tradition maintained throughout the colonial era. Terrestrial carnivores include bobcat (*Lynx rufus*) and mountain lion (*Puma concolor*), each represented by one phalanx at CA-MRN-202. Since no other parts of the skeleton from these two animals were identified, the bones (and paws) might have arrived on site attached to animal pelts used to keep warm in the chilly coastal environment.

Mule deer (*Odocoileus hemionus*), indeterminate medium and large Artiodactyla, rabbit (including *Sylvilagus bachmani* and *Lepus californicus*), and elk (*Cervus canadensis*)—represented by a single calcaneus bone collected from CA-MRN-363—round out the Toms Point mammalian taxa. Only one element was identifiable as deer, which suggests that either deer were not hunted by people associated with the trading post or that deer bones were heavily processed (e.g., for extracting marrow). In contrast, large numbers of deer bone were recovered from the contemporaneous Petaluma Adobe where Indigenous peoples ate venison and collected deer hides even with access to beef (Silliman 2004:161–62). Still another possibility might be that deer were rare in the local environment due to overhunting and/or habitat loss from grazing livestock introduced in the late 1700s. Indian vaqueros accompanying Lieutenant Joseph Warren Revere on a hunting expedition at Point Reyes in 1846 dispatched six elk, which amounted to four hundred pounds of rendered tallow. "The superior hardness, whiteness and delicacy of the elk's tallow" came at a price, however, as the hunting party "passed many places, on [their] way back, where mouldering horns and bones attested to the wholesale slaughter which had been made in previous years by the rancheros of the neighborhood" (Revere 1947 [1849]:68).

As Tomales Bay is on the Pacific Flyway, it is not surprising that many of the identified avian species at CA-MRN-202 include migratory birds such as geese (*Anser caerulescens, A. albifrons,* and *Branta canadensis*) and scoter (*Melanitta* sp.), which winter in Tomales Bay. Several species of duck—including canvasback (*Aythya valisineria*), mallard (*Anas platyrhynchos*), northern shoveler (*Anas clypeata*), and cinnamon teal (*Anas cyanoptera*)—pelican (*Pelecanus occidentalis*), gull (*Larus* sp.), pied-billed grebe (*Podilymbus podiceps*), and other diving birds (e.g., loon and cormorant) are also present in the faunal assemblage from CA-MRN-202 and were probable sources of food. Of the small sample of eleven bird bones from CA-MRN-363, only one could be assigned to a species: the radius of a Brandt's cormorant (*Phalacrocorax penicillatus*). Native laborers at Wood's trading post are said to have captured "brant" geese "by using slip knots made of grasses and pegging them down in the mud [with] a little grain as bait" (Lauff 2016 [1916]:55). Nets, slings, traps, and possibly bow and arrow (for larger birds) would have all been employed to capture birds (Lightfoot et al. 2009:241–45). As seen in illustrations created by early 1800s visitors to the region (see Hudson and Bates 2015), Coast Miwok people also collected bird feathers to decorate baskets and ceremonial regalia, to make the fletching for arrows, and for feather capes. Indeed, a solitary hawk (*Buteo* sp.) wing bone collected from CA-MRN-202 might be best explained as part of a toolkit for engaging the Coast Miwok ceremonial world (Collier and Thalman 1996:161).

Fish remains from CA-MRN-202 and -363 reflect nearshore fishing activities with a focus on small schooling taxa, such as Embiotocidae (surfperches), Clupeidae (sardines and herrings), and Atherinopsidae (neotropical silversides) (Schneider et al. 2018:58–59). Other fishes inhabiting nearshore waters include bat ray (*Myliobatis californica*) and Pacific herring (*Clupea pallasii*), which could probably be found during the winter spawning in the beds of eelgrass skirting Toms Point. Collected from CA-MRN-202, pile perch (*Rhacochilus vacca*) and cabezon (*Scorpaenichthys marmoratus*) dwell within rocky intertidal areas and kelp beds, suggesting that people crossed Tomales Bay to be able to fish from the ocean. They may have coordinated these trips with abalone collection.

What tools might someone use to capture fish? For schooling fishes, nets could be cast from the shore or tossed from a tule balsa. Spears could be used for larger animals, and fishing lines could also be cast from shore. With time, metal fishhooks were also incorporated into fishing kits. Among the glass beads, needles, mirrors, knives, and other "trinkets for trading" described by Revere (1872:173–74) during his 1849 kidnapping expedition north of Bodega Bay, fishhooks were especially "coveted . . . the sight of which . . . [Native people] greatly marveled, never before having seen steel or iron hooks." Collected from CA-MRN-202, a slender wrought iron spike bent into a hook might have been used by an intrepid Coast Miwok hunter seeking even bigger fish—such as sturgeon (see Lightfoot and Gonzalez 2018:81)—dwelling in deeper water (figure 14a).

Large quantities of marine shells (bivalves, gastropods, and crustaceans) are associated with all three sites at Toms Point: approximately 3.2 kilograms at CA-MRN-201 (from surface collection units only), just over 8 kilograms at CA-MRN-202 (from eleven excavation units), and 5 kilograms at CA-MRN-363 (from a single excavation unit). I assume that most shell fragments reflect the leftovers of past meals; however, one abalone button (from CA-MRN-202), two *Olivella biplicata* beads (from CA-MRN-201 and -202), and a long history of clamshell bead manufacture in the region are reminders of other important cultural practices besides catching animals and preparing

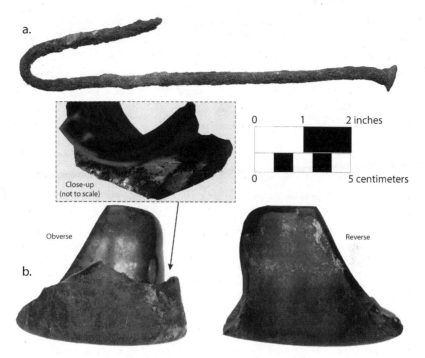

FIGURE 14 Artifacts collected from CA-MRN-202 include (a.) a metal spike transformed into a possible fishhook, and (b.) a glass bottle base modified along one edge and hafted to create a tool.

meals. Identifiable clam species include Washington (*Saxidomus nuttalli*), Pacific gaper (*Tresus nuttalli*) and Pacific littleneck (*Protothaca staminea*) clams. Mussel shells include California mussel (*Mytilus californianus*) and bay mussel (*Mytilus trossulus*) species. The Olympia oyster (*Ostrea lurida*) is also native to Tomales Bay but is represented by only a few small fragments at CA-MRN-202 and -363. In addition to bivalves, gastropods include red abalone (*Haliotis rufescens*), purple olive snail (*Olivella biplicata*), whelk (Muricidae), and other unidentifiable species. Crustaceans are represented by fragments of barnacle (Archaeobalanidae) and crab (Cancridae) shells.

Examining the marine shell assemblages, at least two patterns emerge. First, the surprisingly large clamshell assemblage—including several whole clam valves at CA-MRN-363—contrasts with the comparatively small number of abalone shells, which appear to be overemphasized in historical descriptions of the sale of "large quantities" of abalone shell to French merchants (Munro-Fraser 1880:123). Perhaps the nineteenth-century occupants of Toms Point were amassing clams instead of abalone (see chapter 5)? Second, for the

older CA-MRN-363 site, small amounts of mussel and oyster shells (one fragment of each) suggest that Tomales Bay clams were highly prized for thousands of years. At the same time, and quite unlike many San Francisco Bay
shellmounds, the collection of mussels appears to be a recent occurrence at
Toms Point, based on higher mussel shell weights in two areas of Toms Point
occupied in historic times: CA-MRN-202 and CA-MRN-201 (Locus A).

The bones and shells of wild animal species dominate all three zooarchae-
ology assemblages from Toms Point. Domesticated species (chicken, sheep/
goat, cattle, horse/donkey, and pig) were also collected from CA-MRN-202
but not in the quantities one might expect for a place enmeshed in the herd-
ing and processing of domesticated livestock during the mid-nineteenth century. With a NISP of six and a minimum number of individuals (MNI) of
one, chickens (*Gallus gallus*) were sometimes consumed at CA-MRN-202.
While the remains of domesticated ungulates outnumber the remains of wild
ungulate species (e.g., deer), they still appear in small quantities: sheep/goat
(Caprinae; NISP=1, MNI=1), cattle (*Bos taurus*; NISP=20, MNI=2), horse/
donkey (*Equus* sp.; NISP=1, MNI=1), and pig (*Sus scrofa*; NISP=65, MNI=4).
Small numbers of domesticated species reinforce the idea that Wood's trading
post rested on a solid foundation of Indigenous knowledge. Literally. Layered
on top of a much older deposit and in close proximity to two other ancient
sites (CA-MRN-201 and -363), Coast Miwok knowledge of the tides and
shellfish beds, plant communities, and the collection native animal species
buoyed the settler project and its Native workforce. Moreover, the people of
Toms Point were not entirely averse to incorporating sheep (for wool or meat),
poultry, beef, and pork into their foodways repertoire.

Lithics

Even after colonists introduced new technologies in the late 1700s, California
Indians continued to make and use tools that were familiar to them. Ground
stone and flaked stone artifacts are among those tools with protracted histories of manufacture and usage despite the introduction of metal cutting
implements and other processing tools. At Toms Point, Gerkin (1967:8) reported the fragments of an estimated twelve "large heavy mortars," including
straight-sided and rounded examples which date to the Late Period and earlier
(Beardsley 1948). Nearly all other ground stone artifacts collected from CA-
MRN-201 (n=3), -202 (n=32, mostly from the upper thirty centimeters of
the deposit), and -363 (n=12) are fragmentary. Tools identified in the ground
stone collection from CA-MRN-202 include one complete handstone, one

handstone fragment, one rim fragment from a micaceous vessel, and two mortar fragments.

Flaked stone artifacts include formal tools and debitage from obsidian, chert, and other lithic raw materials (basalt and quartzite). Earlier identifications made by Gerkin (1967:9) counted more than 600 pieces of obsidian and chert debitage from CA-MRN-489, as well as 11 chert tools and 539 obsidian tools, including 208 obsidian projectile points diagnostic of the Middle Period, Late Period, and colonial era. Origer (1982:172) analyzed twenty of the projectile points in Gerkin's collection as part of a regional obsidian hydration study and found that the tools dated from 2836 to 312 BP, or 2.8 to 0.9 microns (mean = 1.3 µm, or 614 BP).

Lithic tools collected from the surface of CA-MRN-201 include one obsidian corner-notched projectile point (missing distal end) from Locus A, as well as one chert biface fragment and two chert drills from Locus B. Excavations at CA-MRN-202 produced six obsidian tools, including two cores, one biface, one biface fragment, two projectile point fragments, including the distal end of an obsidian corner-notched point and the proximal end of a side-notched point. Three obsidian biface fragments, two obsidian cores, and one basalt flake tool were collected from CA-MRN-363. In addition to formal tools, lithic debitage from CA-MRN-201 includes chert, or cryptocrystalline silicates (CCS, or fine-grained sedimentary rock) (n=61), obsidian (n=63), and other materials such as basalt and quartzite (n=10). Most lithic debitage, including over 90 percent of obsidian flakes, was collected from the older Locus B of CA-MRN-201. Debitage from CA-MRN-202 includes obsidian (n=53), chert and CCS (n=36), and other materials (n=19). A larger assemblage of obsidian (n=1,071), chert and CCS (n=129), and other (n=38) flakes were collected from CA-MRN-363. All of the obsidian—tools and debitage—from CA-MRN-201, -202, and -363 were geochemically sourced (see below).

Glass and Other Imported Material

Assemblages of imported material collected from CA-MRN-201 and -202 include glass (beads and window, bottle, and container glass fragments), ferrous and nonferrous metal, and ceramic artifacts diagnostic of the mid-nineteenth century. This discussion focuses on glass artifacts, especially flaked bottle glass. Other imported materials collected from CA-MRN-202 and CA-MRN-489 are examined elsewhere (Panich et al. 2018d, 2020). Much of the glass, metal, and ceramic materials probably arrived onsite via overland routes when the mid-1800s trading post operated; however, mass-produced glass, metal, and ceramic objects would have also filtered into the Tomales Bay region during the mission period and even earlier in time considering the two sixteenth-century shipwrecks at Point Reyes. Moreover, I consider still other "sources" of imported materials—including the 1852 *Oxford* shipwreck and an untold number of other ships that wrecked on the California coast. For example, reports of the *Oxford* wreck explained that the ship "lies upon the same spit that wrecked the Dutch barque *Helena*, in 1849" (DAC 1852b:2). A public auction of *Helena*'s salvaged cargo held at Bodega Bay included: "wines and liquors, champagne, brandy, gin, sherry and liqueurs, cheese, a variety. of manufactured goods, and a ship's long boat, half-decked. . . . The above goods, being a portion of the cargo saved from the wreck of the Danish ship 'Helena,' are more or less damaged, and will all be sold . . . to the highest bidder for cash" (*Weekly Alta California* 1849:2). The three archaeological assemblages from Toms Point encourage deeper consideration of the assorted social and economic networks that intersected and encompassed this seemingly isolated place.

For CA-MRN-201, imported material is confined to Locus A. These items include ferrous metal, nonferrous metal, and glass beads and fragments. Ferrous (e.g., nails, pieces of an iron stove, a stirrup, a mule shoe, and numerous metal fragments) and nonferrous (e.g., tin ware fragments, buttons, a lead cap for a gunpowder container, copper alloy percussion caps for muzzleloader firearms, and lead shot) metal artifacts were also collected from CA-MRN-202 (figure 15). Additional imported materials from CA-MRN-202 include ceramic fragments (e.g., porcelain, shell-edged earthenware, salt-glazed stoneware), Prosser (high-fire ceramic) and bone buttons, bone comb fragments, kaolin or white ball clay pipe fragments, glass beads, and hundreds of window, bottle, and container glass sherds.

Glass bead type identifications follow Kidd and Kidd (2012 [1970]). Seven glass beads from CA-MRN-201 include six compound beads—including white-over-white (n=5, IVa11 and IVa13) and red-on-green (n=1, IVa6) beads—and one simple white bead (IIa14). All of the glass beads from CA-MRN-201 are drawn. For CA-MRN-202, glass beads reflect drawn (n=65) and wound (n=3) manufacturing techniques. Of the drawn beads, there are eighteen simple beads colored green (n=1, Ia11), dark purple or "black" (n=2, IIa7), and white (n=15, IIa14). The remaining forty-seven drawn beads are compound red-on-green (n=1, IVa6), red-on-white (a.k.a., *Cornaline d'Aleppo*) (n=6, IVa9), white-over-aqua blue (n=1, IVa14) with twelve engraved lines (four groups of three lines equidistant around bead circumference), and white-over-white (n=39, IVa11 and IVa13). The three wound glass beads from CA-MRN-202 include two simple beads colored white (n=1, W1b2) and irides-

FIGURE 15 Clamshell, abalone shells, pig bones, ceramic and glass fragments, and a panel from an iron box stove litter the floor of one CA-MRN-202 excavation unit. Photograph by Lee M. Panich.

cent dark brown (n=1, W1c), as well as one compound red-on-white bead (n=1, WIIIa; see Karklins 2012 [1970]:70–71).

Broken glass (n=14) from CA-MRN-201 can either be attributed to bottles or other types of containers. For CA-MRN-202, glass sherds from bottles (n=264), other containers (n=177), and window, or "flat," glass (n=156) are found primarily in the upper thirty centimeters of the deposit. Glass from CA-MRN-201 includes unmodified glass fragments (n=5), one modified glass fragment, and glass flakes (n=8). Glass artifacts from CA-MRN-202 include unmodified glass fragments (n=519), modified glass fragments (n=18), glass flakes (n=49), and tools (n=11). For both sites, bottles include amber (n=7), colorless (n=15), green (n=16), light green/aqua (n=3), and dark green (n=232) glass. Predominately used for liquor, wine, or ale, dark green, or "black," glass was manufactured throughout the nineteenth century and especially before the 1890s (Lindsey 2019), which most likely reflects import and consumer practices at the trading post. Additionally, all of the dark green glass (57 percent of the glass fragments) from CA-MRN-201 is culturally modified, and, while only 13 percent of the glass fragments from CA-MRN-202 exhibit deliberate modification, 93 percent (n=73) of the seventy-eight intentionally modified glass artifacts (flakes, tools, and modified fragments) from this site are dark green (see also Layton 1990:184; Lightfoot and Gonzalez 2018:70; Silliman 1997:160, 2004:126).

Additional diagnostic glass from CA-MRN-202 includes one colorless glass bottle finish exhibiting a two-piece mold and crudely applied oil or ring finish dating from the 1830s to 1920s (Lindsey 2019) and two fragments of amber glass (likely from the same bottle) embossed with the letters "AM" and "WOLFE'S" from an Udolpho Wolfe's Aromatic Schnapps bottle. This "medicinal gin tonic, diuretic, antidyspeptic and invigorating cordial" was produced in Schiedam, Netherlands, beginning in 1848 (Fike 2006 [1987]:187). It is unclear whether the bottle arrived at Toms Point via the *Oxford*, the *Helena*, or by some other means.

From Refuge to Recourse

AMS radiocarbon dating, chemical sourcing of archaeological obsidian, and flaked glass analysis help to further contextualize the short-lived trading post within wider historical currents, including the longstanding relationships between Native people and the Toms Point landform and between this place and a broader Indigenous hinterland.

Providing temporal control for Toms Point are thirty AMS radiocarbon assays, including radiocarbon determinations from CA-MRN-201 (n=8), -202 (n=15), and -363 (n=7) (table 3). To account for the marine radiocarbon reservoir effect, dates derived from shell samples were calibrated using a Delta-R correction value of 259 ± 48 (see Panich et al 2018c). For CA-MRN-201, AMS radiocarbon assays on clamshell fragments collected from Locus A (n=4) and Locus B (n=4) confirm the observation that there are two temporally and spatially distinct areas of the deposit. Four conventional dates for Locus A range from 957 ± 20 BP to 826 ± 31 BP, or two-sigma median ages of 350 cal BP (1600 cal CE) and 192 cal BP (1758 cal CE). Minimally, this suggests occupation during the Late Period Phase 2 and colonial era. Diagnostic artifacts extend occupations at the site into the nineteenth century. Locus B produced four much older conventional dates ranging from 4775 ± 31 to 2769 ± 27, which calibrate to two-sigma median ages of 4711 cal BP (2762 cal BCE) and 2180 cal BP (231 cal BCE). Bearing in mind that these data are associated with surface collected marine shell, it is interesting to note that the glass beads, flaked glass, and other imported material are confined to one small area of a larger and considerably older Early Period site.

Examining CA-MRN-202's upper deposit (0–250 centimeters), thirteen shell, bone, and charcoal samples returned conventional AMS radiocarbon dates ranging from 968 ± 20 BP to 73 ± 24 BP, or two-sigma calibrated median ages of 358 cal BP (1592 cal CE) and 93 cal BP (1857 cal CE). A profile excavation at the base of the site deposit (262 centimeters) produced two conventional ages of 1545 ± 34 BP and 1541 ± 37 BP, or median two-sigma calibrated dates of 1456 cal BP (494 cal CE) and 1448 cal BP (502 cal CE). In sum, CA-MRN-202 includes mixed nineteenth-century trading post and mission-era deposits above a Late Period Phase 2 occupation, which is on top of an even older and deeply buried Middle Period deposit.

For CA-MRN-363, seven AMS radiocarbon determinations are associated with six shell samples and one bone sample collected from the excavation unit at depths of zero to fifteen centimeters (n=1; shell), thirty-five to forty-five centimeters (n=1; shell), forty-five to fifty-five centimeters (n=2; shell and bone), fifty-five to sixty-five centimeters (n=1; shell), sixty-five to seventy-five centimeters (n=1; shell), and eighty-five to ninety-five centimeters (n=1; shell). Conventional radiocarbon ages for all seven AMS assays range from 4078 ± 28 BP to 2744 ± 25 BP, which calibrate to two-sigma median ages of 3767 cal BP (1818 cal BCE) and 2828 cal BP (879 cal BCE). Four of the seven shell assays associated with sediments at thirty-five to seventy-five centimeters below ground surface (i.e., from the fifty-centimeters deep shell layer discussed above) produced dates of approximately 3700 years ago (3731, 3738, 3761, and 3767 cal BP [two-sigma]), which strongly support occupation during the Early Period. Considering the unequivocally longer Indigenous history evident at Toms Point and returning to Nels Nelson's (1909b) observations of early twentieth-century Coast Miwok families who lived on or near shellmounds, I surmise that local Coast Miwok people—with knowledge of their homeland and the locations of ancient places—determined where George Thomas Wood could and could not establish his trading post.

Flaked stone artifacts add further texture to Indigenous history at Toms Point. One of the more striking aspects of the intertidal lithic assemblage amassed by Gerkin (1967) is the large number of obsidian projectile points that are diagnostic of the Middle, Late, and postcontact periods. Of the more than two hundred projectile points, there are leaf-shaped points (e.g., Excelsior and Houx Contracting Stem) generally characteristic of the Early and Middle Periods (Justice 2002:265, 269). Small, serrated "Stockton" (n=53) points and small, triangular, and corner-notched "Rattlesnake" (n=97) projectile points are Late Period and postcontact types (Justice 2002:353–59, 403). Unlike the Gerkin collection, only one Rattlesnake point fragment was

Table 3 Summary of AMS radiocarbon assays from Toms Point (CA-MRN-201, -202, and -363).

Site (MRN-)	Sample No.[a]	Material	Depth (cm)	ΔR	14C Age (BP)	2σ Cal Age Ranges (CE)	2σ Cal Median Age (CE)[b]
201	DAMS-20852	shell	surface	259 ± 48	882 ± 19	1540–1825	1682
201	DAMS-20853	shell	surface	259 ± 48	826 ± 31	1645–1946, 1921–1950	1758
201	DAMS-20854	shell	surface	259 ± 48	957 ± 20	1494–1692	1600
201	DAMS-20855	shell	surface	259 ± 48	837 ± 21	1633–1899, 1933–1950	1746
201	DAMS-20856	shell	surface	259 ± 48	4203 ± 39	2176–1810 BCE	1987 BCE
201	DAMS-20857	shell	surface	259 ± 48	2769 ± 27	364–78 BCE	231 BCE
201	DAMS-20858	shell	surface	259 ± 48	4330 ± 25	2332–1985 BCE	2159 BCE
201	DAMS-20859	shell	surface	259 ± 48	4775 ± 31	2887–2591 BCE	2762 BCE
202	DAMS-13192	charcoal	80–90	…	73 ± 24	1694–1727, 1812–1863, 1866–1919	1857
202	DAMS-13193	charcoal	90–100	…	86 ± 26	1691–1729, 1810–1923	1844
202	DAMS-13194	charcoal	60–70	…	153 ± 25	1667–1706, 1719–1783, 1796–1819, 1824–1825, 1832–1883, 1914–1949	1773
202	DAMS-13195	charcoal	40	…	121 ± 24	1681–1739, 1744–1763, 1802–1895, 1903–1938	1834

202	DAMS-13196	bone	30–40	...	171 ± 25	1662–1695, 1726–1814, 1837–1842, 1852–1868, 1874–1875	1767
202	DAMS-20860	shell[c]	40–50	259 ± 48	902 ± 20	1532–1808	1658
202	DAMS-20861	shell[c]	30–40	259 ± 48	814 ± 19	1661–1902, 1928–1950	1768
202	DAMS-20862	shell[c]	40–50	259 ± 48	968 ± 20	1491–1685	1592
202	DAMS-20863	shell[c]	60–70	259 ± 48	780 ± 18	1692–1910, 1920–1950	1801
202	DAMS-20840	bone	30–40	...	73 ± 32	1690–1729, 1810–1925	1847
202	DAMS-20841	bone	40–50	...	156 ± 57	1661–1894, 1905–1950	1793
202	DAMS-20842	bone	60–70	...	109 ± 25	1683–1736, 1805–1934	1837
202	DAMS-20843	bone	262	...	1545 ± 34	423–587	494
202	DAMS-20844	bone	262	...	1541 ± 37	424–595	502
202	DAMS-20845	shell	230–250	259 ± 48	844 ± 22	1617–1898, 1934–1950	1738
363	DAMS-20846	shell	0–15	259 ± 48	3948 ± 33	1826–1495 BCE	1655 BCE
363	DAMS-20847	shell	35–45	259 ± 48	4047 ± 23	1923–1632 BCE	1782 BCE
363	DAMS-20848	shell	45–55	259 ± 48	4078 ± 28	1971–1661 BCE	1818 BCE
363	DAMS-23779	bone	45–55	...	2744 ± 25	969–962, 933–826 BCE	879 BCE
363	DAMS-20849	shell	55–65	259 ± 48	4053 ± 25	1932–1637 BCE	1789 BCE
363	DAMS-20850	shell	65–75	259 ± 48	4073 ± 27	1963–1657 BCE	1812 BCE
363	DAMS-20851	shell	85–95	259 ± 48	3777 ± 24	1598–1315 BCE	1456 BCE

[a] DirectAMS (DAMS) radiocarbon dates funded by grants from the American Philosophical Society and the National Science Foundation.

[b] Median probability ages calculated using Calib 7.1 online radiocarbon calibration program (Stuiver et al. 2020).

[c] Shell samples dated by Apodaca (2017).

collected from CA-MRN-201 in 2016, and two point fragments—a piece of a corner-notched point and part of a desert side-notched point—were collected from CA-MRN-202 in 2015 and 2016. Tempting as it may be to hypothesize why so many projectile points were removed from the intertidal zone, the most likely explanation for this patterning centers on the 1964 earthquake and tidal wave which redeposited part of CA-MRN-202 and, with it, the remains of 1,500 years of human habitation into Tomales Bay.

Regardless of postdepositional processes at CA-MRN-202, postcontact manufacture of stone tools and the presence of hundreds of obsidian projectile points from the adjacent intertidal zone support two key points. First, while the nature of obsidian procurement may have changed after contact, it did not end. Coast Miwok women and men at the mid-1800s trading post continued to use lithic technology for a variety of tasks even with access to imported metal tools and glass bottles. In fact, fewer decortication (n=7) and percussion (n=1) flakes (15 percent of debitage) and more bifacial thinning (n=10) and pressure (n=17) flakes (51 percent of debitage) identified in the CA-MRN-202 obsidian debitage suggest that Native people may have placed more emphasis on finishing imported flake blanks and/or sharpening existing tools. In comparison, obsidian debitage from the much older Locus B area of CA-MRN-201 reflects all stages of reduction—including decortication (n=2) and percussion (n=18), biface thinning (n=13), and pressure flaking (n=18)—suggesting retouch and some access to obsidian cobbles (i.e., raw material). Similar to CA-MRN-201's Locus B, CA-MRN-363's larger numbers of biface thinning (n=136) and pressure (n=329) flakes—43 percent of obsidian debitage from this site, compared to fewer decortication (n=21) and percussion (n=51) flakes—suggest emphasis on sharpening existing tools and processing imported flake blanks. The large number of flake fragments, angular shatter, and unidentified flakes (n=534) from CA-MRN-363 further supports my interpretation, especially if Native people are regularly sharpening their stone tools for processing catches of shellfish, fish, sea mammals, and terrestrial fauna.

A second and related point is that through time California Indians made stone tools and conveyed tool blanks and/or lithic raw material over great distances. "Time, effort, and connections" (Silliman 2004:186), continued to be factored into Native peoples' daily and annual routines. As with the China Camp materials (chapter 3), X-ray fluorescence (XRF) analysis of obsidian artifacts connects Toms Point to a larger region and longer record of commerce and persistent mobility. Tools and debitage from CA-MRN-363 reflect far-reaching exchange economies. Approximately 98 percent of obsidian tools and debitage collected from this site come from two key sources north of San

Francisco Bay: Napa Glass Mountain (n=559) and Annadel (n=391) quarries. Smaller numbers (n=6) of obsidian flakes are sourced to the Clear Lake region (Borax Lake and Mt. Konocti quarries). Two pressure flakes, possibly removed by someone resharpening a tool, are sourced to an obsidian quarry (Bodie Hills) east of the Sierra Nevada mountain range—an unusual, but not unheard of, pattern for the California coast during the Middle–Late Period transition and after (e.g., Allen 1998:82; Hughes 2018:71). At CA-MRN-201, nearly two-thirds (n=41) of the obsidian comes from Napa Glass Mountain, and the remainder of obsidian artifacts (n=23), including one projectile point, are from the Annadel source. The same may be said of CA-MRN-202, where approximately one-third (n=21) of the obsidian tools and debitage from this deposit are derived from the Annadel source with the balance arriving from Napa Valley. Through time, while the amount of obsidian carried to Tomales Bay certainly declined, Napa and Annadel obsidian remained a fixture in the persistent stone tool technologies of Toms Point occupants before and after contact.

In addition to fashioning and using flaked stone and ground stone tools, Coast Miwok people also repurposed discarded glass bottles to create sharp cutting implements, even with continued access to chert and obsidian tools and raw material. Flaked glass is frequently reported at California colonial period sites (e.g., Allen 1998; Layton 1990; Silliman 2004; White 1977) and at other sites around the world (e.g., Harrison 2000, 2002, 2003). Researchers have also documented their association with Indigenous laborers taking part in maritime industries (e.g., Ainis et al. 2017; Lightfoot and Gonzalez 2018; Martindale and Jurakic 2006; Russell 2012; Silliman 1997). In Australia, for example, glass tools—among them an adze made from a telegraph insulator— were found in the camps of late nineteenth-century sealers (Walshe and Loy 2004). Flaked glass tools—bifaces, projectile points, scrapers, and burins— were also manufactured for sea mammal hunting and processing tasks tied to the Russian-American Company (Ainis et al. 2017:96–97; Lightfoot and Gonzalez 2018:64–72; Silliman 1997:160–63).

Flaked glass artifacts are poignant examples of Indigenous resilience, as well as examples of the skill required to creatively pair imported Euro-American materials with preexisting technological traditions. Yet, most archaeological analyses of chipped glass tend to focus on functionality, including close study of the mechanics of glass knapping and the purpose of specific tools in contexts of expediency (e.g., cutting, gouging, and scrapping tasks). In this case, lithic debitage analysis has been fruitfully applied to glass flaking debris in order to assess stages of glass reduction. Importantly, as Harrison (2003:331) also reminds us, instead of focusing on what tools people were making and using, archaeologists might also think about how people used them. For Toms Point, where obsidian projectile points and other stone tools were manufactured and used for the past four thousand years, why did Coast Miwok people choose to create and wield glass tools?

The small assemblage of flaked glass artifacts from CA-MRN-201 includes eight glass flakes and one modified glass fragment. The modified glass artifact comes from the side of a straight-sided (molded) light green/aqua bottle and it features retouch along the inner curve of the fragment (figure 16h). The pieces of flaked glass debitage measure approximately one to four centimeters long, and flake types generally reflect early stages of reduction, including decortication (n=1), percussion (n=2), and bifacial thinning (n=3). There are also two flake fragments. One especially clear example of a bifacial thinning flake was produced from the base of a dark green glass bottle; it exhibits "cortex" and multiple flake removals on its dorsal side (figure 16b). While the sample size is small (and compiled from surface collection units without the use of excavation screens), the artifacts support the basic picture of expedient glass tool production at CA-MRN-201 with emphasis on producing a sharp edge from a piece of broken glass.

Unlike CA-MRN-201, small pressure flakes are better represented in the collection of flaked glass debitage from CA-MRN-202. On the one hand, decortication (n=2), percussion (n=5), and bifacial thinning flakes reflect early stages of bottle reduction (figure 16a). Pressure flakes (n=17), on the other hand, suggest additional stages of reduction or retouch associated with sharpening glass tools before or after use (figure 16c). Flake fragments, shatter, and unidentified flakes (n=17) round out the flaked glass debitage from this site. Eleven glass tools from CA-MRN-202 include six expedient tools made from glass sherds, four projectile point preforms, and one hefty bottle base that exhibits extensive retouch along the inner margin (facing the push-up) of the bottle's outer surface (figure 14b). A faint horizontal line of residue is also evident along the outer surface of the bottle base's tall push-up. This may be the place where the object was hafted, or attached, to a handle and then used like an adze for woodworking or processing animal hides. Gerkin (1967:9) collected four dark green bottle bases exhibiting similar modification and two glass flakes from the intertidal zone, but these objects could not be relocated.

I distinguish glass "tools" from "modified glass" based on the amount of retouch exhibited on the artifact. That is, while several fragments of glass have some evidence for light retouch (e.g., one to two flake removals), other glass sherds demonstrate more extensive flaking and represent objects that could conceivably be used as tools. Six artifacts with extensive retouch along one margin of the glass sherd (n=13) are interpreted as expedient tools

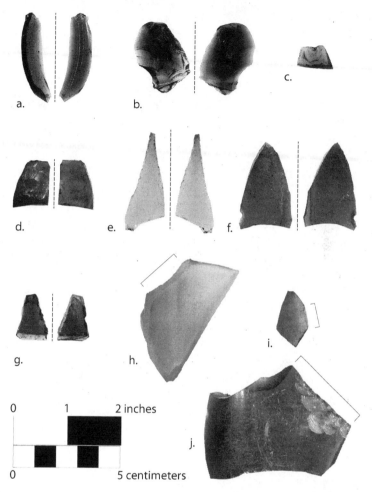

FIGURE 16 Examples of flaked glass artifacts from Toms Point (dark green glass, unless otherwise noted). Debitage: (a.) decortication flake from a bottle base (CA-MRN-202), (b.) bifacial thinning flake (CA-MRN-201), and (c.) pressure flake (CA-MRN-202). Projectile point preforms (all from CA-MRN-202): (d.) fragment with flaking extending across dorsal surface, (e.) colorless glass artifact with retouch along two longest margins, (f.) specimen with a side notch, and (g.) the distal end of a projectile point preform with retouch along the two longest margins. Other glass tools (brackets indicate margin with intentional retouch): (h.) light green/aqua artifact from CA-MRN-201 and (i and j.) two additional glass tools from CA-MRN-202 with retouch along one margin.

(figure 16i–j). Much like flake tools made from chert and obsidian flakes, a piece of broken window glass or bottle glass could be quickly knapped to create a sharp and fortified edge useful for scraping, cutting, and other repetitive processing tasks (see Silliman 2004:187). Other intentionally modified glass fragments from CA-MRN-202 include four projectile point preforms, including three objects created from dark green bottle glass and one fragment of colorless flat glass (figure 16d–g). Flaked glass—including glass projectile points and preforms—have been reported at other Marin County archaeological sites (e.g., Slaymaker 1977:143), as well as other sites on the Central California coast (e.g., Layton 1990:184; Lightfoot and Gonzalez 2018; Silliman 1997; see also Hudson and Bates 2015:78–87). One artifact from CA-MRN-202 shows flake removals extending across the dorsal surface, and the triangular sherd of colorless flat glass shows extensive retouch along its two longer margins. Another triangular glass sherd has one side notch and a curved base reminiscent of desert side-notched projectile points, and a fourth artifact with retouch along its two longest margins may have been the distal end of a projectile point preform that snapped in two during the reduction sequence.

Typological and attribute analyses are useful for understanding how glass tools were created, maintained, and used; yet, what are some of the other explanations for glass tool manufacture and use at Toms Point? Sharp glass tools would have certainly been useful for daily cutting and processing tasks associated with a nineteenth-century trading post, particularly one engaged in the hide and tallow trade. Considering glass artifacts as more than "just another lithic resource" to be incorporated within an Indigenous economy (Martindale and Jurakic 2006:425), flaked glass can also reflect symbolic shifts taking place in colonialized Indigenous societies as well as the "practical politics" of Indigenous peoples actively differentiating and asserting their cultures and identities (Silliman 2001a). Viewed as "objects of survivance," or objects "made in the crucible of colonialism but with the full agency of Native Americans" (Montgomery and Colwell 2019:31), flaked glass tools reflect Native peoples' experiences of colonialism and their continued reliance on traditional technologies to make and use expedient tools to meet the demands of a free market enterprise. Flaked glass tools might further represent the pathways Native laborers created for their families and traditions while demonstrating tacit knowledge of foreign materials and imposed values.

In a similar way, the bones of pigs collected from CA-MRN-202 might, on the one hand, reflect changing foodways preferences and a newly acquired taste for pork. On the other hand, as Silverman (2003:514) suggests, we should also consider the possibility that Native people were keeping pigs and other livestock as a "quiet" revanchist strategy for enhancing customs and claiming land. For the flaked glass assemblage, tools made from broken glass could be symbolic of the ancient places and technological traditions layered below the feet of Coast Miwok people who were responding to new circumstances and materials. As mnemonic objects, glass tools recalled and reasserted a history and identity. Moreover, recycling glass bottles into tools might also signal familiarity with introduced goods as well as the desire for distinction by transforming the bottles "in a manner that was both unfamiliar to Europeans and somewhat contrary to the consumer aesthetic of the market economy" (Martindale and Jurakic 2006:425). Repurposing "trash," a lasting byproduct and highly visible symbol of settler claims to Indigenous land, reveals how Native people could in fact assert their culture and identity by skillfully redeploying imported material—and reconfiguring foreign rules about how glass should be used and disposed—within a living cultural tradition (i.e., flintknapping). Modernity is called into question once again.

Summary

When George T. Wood established a home and business at Tomales Bay during the 1840s, Coast Miwok people had by that time already experienced approximately six decades of colonial invasion by missionaries, merchants, and other representatives of England, Spain, Russia, Mexico, and the United States. By the 1840s, Coast Miwok families residing at Rancho Nicasio were engaged in a legal battle with the Mexican government over their sovereign claim to eighty thousand acres and the ancient village of Echa-tamal. Other Coast Miwok people remained living around the former mission of San Rafael, but also rotated between visits with family members at Echa-tamal and Tomales Bay (Schneider 2015b:706). Some would relocate north and find work at the RAC colony of Ross until it closed in 1841, and many others labored at one or more of the numerous rancho estates established throughout the region. Those who made the decision to interact with Wood, in other words, were probably not unfamiliar with his interest in laying claim to a section of coastline for personal profit. In fact, some Coast Miwok people residing at the northern end of Tomales Bay may have held personal memories—or had heard stories from relatives and friends—about encounters with a Franciscan padre, an English marine, a Spanish soldier, a Russian merchant, a Native Alaskan hunter, or a horseback vaquero. Varied accounts of strange languages, modes of dress, and encounters were likely to share a common negative theme: outsiders seeking to exploit Coast Miwok people and Coast Miwok lands.

Rather than being ejected outright, however, George Wood was allowed to remain in Marin. Considering the history of colonial encounters for the region, here we might consider instead the potential advantages Coast Miwok people saw in allying with Wood and the coastal enterprise. Like the missions, ranchos, and other colonial experiments that came before, Wood's trading post operated fundamentally on Native ground (DuVal 2006). It is through this critical lens that we must peer. George Wood's Coast Miwok spouse and in-laws "might not have considered his European family a barrier to the new marriage," as Sousa (2015: 716) notes for interethnic unions at Sutter's Fort (1839–48) but rather one route for sustaining community and connections to Native homelands at a time when self-identifying as "Indian" was lethal (see also Hull 2011). A place of history and memory, Toms Point also provided Coast Miwok people space for recourse and asserting their relevance in a changing world.

Several aspects of the Toms Point archaeological assemblages analyzed to date—especially the chronometric data, stone tools and other diagnostic artifacts, and flaked glass assemblage—speak to the ways Indigenous people sought refuge at Tomales Bay during the turmoil of the mission and post-mission era. They also found recourse. Undoubtedly during their engagements with assorted colonial institutions and representatives between the late 1700s and the late 1800s, Coast Miwok people persisted—their culture and identities transformed and persevered—especially when confronted with the sharp realities of survival. To what end did Coast Miwok people persist? Memory, mobility, and an unassailable sense of place motivated Coast Miwok to find places of refuge and recourse. In these spaces, they made choices about their future in keeping with treasured pasts and the contingencies of the present. The ability to not only resist but to also rebuild is central to the resilience concept discussed more in the next chapter. Resilience is at the heart of a Coast Miwok sense of belonging upheld from the past to the present day.

Note

1. "Huezos de abalorios del que ellos hazen" (Wagner 1931:344), or "bone beads that they make" (my translation), is probably a reference to white clamshell disk beads.

5

Seeing Resilience

We called ourselves liwánwali (liwa—water, wali—spirit).
—TOM SMITH, 1931

We [Nicasio people] call the Tomales and Bodega people tamalko (coast people).
—MARIA COPA, 1932

IT WASN'T ENOUGH for a meal, but it was fun. One afternoon of clamming at Bodega Bay, where my family gathered after the New Year to hunt Washington clams (*Saxidomus nuttalli*) and eat cioppino, resulted in sore limbs and a handful of littleneck clams. Although the "Washingtons" remained elusive for us that day, I was able to find a few random valves in the mudflats—the leftovers of some other creature's New Year's feast. In lieu of preparing a meal, I could instead break the shells and then rough-out, drill, and polish the shell fragments to make clam beads—"our money," as Tom Smith, a member of my extended family, referred to clamshell disk beads. To produce a few beads is a challenge, but to make them from the shells of an animal you collected from the bay is quite another process. To be able to read the tides, locate the clam beds, identify the animal's tiny siphon holes, dig for the deeply buried clams and dislodge them from their homes without breaking your back, and process the catch is another procedure altogether that is usually, admittedly, forgotten when handling a single clamshell bead a little smaller than the size of a US dime. Our tools—shovels and hand rakes—may have differed from the digging sticks wielded by our ancestors, but we made sure to leave an offering of tobacco for the clams we had hoped to collect. We carried fishing licenses issued by the State of California, whereas Tom Smith and kin privately owned the rights to collect from designated clam beds. My family and I may have ultimately struggled to locate Washington clams, but the scattered shells and shell fragments that we took home were enough to fuel a one-thousand-year-old tradition for another year. The setting and tools may have differed from the world that Tom Smith and Maria Copa experienced and remembered when they were interviewed by anthropologist Isabel

Kelly in the early 1930s (see Collier and Thalman 1996), but the relationships and interactions with our shared homeland and homewaters reach across time.

The goal of this chapter is to draw connections between the archaeology conducted at the China Camp and Toms Point study sites and to further explore the process of resilience I see sustaining Coast Miwok people throughout subsequent phases of colonial intrusion and upheaval. Three core themes—refuge, recourse, and resilience—are introduced in this book. Refuge seeking, the focus of chapter 3, casts light on active and power-laden space, an Indigenous hinterland beyond the walls of colonial missions, forts, and ranches where California Indians rebuffed colonial attempts to extinguish their cultures and erase their ties to place. Purposeful trips to and interactions with shellmounds—living, working, and eating on them—constitute incorporated memories, or routinized acts of remembering the past, as well as powerful inscriptive commemorations with the capacity to refuse colonial imposition and construct a future. In chapter 4, I introduced the idea that Native people sought to distance themselves from colonial intrusion. They also simultaneously sought recourse through strategic engagements with other people, modes of living, and materials introduced to California during the colonial era. The distancing and familiarizing strategies practiced by nineteenth-century Coast Miwok communities were reinforced by place, memory, and mobility—key ingredients that mobilized Native people to evade and participate in colonial programs, reconnect with relatives and make and undo communities, and to create and reinvest in meaningful places and histories. Resistance and rebuilding, I argue, undergird a process of resilience. During the late nineteenth and early twentieth century, shellfishing and fishing can be counted among the suite of cultural practices representing resilient Coast Miwok people and their "large families" picking up the pieces of their lives and reformulating their communities and sense of purpose amid compounding waves of violence, dispossession, and structural racism introduced by Spanish, Mexican, Russian, and American colonizers (Dietz 1976:22).

Colonial Marin in Comparative Perspective

The two study areas (i.e., China Camp and Toms Point) and six Marin County archaeological sites (i.e., CA-MRN-114, -115, -201, -202, -328, and -363) showcase the role of memory, mobility, and place in the study of Native-lived colonialism in California. These archaeological sites also draw attention to the three central themes discussed throughout this book: refuge, recourse, and resilience.

First, to protect their cultures and identities, colonized Indigenous peoples of California—Coast Miwok people among them—sought refuge and ways to remain connected to their homelands. Archaeological collections from the CA-MRN-114, -115, -201, -202, and -328 shellmounds and critical rereads of the colonial archive call attention to populated landscapes beyond the walls and small foundations of colonial settlements established in the San Francisco Bay region. Within these Indigenous hinterlands, as I call them, are places of memory and protection for Native peoples contending with the assorted policies of cultural erasure Euro-American colonists sought to impose. Quite different from descriptions of imposing mission prisons that policed Native bodies and restricted mobility inside and outside missions, for instance, the archaeological records from a growing number of sites showcase a more complex history that casts Indigenous peoples and places as the main characters in events and processes that shaped Indigenous lives and futures (see Schneider et al. 2020). Illustrated at the outset of this book by the example of the Coast Miwok (Huimen) couple, Julúio and Olomojoia, many Indigenous people did not terminate their relationships to their homeland and home communities after crossing the threshold of a Franciscan mission. More often, those connections remained intact and they endured, especially when considering instances of flight and approved furloughs from the missions. When taken at face value, colonial sources have trivialized the crucial and ongoing relationships that Native people maintained with their homelands, resources, and communities and have rendered them epiphenomenal to a widely shared master narrative of colonial domination and Indigenous victimhood.

By breaking down arbitrary intellectual barriers that have prevented archaeologists from studying long-term Indigenous histories—including the categories that have defined "prehistoric" and "historic" sites, materials, and chronologies, as well as a terrestrial bias in archaeology that hampers discussion of the agency and mobility of coastal peoples—a richer and more dynamic landscape comes into focus. Instead of discussing a vacant borderland on the Marin Peninsula between the competing interests of Spanish/Mexican and Russian imperial powers, an Indigenous hinterland concept suggests a region alive with memory, power, and the continued "strategic exploitation of customary waters" (Reid 2015:4), as well as the messiness associated with resisting and accommodating assorted settler claims. Shellmounds may be counted among the numerous hinterland destinations that Coast Miwok people recalled and returned to for protection and empowerment. Negatively impacted by tunneling rodents, sprawling tree roots, and erosion, and systematically dismantled by modern construction projects and the hands of curio collectors and archaeologists, however, most shellmounds have been ravaged by natural and cultural forces and overlooked by researchers as critical spaces of resilient postcontact Indigenous histories and commemorations (Schneider 2015a, 2015b).

Recentering Indigenous priorities and places in the archaeology of colonialism opens up conversations about change and continuity that are not necessarily tied to assertions of colonial authority or to the experiences of Native people at missions and other colonial settlements. For those who inhabited CA-MRN-114, -115, and -328 during the Late Period and mission period, for example, they continued to trade obsidian and create stone tools; they returned seasonally to collect shellfish and prepare meals; they weaved and used baskets; and they constructed conical bark houses atop elevated ancestral space because those places still mattered. They "go on" (Sarris 2013 [1994]:153). Even while Native people made, used, and adorned their bodies and baskets with abalone pendants and clamshell beads, a single scored and snapped sea otter bone from CA-MRN-115 also suggests that Coast Miwok people were drawn into emerging settler economies. As the obsidian source data from the San Francisco Bay and Tomales Bay sites further suggest, hinterlands were dynamic places where the outer edges of colonial power became increasingly frayed and distorted by hesitation, ambiguity, and the denunciations of Indigenous people (see Richard 2012).

Some Coast Miwok people from communities at Tomales Bay and San Pablo Bay chose to evade Franciscan proselytizers. Others—more than two thousand Coast Miwok people—would receive baptism at Franciscan missions, although many of them, including Chief Marin, probably did so cautiously and largely on their own terms. Coast Miwok also labored at Mexican-era ranchos and took up residence at Colony Ross where they learned to communicate in Spanish, English, Russian, and the languages of other Indigenous compatriots whose lives intersected colonial projects. Given this more complex pattern of rejection, acceptance, and ambiguity, one bottom line is that materials such as glass beads and other "historical artifacts" that archaeologists have come to rely on for spotting contact-era sites and studying Native-lived colonialism might not always be the best cues for identifying Indigenous presence. The three China Camp study sites are a case in point. That some Native people fleeing for their lives or avoiding colonial settlements may have purposefully eschewed the trappings of institutions bent on manipulating and erasing Native bodies could help to further explain why so few postcontact archaeological sites in Marin County produce glass beads (Panich and Schneider 2019)—a crucial idea gaining traction in California archaeology (e.g., Byrd et al. 2018; Eerkens and Bartelink 2019; Ruby and Whitaker 2019).

Closer inspection of animal bones, plant remains, shell artifacts, stone tools, and flintknapping debris give an alternative perspective not normally associated with "prehistoric" shellmounds. As places with deep histories, the six sites I investigated at China Camp and Toms Point should make it clear that a concept of "abandonment" (archaeology shorthand used to maintain the boundary between prehistory and history) does not comfortably apply. All of the sites I studied except for MRN-363 show colonial-era occupations layered above much older deposits. Even with stunning 360-degree views of Tomales Bay, Point Reyes, and beyond, for MRN-363 I have argued that this ancient place, with deposits that predate the Roman Empire, may have factored into decisions about where George Wood could establish a coastal enterprise and where he couldn't trespass. These were and are old, powerful, and memorable places.

Bearing in mind that Coast Miwok peoples actively refused colonial transgressions (see also Nelson 2020), discrete components associated with Indigenous apostates—or any discrete moment in time, for that matter—will be difficult to pinpoint on the basis of AMS radiocarbon dates alone. Yet, the combination of diagnostic artifact types (e.g., clam beads, a five-sided abalone ornament, the cut sea otter bone, Rattlesnake and Stockton series projectile points), radiocarbon dates, geochemical details gathered from unassuming mussel shell "waste" piled up seasonally and steadily over time, and obsidian source provenance data help to further bypass the intellectual barriers that have long prevented serious scholarly inquiry into the protracted and life-sustaining histories of mounded landscapes in the San Francisco Bay region. In the absence of particular forms of evidence, archaeologists might instead pay closer attention to these and other forms of contextualizing data. Such details can help render an Indigenous hinterland comprised of resilient exchange economies, technologies, and foodways, as well as dynamic mobilities, seasonal journeys to resource collecting areas, and purposeful trips to places of refuge. At shellmound refuges, I argue that Indigenous people sought comfort in their relationships and interactions with these deeply layered cultural archives that, as center points, communicated a necessary and relevant past. Coast Miwok people constructed houses, prepared and consumed meals, created tools, and otherwise commemorated their lives.

The second theme I introduce in this book is the concept of recourse. Even while Coast Miwok people sought to distance themselves from colonial establishments by seeking refuge in their homeland, those who engaged missions, merchant ships, Colony Ross, ranchos, trading posts, and other colonial projects simultaneously became acquainted with new materials and ideas. Distance and familiarity could be maintained, I argue, without jettisoning one's culture and identity. Coast Miwok people instead found recourse by balancing their commitments to the past, present, and future. Toms Point (CA-MRN-201 and -202) is one of numerous places where this happened. People found safe haven at Tomales Bay and Point Reyes; yet survival also necessitated becoming acquainted with new people, ideas, and materials filtering into Coast Miwok societies. Just as Coast Miwok people may have returned to shellmounds and other places to keep the past, their sustained relationships to meaningful places and waters ensured a future and generated a sense of belonging for their imperiled communities. Pondering the burned remains of a conical bark house on top of CA-MRN-115 and the three conical homes depicted on an 1862 United States Coast Survey map featuring the Toms Point trading post (CA-MRN-202), what connections did Coast Miwok people seek to draw between the past, present, and future by constructing their houses at these ancient places? Traditions, including a sense of place, may be rooted in the past, Lightfoot (2001:239) observes, "but they are constructed in the present, and as such they may be continually in the process of reconfiguration, as past actions are reinterpreted and modified to meet contemporary demands." Such reconfigurations took place relative to colonial structuring mechanisms. They also reflect local decisions informed by the past—memories of places, people, and histories—and imagined futures (see Hayes and Cipolla 2015).

California tribes living during the nineteenth century are often portrayed as casualties of settler greed, theft of land, and state-sponsored murder. Archaeological study of Tomales Bay reveals another history: one of recovery and possibility, seclusion and experimentation, and the continuation of cultural practices that supported Coast Miwok people for millennia. Toms Point in particular represents an important counterpoint to popular narratives of victimization and the image crafted by anthropologists of static and unbending Indigenous cultures doomed to extinction. Taking a theoretical cue from Silliman (2001b), labor at places like Toms Point was certainly a source of production for Euro-American colonizers. Labor can also be understood as a vehicle for social action among colonized Indigenous peoples who had the capacity to alter their circumstances for good. Described by Charles Lauff (2016 [1916]:54) as a "rendezvous of all of the Indian tribes" in the region, the trading post at Toms Point was one hub among several mills, farms, and ranches throughout the region where Native people congregated periodically to work and to socialize. During the summer months, Lauff (2016 [1916]:54–55) continued, "it was not an uncommon sight to see 1000 Indians along the [Tomales] bay shore. They would come overland with their supplies of hides, tallow, and skins, and would wait for weeks for the arrival of a vessel." Unrecognizable or unseen by white settlers, California Indians likely also brought with them obsidian from sources at Annadel, Napa Valley, and Clear Lake, as well as beads, pigments, bear skins, food, news, potential marriage partners, reciprocal resource collecting rights, and other resources that might be traded for fish, seaweed, salt, and other maritime commodities.

Inland groups visiting Tomales Bay and Bodega Bay during the summer probably also relished the cool coastal air and the opportunity to swim and dig for clams, which provided a great meal and the shells necessary for bead money (Collier and Thalman 1996:203–4; Driver 1936:194; Peri et al. 1985:211–16). Periodic coastal gatherings at Toms Point may have resembled the "trade feasts" documented ethnographically among tribes in the north San Francisco Bay region (e.g., Peri et al.1985:209; see also Merriam 1967:365–66). In this sense, the drudgery of processing cattle carcasses and other hard work at the trading post was punctuated by communal gatherings that included dances and singing, in some cases reciting "Latin hymns taught by the padres" (Lauff 2016 [1916]:55). Native workers at Toms Point could also "talk English fairly well" (Lauff 2016 [1916]:55), a comment that lends additional support to the observation that Coast Miwok people were especially adept at learning new languages and adapting English, Spanish, and Russian vocabulary to their daily routines (see Callaghan 1970). While George Wood may have sought to amass a fortune "by the aid of his Indians" (Munro-Fraser 1880:123), Native people had also ingeniously fit George Wood and the trading post into their own existing social networks. In the post-mission era, Coast Miwoks and other Native people by and large worked under circumstances and conditions not entirely of their own design and the broader constellation of labor demands and job sites scattered across occupied lands resulted in the dispersal of Native families. Yet, seasonal labor might also have been an important option for those seeking to remain connected to their homelands and loved ones. Mobility still mattered.

As archaeological evidence for foodways and technology collected from CA-MRN-201 and -202 further attest, when confronted with the kind of contingencies and uncertainties that made up daily life in colonial California, Coast Miwok people were quite capable of evoking two seemingly incompatible Indigenous and colonial realities. "It was not a difficult matter," Lauff (2016 [1916]:54–55) commented, to keep Native workers "supplied with food, as deer, bear and wild cattle were plentiful . . . the bay was full of fish and clams . . . the hills were alive with rabbits and quail, and in the bays were millions of wild ducks." As seen at CA-MRN-202, past meals of fish, shellfish, waterfowl, and wild plants were supplemented with pork and poultry (Schneider et al. 2018). Similarly, ground stone fragments and obsidian and chert tools and debitage documented at CA-MRN-201 (Locus A) and

CA-MRN-202 suggest time-honored technological customs. The discovery of lithic tools alongside ceramic fragments as well as several examples of broken and modified bottle glass also suggests an adaptable and living tradition. Still other objects such as cupreous metal spikes and sheeting, iron nails and bolts, brass fixtures, and pieces of a box stove were most likely removed from at least one nineteenth-century shipwreck in Tomales Bay and possibly others—unpredictable floating "sources" of material readily folded into an Indigenous domain.

Some imported materials were probably used at the trading post as is. Other items were repurposed: stripped from the copper-bottomed hulls of ships, people rolled sheets of copper into tubular beads; a fishhook was fashioned from an abandoned metal spike; and Native people transformed bottle glass sherds into handy cutting and processing implements. Instead of viewing these objects as the result of opportunistic "scavenging," I understand them as active recontextualizations within preexisting and highly adaptable Indigenous technological, economic, and social pursuits. They are "gestures," or memorials, to the "experience of colonialism . . . the colonial 'West' transformed into the image of its 'Others' . . . [and] an act of ironic inscription in a contested landscape of invasion" (Harrison 2003:329). In the case of the large iron spike-turned-fishhook from CA-MRN-202, this tool is especially exemplary of the long-standing relationships Coast Miwok held with their homewaters and, discussed more below, the creative blending of deep-seated maritime and intertidal traditions with the ingenuity needed to make those traditions sing in uncertain times.

The idea of Indigenous peoples wielding their knowledge of and ongoing relationships to ancient places while they simultaneously refused and adopted aspects of invading colonial cultures introduces another key theme for this book. This third theme, discussed more in the next section, suggests that a process of resisting and rebuilding, or resilience, best describes the experiences of Indigenous Coast Miwok communities facing ongoing and accumulating waves of sustained colonialism. "Resilience" is a concept widely shared by scholars from several disciplines, including educational psychology, Native American and Indigenous studies, and anthropology (e.g., Daehnke 2019; Fixico 2013; LaFramboise et al. 2006). LaFramboise and co-authors (2006) study and apply the term resilience to characterize the positive, or "prosocial," outcomes of Native youth facing adversity and numerous risks on modern Indian reservations. Daehnke (2019:66) uses the term resilience to describe the Chinook Indian Nation's performance of canoe protocols, which are "active, forward-looking" aspects of Chinook cultural heritage as well as celebrations of the past and ongoing responsibilities to nonhuman and human actors. Resilience is also a term used by Fixico (2013) to characterize tribal sovereignty, reinvention, and nation building in the twentieth century. "Resilience is required of anyone who wishes to survive" and is a necessary first step toward rebuilding, or "adjusting again and again" (Fixico 2013:15, 119).

That all three definitions of resilience prioritize the actions of present-day Indigenous nations helps to underscore my effort to write, first and foremost, about a living Native American community and culture that certainly experienced a traumatic past but also exhibits a bright and stunningly long record of perseverance. Conceptually, "persistence" might be one way to describe the postcontact story of Coast Miwok people. This concept correctly exposes the fallacies of essentialist thinking in anthropology as well as the value of seeing change and continuity as integral parts of Indigenous responses to colonialism. For me, however, "resilience" foregrounds refuge and recourse—and, with them, place, memory, and mobility—as central to the story of my community and my ancestors who sustained a sense of relevance and belonging by making careful decisions to resist and rebuild.

From the late 1700s to the late 1800s, Indigenous Coast Miwok people held tightly to many of their traditions—speaking two Coast Miwok languages (Bodega Miwok and Marin Miwok), practicing mobility, collecting resources for food, medicines, and raw material, and manufacturing baskets, beads, and stone tools—and they were quite capable of adopting new materials and creatively integrating them into preexisting cultural practices. Seeing resilience requires necessary adjustments to the categories archaeologists have normally applied when discussing the material choices of postcontact Indigenous peoples. When faced with applying tired adjectives like "prehistoric" and "historic" to describe aspects of the Coast Miwok world, scholars might instead consider shellmounds as relevant and alive in the modern world and fishing boats, Western-style frame houses, bottle glass tools, metal fishhooks, and other imported materials as enhancements of Native claims to place and history. "Old" might become new again, and "new" can be wielded in the service of tradition. As Gitxaała anthropologist Charles Menzies (2015:132) observed when reflecting on the maritime traditions maintained by his family, "when my uncle lights the fire in his smokehouse with a propane torch his smoked fish is still smoked fish. That his fire sits in a pink ceramic bathtub merely adds to the picture." In populated Indigenous hinterlands, Native people commemorated and constructed their communities and identities as the world closed in around them. Purposeful trips to sites of refuge and finding opportunities for recourse helped retrace and reinscribe relationships to the land, to loved ones, and ultimately helped anchor lives uprooted and violated by colonialism. Resilience frames a deep sense of belonging.

A "Lively Business": Seeing Coast Miwok Resilience

The headline for a brief newspaper article published in the spring of 1901 reads, "Terpsichore on Tomales Bay" (*Sausalito News* [SN] 1901:3). For three consecutive days and nights, the story reads, Native families gathered at Tomales Bay—possibly at Lairds Landing situated on the bay's western shore opposite the small hamlet of Marshall—where they danced, shared meals, and socialized. The celebration sparked considerable excitement in the non-Native community as seen in the story published by the *San Francisco Call*, which described the event's dances, meals, and the "wailing chant" of one elderly man seated atop a shellmound who "[wept] for his dead of several generations ago" in terms of the vanishing Indian trope popular at the time (see also Schneider 2018:88). Coverage of the event in the *Sausalito News* focused instead on California Indian fishermen and shellfish collectors, whose attendance at the multiday ceremonial gathering stymied the local economy. "As the clam diggers have been attending the dance for three days and three nights, Tomales Bay clams are a very scarce article in the market" (SN 1901:3). In 1901, Indigenous communities continued to engage with the lands and waters that pertained to them; they maintained a cultural identity distinct from the outside world; and they also continued to pursue livelihoods and a sense of relevance as California's colonial era extended further into a second century.

Whereas outsiders tended to view late 1800s and early 1900s California Indians as a vanishing race or as itinerant and landless labor making do with colonial forces largely beyond their control, archaeology at China Camp State Park and Toms Point have led me to an alternative perspective. Archaeological and historical research support a long-term picture of Coast Miwok resilience. Indigenous people found protection and spaces for self-preservation in their homelands while also creatively making do with colonial oppression as knowledgeable actors capable of mitigating sweeping change. At places like CA-MRN-114, -115, and -328, Native people sought refuge and protection at familiar gathering places. And at Toms Point, rather than view the mixture of imported and locally manufactured materials from CA-MRN-201 and CA-MRN-202 as symptomatic of cultural loss, to me the mid-1800s assemblage of food remains and metal, glass, and stone tools—as well as the Native ground where the trading post operated—are examples of how Coast Miwok communities created recourse in the years following missionization. Responding to waves of colonial invasion, survival meant balancing familiarity and distance, or keeping separate from and knowledgeable of incoming colonial projects.

In the early 1900s, when Nels Nelson surveyed Tomales Bay shellmounds—including sites on Toms Point—Coast Miwok people were observed working near or living on top of these ancient places (see chapter 4). For example, south of Marshall at the community of Fishermens (now called Marconi), Nelson (1909b:13) recorded a shellmound near "where a small group of Indians still live . . . [but] inasmuch as a good deal of refuse of the same nature was found all about the cottages at present occupied by the Indians, the Shell-heap referred to may be a modern accumulation." An "Indian house" and a beach "occupied by huts of some fishermen" accompany two other Tomales Bay shellmounds, and, at another site, Nelson noted "a house, probably occupied by the Indians who were seen digging clams across the Bay at Marshalls [sic] a few days before, is situated immediately to the southwest of the deposit" (Nelson 1909b:17–18). Unbeknownst to Nelson, during the late 1800s and early 1900s Coast Miwok people of Tomales Bay continued to hold memories of and maintain relationships to their homelands, homewaters, and sacred places—the result being a deliberate spatial pattern of Coast Miwok hamlets ("huts") placed immediately above or nearby older shellmounds, as seen on an 1858 plat (a cadastral map demarcating land holdings) for the Point Reyes region (Matthewson 1858) (figure 17). Continued faith in their rightful access to clam beds contributed to the emplacement of Coast Miwok families (see also Lelièvre 2017:102). In this context, the seemingly perfunctory exercise of digging for clams—an "annoyance" to white settlers seeking to claim and restrict access to property around Tomales Bay (Merriam 1967:365)—might instead reflect critical acts of contestation and empowerment. As examples of resilience, fishing and clamming would have been essential for Native families to remain relevant and seen by the outside world, while also privately attached to places that were being wrested away from them by archaeologists and the steady privatization of land and resources.

From the account of "Mílan," who fled Mission Dolores in 1795 to dig for clams to feed his hungry family (see chapter 2), to the nineteenth-century Toms Point trading post where Indigenous people sometimes held a "good old-fashioned clam bake" during warm summer evenings while waiting for merchant ships to arrive (Lauff 2016 [1916]:55), Indigenous communities collected and consumed shellfish and other native foods throughout multiple waves of Euro-American colonization. Long before the first colonists arrived in California, all six archaeological sites examined in this book boast a long record of shellfish collecting. Whether heaped into large mounds like CA-MRN-115 or spread across sprawling sites like CA-MRN-363, I view the shells of clam, mussel, oyster, abalone, and other species as records of past meals and, more urgently, symbols of long-term relationships to place. "It is

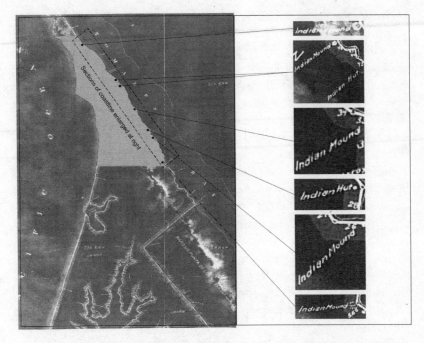

FIGURE 17 An 1858 plat of Rancho Punta de los Reyes Sobrante shows "Indian huts" and "Indian mounds" in close proximity on a section of Tomales Bay's western shore (purposefully obscured to protect the confidential locations of archaeological resources). Courtesy of the Point Reyes National Seashore Museum and Archives.

in the secluded coves of Tomales Bay," another archaeologist observed in the 1950s, "that beachcomber shacks of various Indians or part-Indians exist to the present day, adding their quota of refuse to the shellmound accumulations on which the shacks are built" (Beardsley 1954:19). As places with deep pasts and as "modern accumulations," shellmounds might more accurately reflect ongoing time, or time immemorial (beyond memory), for Coast Miwok alive in the past and present.

Shellfishing and fishing during the late nineteenth and twentieth century represented one source of income for households that remained anchored to the shoreline of Tomales Bay. Pieced together with seasonal jobs at ranches, farms, orchards, domestic settings, and other work sites, shellfishing and fishing closed the circuit in which Native families cultivated relationships of avoidance and proximity by staying mobile and rotating between different community hubs throughout the broader region (e.g., Bauer 2009). Of the Native people and occupations listed in the 1880 census for Nicasio and Point

Reyes Townships, for instance, women typically worked as housekeepers and men worked as ranch hands, fishermen, and clam diggers (United States Census Bureau 1880). Children attended school but sometimes only through sixth grade, as John Carrio remembered in the 1980s, since many families depended on their children to work for additional income (e.g., Anonymous 1989). For those traveling between job sites, they might earn nominal wages by performing manual labor throughout the year. Mobility, as seen during the 1800s, also afforded opportunities to visit with dispersed family members, relay news and information, convey food and resources, and recall the contours of a homeland—its natural resources, cultural places, and history—by continually traversing a region that most outsiders assumed had been emptied of Coast Miwok people. Long hours, hard work, and paltry compensation drove additional wedges between different Native families; these intended constraints, however, may have inadvertently led to new forms of community interaction and place-making practices (see also Law Pezzarossi 2015). Closer inspection of settler economies can tell us about the daily lives and decision-making of Indigenous people. Fishing and clamming at Tomales Bay can also reveal important narratives of place, memory, and mobility—a story of Indigenous resilience—hidden in plain sight.

Beginning in the 1850s, shallow draft schooners put in at Tomales Bay and collected potatoes, butter, clams, livestock, and other products from wharves constructed at Keys Creek, Lairds Landing, Sacramento Landing, and Marshall and transported them to San Francisco merchants, who in turn sent grain and supplies back to West Marin (Avery 2009:41–43). By the 1870s, everything from people to locomotives came into Tomales Bay by steamer (Mason 1976a:38). Weekly—and later, daily—shipments carried numerous sacks of fresh Tomales Bay clams to San Francisco markets. "Importations" announcements appearing in forty-three issues of the *San Francisco Examiner* published between January 5, 1870, and December 30, 1871, list minimally 2,239 sacks and 129 casks of Tomales Bay clams arriving at the port of San Francisco. During an interview at Marshall in 1939, Julia Elgin remembered that "a schooner used to come into Tomales Bay maybe every week or [less] often to buy clams from the old Indians at 2.50 per sack. It only took the old Indians a short time to dig a sack full" (Harrington 1942:28). Applying a rate of $2.50 for every "sack" of clams, an image emerges of an important cash crop. Shellfish, the humble majority of most faunal assemblages from thousand-year-old San Francisco Bay shellmound sites, continued to support Indigenous peoples into the twentieth century.

Not every sack of clams was destined for San Francisco markets and dining room tables. Clams gathered during "clam tide," the term used by

one newspaper to describe the rush of California Indian clam diggers to the
mudflats at low tide (*Marin County Journal* 1877:3), were also sold locally to
tourists, grocers, and other families. In the early 1900s at Pierce Ranch "on
Sunday morning the clubhouse backdoor became a marketplace where Indian
squatters peddled clams at 50 cents a sack" (Mason 1976b:79). Passengers
riding the North Pacific Coast Railroad also witnessed the brisk sale of clams
during brief train stops. The Fishermens (Marconi) and Marshall stations on
the eastern shore of Tomales Bay doubled as impromptu markets (figures 18
and 19). As one train passenger observed, "At Marshalls [*sic*] the scene is en-
livened by the appearance of numerous little huts which dot the shore. These
are occupied by Indians, the relic of a fast-fading nation whose plumes and
feathers are drizzled and torn and who manage to eke out a scanty existence
by digging clams" (*San Francisco Examiner* 1883:1). Besides selling directly to
ships and tourists, many clam diggers took their catches to local businesses
and sold them in exchange for store credit and to be able to access fresh
meat, eggs, produce, and other dry goods. The shops would then sell sacks of
clams at a markup to purveyors for restaurants and markets in San Francisco,
Oakland, and other cities. Shopkeepers at one store in Marshall, for instance,

> buy from the fishermen who live along the shore for a mile or two below
> Marshall's [*sic*], in what is known as Fishermen's [*sic*], the products of their
> nets and seines, and the clams they dig. As the price of clams at Marshall's
> [*sic*] is considerably lower than in the French restaurants, and the price of
> goods at [the store] in no wise suggests a bargain sale at the Emporium,
> there is a wide margin of profit in the business, which is all the greater if
> the clam digger or the fisherman takes his pay in cash and spends it over
> the bar buying 'rot gut,' at the price of the very best Bourbon. (*Marin
> County Tocsin* [MCT] 1907:1, 4)

Native clam peddlers may have "transacted a lively business" (*Petaluma Daily Morning Courier* [PDMC] 1902:1), but discrimination and anti-
miscegenation rhetoric characteristic of the Gilded Age ate away at the livelihood of mixed heritage families of Coast Miwok and European immigrant
descent. In 1879, for example, a "drunken Mexican" later identified as an
"Indian clam peddler" was beaten "to a pulp" by a white detective (*Petaluma
Courier* 1879a:3, 1879b:3). What prompted the beating is unknown, but it
was an especially dangerous time to be an Indian (see Goerke 2007:180–83;
Smith 2014:6–7). The detective was in Marshall investigating the death of
Paul Rieger, a white San Francisco merchant who, during a fishing excur-
sion to Marin County in 1879, was murdered by "Salvador," an Indian from

FIGURE 18 "Fisherman's M.P. 43½," circa 1900. View of Fishermens (now Marconi, CA) looking south. The North Pacific Coast Railroad stop is visible below the tall tree at left. Roy D. Graves Pictorial Collection. Courtesy of the Regents of the University of California, the Bancroft Library, UC Berkeley.

FIGURE 19 Drying fishing nets and other gear in front of Marconi station, Tomales Bay, sometime between 1907 and the 1930s. Courtesy of the Tomales Regional History Center.

Nicasio. After killing Rieger and five others, Salvador fled to Tomales Bay but was later apprehended and executed (*San Francisco Chronicle* 1879:1).

Newspaper articles describing Native people living and working at Tomales Bay between the late 1800s and early 1900s often used racial epithets—such as "half-breed," "redskin," and worse—and overemphasized Native drunkenness and violence. In one racist characterization of Fishermens, the community is described as being:

> composed of an international aggregation, of which the basic principle seems to be Indian blood, with Italian, Spanish, Austrian, Swiss, and other nationalities added. Spanish is the language of the community, though every one speaks English and understands it thoroughly. But with all the mixture there is a very large percentage of Indians, and as I have already said, nearly all the younger generation has Indian blood in their veins. . . . So far as race goes, things are reversed at Fishermen's [*sic*] from what they are popularly supposed to be in the rest of the United States, for we are told that Europe is the mother of America, while at Fishermen's America seems to be the mother while all Europe is represented in the paternal side of the juvenile population. (MCT 1907:4)

The 1906 earthquake that destroyed much of the city of San Francisco appears to mark a turning point in the clamming economy and in the lives of Indigenous families at Tomales Bay. According to one account, a drop in sea level following the earthquake prevented people from using boats to access clam beds. "In consequence of the great earthquake the [Native] and Spanish population about Marshalls and Tomales bay have been practically thrown out of employment. A large number of these people were engaged in supplying clams for the market . . . in many instances the former clam diggers have been reduced to poverty" (*San Francisco Call* 1907:11). When the land lurched as much as seventeen feet in some areas, landslides triggered by the earthquake occurred on the ridges above Tomales Bay, tidal mud liquefied, and clam beds were buried in silt (Avery 2009:109). In addition to these impacts, the underlying actions of non-Natives who had settled around the bay were also to blame for the devastation of clam beds and the eventual curtailment of shellfish collecting. Herds of grazing livestock owned by numerous Tomales Bay dairies—twenty of them by 1860 (Avery 2009:51)—devoured and trampled grasslands causing creeks to erode and sending runoff and other waste into the bay. An estimated two thousand tons of sediment per square mile washed into Keys Creek (just below Toms Point) alone each year between 1852 and

1902 (Avery 2009:56). Accounting for the numerous creeks that drain into Tomales Bay, one can imagine the broader impacts of ranching, erosion, and sedimentation to the watershed.

In addition to the ecological harm caused by settler farms, dairies, logging, and other extractive enterprises, by the 1870s, polluted San Francisco Bay waters and the high price of tideland sent oyster farmers in search of cleaner water. Installation of the North Pacific Coast Railroad in 1874 facilitated access to Tomales Bay, and by 1875 the first oysters were being farmed and shipped to cities; highly profitable commercial oyster farming accelerated after 1907 and soon "angered local fishermen" when company fences carved up favored tidelands (Avery 2009:90–96). In 1915, for example, the Tomales Bay Oyster Company, owner of "many acres of tide land on Tomales bay" staked off for growing non-native oysters, used the courts to begin administering penalties for trespassers, including "many clam diggers, who at different times have invaded the oyster beds, broken and removed [equipment], and destroyed vast quantities of the young oysters" the company complained (PDMC 1915:8). As the Tomales Bay ecosystem unraveled, "clam diggers" were ironically blamed for the declining health of clam beds (see Baker 1992). Courts imposed catch limits and exacted fines fearing "a fate for the Great Washington clam similar to that which has overtaken the abalone in the vicinity of Bodega Bay" (*Santa Rosa Press Democrat* 1925:9). A strong oyster lobby and a deadly red tide in 1929, which killed four and put "more than 200 Indians who have made their living digging clams and mussels on the shores of Tomales Bay . . . out of work" due to a quarantine (*Oakland Tribune* 1929:1), placed an additional burden on Native families who had looked to clams as a source of food and income. The low price of clams during the Great Depression and harvest limits, which undermined the traditional ecological practice of aerating beds and removing older clams to encourage younger clams to grow (Baker 1992:29), marked the beginning of the end of for-profit clamming at Tomales Bay. As Coast Miwok elder Sam Carrio recalled in an interview during the 1990s, at that time "we didn't get but three cents a pound. That's a few bucks for a hundred pound gunny sack. Lord, we'd push a skiff around all day just for that. The harvest limit killed that business" (Baker 1992:29).

"Resilience" is probably not a word that many Coast Miwok people uttered when their clam beds diminished and disappeared, when alcoholism and violence ripped families and communities apart during the nineteenth and twentieth century, or when children were forcibly taken from their families and placed in distant boarding schools (Compass 1998:78). Resilience does not immediately leap to my mind when seeing a derogatory term, "digger," listed as the tribal identity for my relatives in the 1900 federal census for Bodega Township (United States Census Bureau 1900). In this case, the "legacies" of colonialism are abundantly clear (Lightfoot 2005). The accumulating and ongoing structuring effects of multiple waves of colonial violence continue to oppress Indigenous peoples long after initial encounters with missions, ranchos, and other settler projects. Rather than foregrounding these and other hardships to define the experiences and boundaries of Coast Miwok history, however, what happens when we also "write about what makes us strong" (Coté 2010:13)?

Amid environmental collapse and structural racism, Coast Miwok people endured and remained as adaptable as their predecessors had been with roaming missionaries, rancheros, and merchants during the previous century. Recalling her childhood during the 1940s, Kathleen Smith (Bodega Miwuk and Dry Creek Pomo) writes aphoristically: "we were poor . . . but not impoverished, and certainly rich in experiences and the beauty of nature" (Smith 2014:2). Coast Miwok peoples continued to look to the water and land for food and medicine while also shaping the local economy. By 1919, one year before the United States Bureau of Indian Affairs established the 15.45-acre Graton Rancheria for "landless Indians" of Marshall, Bodega, Tomales, and Sebastopol, the Smith family was pioneering the commercial fishing industry at Bodega Bay. From humble beginnings operating a single rowboat fitted with a sail, the Smith Brothers fishing fleet eventually expanded to include twelve ships and a wharf (LeBaron et al. 2011). Other Coast Miwok fishing vessels included the *Point Reyes,* owned by the Roccas of Tomales Bay, and the *Nicky D*, piloted by Captain Joe Damato of Bodega Bay (Morales and Ortiz 2019; Schneider 2019; see also Coté 2010:59–60). Harkening back to the nameless Coast Miwok tule boat pilot who carried Captain Goycoechea's message to Juan Bautista Matute at Bodega Bay in 1793 (see chapter 4), many families also owned and operated small watercraft for personal use and to ferry ranch supplies, tourists, and sport fishermen across Tomales Bay during the early 1900s (Compass 1998:83).

As Coast Miwok families continually reapplied the resourcefulness necessary to survive, parents also remembered to teach their children about the stories and places that matter. From the 1860s to the 1950s, Lairds Landing was the home of the Felix, Campigli, and Sousa families—the descendants of Coast Miwok families as well as European and Filipino immigrants. As tenants of K Ranch paying rent to live in their ancestral lands, the Felixes, Sousas, Campiglis and many other families continued to hunt and collect traditional resources (Avery 2009, Appendix A; see also Compass 1998:82–84). They also lived in Western-style frame houses, grew potatoes, tended livestock, labored at nearby farms and ranches, and applied their knowledge of the sea to the regional economy by ferrying visitors across Tomales Bay, leading fishing excursions for tourists, and collecting and selling oysters and clams to local businesses. I suspect that on any given day, the blending of such pursuits mattered little compared to the power of remaining in familiar lands and keeping tradition through oral histories and teaching through example the wisdom and lessons of generations past. As Theresa Harlan, a Felix and Campigli descendant, explains: "What I know about my mom's life at Tomales Bay, I learned at the kitchen table playing card games or listening to her talk and laugh with relatives . . . [and one of her fondest memories was] following her dad . . . as they dug for clams. She loved to crack open a clam, wash the sand off in the bay, and eat it right there on the beach" (Harlan 2006:10). Just as archaeology in Marin County has not adequately accounted for change and continuity among postcontact Indigenous peoples, seeing Coast Miwok resilience requires expanded consideration of memory, mobility, and the places that operated in the service of resistance and rebuilding.

Summary

Narratives of Indigenous cultural loss or change-as-loss prevailed in academic and popular discourse throughout the twentieth century. Anthropologists like Alfred Kroeber and his colleagues and students advanced a history of Indigenous peoples laden with essentialist concepts that determined what Native people should look like and also defined the time periods and places where they could be found and appropriately studied. Among the forces most detrimental to Indigenous people and places discussed throughout this book, anthropology and archaeology have negatively impacted the writing of California Indigenous history. "We are thrust back into the past when we deal with you or the knowledge you preserve," Vine Deloria Jr. stated succinctly at a 1973 American Anthropological Association conference symposium comprised of anthropologists and Native American scholars (Deloria 1973:94). Commenting specifically on the Mewan family of languages, which includes Coast Miwok, one anthropologist offered the following conclusion on the "present status" of Miwok peoples:

[They] are already extinct or are represented by only one or two survivors. The conclusion is obvious, namely, that the resisting power of the tribes depends, not on numbers, not on extent of territory, not on aggressive or defensive habits, but solely on degree of accessibility to the whites. Contact with whites is deadly; the Indians cannot hold out against it, and the rapidity of their disappearance is directly proportional to the closeness and duration of the contact. (Merriam 1907:356)

This kind of essentialism persists in the present day, and it is the outgrowth of a much older mentality and outmoded style of writing that minimize the history, contributions, and presence of Indigenous people in the United States (O'Brien 2010). Nowhere in an interview with Merrel Rocca in 2015 does he self-identify as the "last Coast Miwok" on Tomales Bay, as the headline reads for an online article about Rocca (Levin 2015). Instead, interspersed with comments about his La-Z-Boy, the Winnebago where he watches *Buffy the Vampire Slayer*, and other modern amenities in his Marshall home, Merrel Rocca summarizes his family's history:

My grandmother grew up in this A-frame across the road, it was built in 1864. I didn't even know my grandmother was half Indian, Coast Miwok. She never mentioned it until she was on her deathbed. Then she filled out all the papers, so now we're connected with the new casino they built in Rohnert Park. We got two free days there before it opened up. Me and my friend were invited to the opening party. We got to eat all the food that was in there. They brought it to us, we didn't have to move. God, they brought these pot stickers . . . the Indians throw fun parties. (Levin 2015)

In another forward-looking comment that expands on the concept of resilience and the poignant sense of belonging permeating the discussions and analyses presented in this book, Rocca continues:

I've got my own oysters, growing on the dock across the road. When the wind blows, a lot of the times one of the Hog Island sacks will break away and they're floating, and I just pick them up. Free oysters.

I've been looking at this bay for years and years and years. Sometimes I take it for granted, but usually when I'm gone and I come back, it's like, wow, like new again. That's a good view. And one of these days, they're going to charge me for it. Don't laugh. They do that. (Levin 2015)

Throughout this book, I use the term "resilience" to describe the experiences of Coast Miwok people during the colonial era. In adopting this concept, I seek to enhance rather than replace discussions of Indigenous change and continuity, or persistence, through a more concerted effort to center living and future-oriented Native American communities in the study and writing of Indigenous histories. For Indigenous communities encountering and counteracting the very worst expressions of Euro-American colonialism in California, they made careful choices about how to modify and retain aspects of their cultures and identities but also remained resilient—they resisted colonial authority and rebuilt their communities—to remain relevant.

Conclusion

Change is not just about seeing and feeling the differences. Change also gives us the opportunity to learn from the differences and to think. Change then gives us the opportunity to make our lives better.

—GREG SARRIS, 2017

"COAST MIWOK" DOES NOT immediately spring to mind when viewing the *Point Reyes* fishing boat beached on the shore of Tomales Bay near the town of Inverness. Constructed in the 1950s and piloted by members of the Rocca family—present-day residents of Tomales Bay and descendants of Coast Miwok people and European immigrants—the nonoperational gasoline-powered fishing vessel represents the long-term Indigenous resistance and rebuilding I examine in this book. The boat also symbolizes the marginalized, or hidden, heritage of Marin Peninsula's First Peoples whose enduring relationships to their homelands and homewaters have been threatened and continually called into question since the late 1700s by successive waves of colonial intrusion. Partially buried by the sand, with Tomales Bay forming a stunning backdrop, the boat is a frequent subject for photographers (figure 20). It adds an element of age and human history to this rural corner of western Marin County and to a region greatly admired by locals and tourists for its natural beauty and, perhaps ironically, considering the region's role as a safe haven for Indigenous peoples, a sense of isolation from the greater San Francisco Bay Area. For many, the *Point Reyes* might represent a monument reflecting the vague passage of time—a vestige of the "old days"—or a quirky prop for photographs and paintings validating peoples' visits to the region. News coverage generated in the aftermath of an accidental fire that destroyed much of the boat in 2016 suggests that most outsiders would probably also struggle to connect the *Point Reyes* to the Roccas who continue to occupy their family home on the opposite shore (Schneider 2019). As material culture, the *Point Reyes* boat represents yet another example of such commonly overlooked

FIGURE 20 Tomales Bay frames the *Point Reyes* fishing boat.

themes as refuge, recourse, and resilience examined in this book primarily through the China Camp and Toms Point archaeological assemblages, as well as needed adjustments to the archaeology of Indigenous history and presence in California.

Place, Memory, Mobility

I started this book with the story of a Coast Miwok family—Julúio, Olomojoia, and their daughters Rosenda, Manuela Antonia, and Jacinta—who paddled a tule boat from their home at present-day Sausalito in the spring of 1783, crossed the Golden Gate, and continued on to Mission Dolores. By the following fall of 1784, Rosenda passed away and the world Julúio and Olomojoia hoped to construct for themselves and their children started to erode. Both parents and their children died by 1796, their names added to the growing list of Native deaths recorded by Franciscan padres stationed at Mission Dolores. Their deaths represent a darker and more widespread pattern of unimaginable pain and catastrophic suffering experienced by Indigenous peoples at every mission established in California. Reflecting on the challenges my ancestors faced in the past and on my enrollment in a federally recognized Native American tribe, I am reluctant to dwell on a history of death, violence, and cultural extinction. Instead, I am motivated to discuss a different outcome for Coast Miwok peoples. As an Indigenous archaeologist, I seek to pen a different history of my community and about Julúio, Olomojoia, their daughters, and the several thousand Coast Miwok speakers whose lives intersected with colonial missions, ranchos, and other Mexican, Russian, and American settlers who insinuated themselves and their enterprises into Marin and southern Sonoma County. Place occupies the center of my writing and thinking, and I believe that greater attention to places and cultural landscapes will help further improve archaeological study of Indigenous-colonial encounters. As seen in Julúio and Olomojoia's multiple trips between the San Francisco and Marin Peninsulas and considering the numerous examples of flight and approved furlough at missions, Coast Miwok people stayed connected to their communities and loved ones even as colonial power endeavored to tear their families apart. Place called them back. A sense of place formed the glue for reassembling shattered lives.

Many other Native people were born at missions and chose to build communities around these newly formed colonial hubs (Hull and Douglas 2018). In doing so, by assembling around a growing assortment of newer establishments, trips home may have become less frequent. This pattern does not undercut the theme of Indigenous resilience, however. Based on my research, Coast Miwok people often still retained knowledge of villages, resource collecting areas, and other destinations within Indigenous hinterlands that could serve to refortify their cultures and identities over time. As seen in the carbon and oxygen isotope data gathered during the study of archaeological mussel shells, for example, shellfish collecting continued to take place because missions were not as rigorously policed as Franciscan padres—and early anthropologists studying the impacts of missions on California tribes—led us to believe. More essentially, this activity continued because Coast Miwok people remembered places to gather resources and wild foods that could help improve their lives. Mission reports and sacramental registers indicate that Native people regularly departed missions to practice their cultures—they danced, gambled, prepared and consumed meals, formed relationships, and buried deceased family members—beyond the walls of colonial settlements. In still another convincing example of the centrality of place and the enduring memories, pull, and power of ancestral places to bring people together in times of great uncertainty, five Coast Miwok men appealed to the Mexican Government in 1839 for Rancho Nicasio because those lands "pertained" to their ancestors and to their "large families" (Dietz 1976:22). California

Indians made choices and, as we see on the Marin Peninsula, their ability to set their own agenda challenged, unraveled, and altered colonial designs.

Memory and a sense of place were continually "enacted and lived" (Daehnke 2017:181). I have argued that future-oriented Coast Miwok and Southern Pomo women and men found ways to remain connected to meaningful landscapes and waters by traveling across them and engaging with their cultural and natural attributes. By recognizing the limitations of archaeological research that to this day primarily focuses on colonies for studying colonized Indigenous communities, we can instead cast additional and needed light on the assorted techniques (e.g., mobility and resource collecting) Native people practiced to be able to retain access to homelands. Usually viewed through the lens of evolutionary theory, there is more to mobility than food collecting, village placement, and reproductive success. Prior to European colonization, most Native peoples of California—Coast Miwok speakers among them—traveled seasonally to access different plants and animals available throughout the year; they made trips to attend dances and other social events; to enjoy cooler or warmer locales; and they regularly moved between larger villages and smaller encampments within defined territories. An enhanced perspective of mobility identifies this practice as a protracted tradition that enabled resistance and rebuilding efforts throughout the colonial era. Policy aimed at controlling the movements of Native people at missions, for example, softened over time and especially when resource-strapped Franciscan padres realized the value of proselytes who could live and provide for themselves in the open country. This idea of "process" was also documented at nearby Rancho Petaluma where Coast Miwok and other Indigenous laborers incorporated ranch labor into their ongoing seasonal rounds (Silliman 2004). Those who worked at the Toms Point trading post probably fit this coastal hub into an intact social circuit of dispersed but interconnected families (Schneider and Panich 2019). Mobility can also be seen in the twentieth century when United States soldiers were continually tasked with "gathering in" California Indians who defiantly traveled off reservation lands to find work and visit family (e.g., Barrett 1908:50). Colonial imposition certainly constrained mobility, but it did not end mobility. As a tradition, Coast Miwok travelers applied and redefined mobility to buffer the impacts of the colonial era—including, evading and accessing settler places, conveying material (e.g., obsidian) and information, and remaining connected to family and kin networks—and by remaining mobile they retraced the contours of home with every footstep. Taken together, theoretical concepts of place, memory, and mobility frame and inform my analysis of refuge, recourse, and resilience in colonial California.

Refuge, Recourse, Resilience

Writing from the perspective of an enrolled citizen of a sovereign and federally recognized community of Coast Miwok and Southern Pomo people
who descend from just thirteen individuals whose names and identities were
recorded in 1852, this book is not intended to be a recapitulation of the
impacts of and responses to different episodes of colonial invasion. Colonial
trespass, Indigenous population decline, and the theft of traditional lands
and waters are well-trodden themes in conventional accounts of California's
coastal peoples, and they continue to be rehashed in academic and popular
conversation. As explored in chapters 1 and 2, histories based predominately
on colonial archives and archaeology conducted at colonial sites can be inhib-
ited by biases that color perspectives on how and where Indigenous peoples
persevered. What we risk is seeing Native resistance and survival as measures
of the relative strength or weakness of colonial power, rather than the product
of genuine agency or even creative collaborations between "dynamic participants in the structuration of the colonial encounter" (Liebmann and Murphy 2010:10). Just as the notes and records prepared by Franciscan padres—
colonists fundamentally motivated to eliminate Indigenous cultures—are
prone to portraying Native peoples in a negative light (or to ignore aspects
of Native cultures that stubbornly undermine perceived colonial authority),
extensive urban development in the San Francisco Bay region has also greatly
reduced the number of Native spaces that might help articulate alternative
histories of colonialism. Shellmounds in Marin County have been leveled,
excavated, and pothunted. The "shell-dirt," plant and animal remains, tools,
and Native remains were also frequently repurposed as road base, fertilizer,
chicken feed, or as curios in museums and private collections. Consequently, it
may be more difficult to locate and narrate shellmound remnants as anything
other than "prehistoric" sites, even though many remain important gathering
places for postcontact Indigenous communities, places of refuge, and sites of
empowerment and memory that California Indians continue to visit and fight
to protect (e.g., Gould 2018).

This book is also not intended to be a study of the ongoing legacies of colonialism, or the lingering and impactful aftereffects of past colonial encounters that continue to structure and disadvantage modern Native American
tribes seeking political and economic redress (see Lightfoot 2005). Identifying
the numerous and compounding impacts of colonialism and its aftermath are
unquestionably important for understanding the unique experiences of California tribes, especially when reflecting on the many communities, including
Coast Miwok descendants (Smith 1993), who proudly proclaim, "We are still

here!" This powerful statement of Native presence, however, is undermined by terminal narratives of Indigenous culture change or change-as-loss and by the continued overemphasis on the sweeping effects of epidemic diseases, violence, and death for Native communities. Explaining survival in terms of an unusual exception to totalizing and unbending colonial authority is different from viewing survival because of colonialism and the resourcefulness, agency, and strength of Indigenous communities to continually and purposefully reassert their interests. Perhaps unintentionally, "still here" statements are concealed by the idea of a colonial legacy, which correctly identifies colonialism as an ongoing process that continues to impede tribal sovereignty but puts archaeology—more than tribal empiricism—in a unique position to expose and evaluate those impediments in the past and present. As a discipline rooted in a Western epistemology, archaeology has come to depend on particular forms of "evidence" to track and validate postcontact Indigenous practices and presence (Schneider and Hayes 2020). Alternatively, seeing "resilience" acknowledges persistent structural inequalities and the disciplinary limitations of archaeology, and it reflects my efforts as a tribal member and archaeologist to identify overlooked Indigenous peoples, places, mobilities, and belongings as products of resistance and rebuilding in the past and ongoing sources of placemaking. This idea forms the core of my book and research centered around Indigenous people, Indigenous places, and Indigenous choices.

Critical rereads of documents and archaeology conducted outside of mission walls can shed light on undertheorized practices of refuge and self-preservation. In chapter 2, I emphasized the mission "process" and presented examples of paseo, extramural living arrangements, and flight to show that missions were and are constructed and emergent places. This different interpretive lens opens the figurative doors of porous mission edifices to Indigenous hinterlands, bringing into focus landscapes of refuge and possibility. My research at three archaeological sites in China Camp State Park are discussed in chapter 3 and help further elaborate on how some Native people remained connected to their homelands. This too, however, required careful and collaborative selection of field and laboratory methods to detect, collect, and identify materials that might otherwise be missed or misinterpreted. Reanalysis of an existing collection, nondestructive geophysical survey, and targeted excavations of buried features to collect samples for geochemical and chronometric study helped document the persistence of stone tool technology, seasonal shellfish collecting, and architectural traditions. Moreover, the conspicuous absence of mass-produced materials (e.g., glass beads) from the three shellmounds should encourage—not intimidate—archaeologists to reassess their assumptions about what places and handiworks are normally studied to dictate the presence or absence of Native people. For CA-MRN-114, -115, and -328, I argue that clam beads, obsidian projectile points, charred basketry, and marine shell isotope data chronicle a story of continuity and presence, not absence. These materials also serve as reminders for archaeologists to continue dismantling the scholarly divide between prehistory and history and further reassess the evidence normally relied on to discuss Native peoples on both sides of that harmful rift.

In addition to seeking refuge, Native people found recourse. They leveraged enduring cultures and senses of place to survive and reconstitute their communities after the 1830s. Discussed in chapter 4, Coast Miwok survivors alive at this time created outlets—and a future—for their culture and families amid new relationships, settings, and activities. Founded by George Wood in 1849, for example, the trading post at Toms Point operated during California's gold rush, a moment when upwards of three hundred thousand people poured through the Golden Gate in search of fortune. For those who had already miraculously survived the missions, kidnapping and coerced labor constantly retested Indigenous resolve. The gold rush also ushered in one of the most destructive eras in California Indian history characterized by environmental destruction and the cataclysmic loss of life attributed to genocide, or the intentional, financed, and indiscriminate killing of Native children, women, and men (Lindsay 2012). As the world rushed to California and new laws increasingly devalued Indigenous lives and land rights, many Native families—called "half-breeds" and worse—understandably hid themselves and their identities. They "kept the language silent," as one Graton Rancheria elder, Jeanne Billy, recalled her grandmother (and my great-great-grandmother) doing in the early 1900s (quoted in Smith 1993:12).

In the secluded coves of Tomales Bay and at other remote communities like Nicasio, Coast Miwok families would also carefully reassemble the pieces of their former communities in the company of lands and waters that had sustained them for millennia. George Wood may have sought wealth "by the aid of his Indians" at Toms Point (Munro-Fraser 1880:123), but Indigenous knowledge seems to have permeated this small trading post. Knowledge of the land and four-thousand-year-old places like CA-MRN-363 may have determined where Wood could locate the intrusive outpost. Catches of shellfish, fish, and waterfowl taken from Tomales Bay waters fed the small Toms Point community, and the shells of abalone pried from rocks within familiar collecting grounds around the Point Reyes Peninsula could also be sold to passing ships. The skilled labor of Coast Miwok blacksmiths, hide workers, and carpenters fueled the trading post, but their use of obsidian, chert, metal, and bottle glass tools simultaneously prolonged technological traditions still germane even in such "modern" social conditions. Coast Miwok people also traveled between Tomales Bay and gathering places and work sites in the broader region (Schneider and Panich 2019). Their labor was exploited, but their mobility, evening dances, tool choices, and traditional foods and medicines still conveyed a sense of history and place, as well as a place for Coast Miwok history in the future.

Amid extended periods of sorrow can be found defiant moments of refusal and celebration central to the process of resilience I foreground in this book. The "resilience" concept I introduce and discuss in chapter 5 reflects the various ways Coast Miwok communities endured and survived by simultaneously maintaining distance and familiarity with colonial peoples, places, and materials. As narrated through six archaeological assemblages from China Camp and Toms Point, Native people sometimes vehemently avoided colonial interlopers by voting with their feet, casting off introduced materials, and seeking refuge in familiar lands. They would also find recourse and a future by creatively participating in colonial projects that fundamentally sought to exploit and supplant Indigenous peoples as well as take Indian land.

For instance, while some 2,800 Coast Miwok people interacted with missions and missionaries, others could and did pursue opportunities to flee missions and visit or continually reside at home. Later, Coast Miwok individuals labored under questionable circumstances at private ranchos, mills, orchards, and trading posts like the one operated by George Wood at Tomales Bay; yet, the steady demand for California Indian ranch hands, hide workers, mill operators, and farmers was also folded into a calendar and circuit of places visited throughout the year. Into the late nineteenth and early twentieth century, Coast Miwok families continued to ply their culturally and locally specific knowledge of Tomales Bay in novel ways. As Bauer (2009:59) argues, California Indians during this time used mobility and wage labor to "take control of their work activities and define community." The sense of community and belonging stems from inviolable connections to place—an idea best captured in the examples of twentieth-century Coast Miwok families living on or near ancient Tomales Bay shellmounds and confidently reasserting Indigenous history and wisdom in the performance of fishing from customary waters and digging for clams in beds maintained for centuries.

"To Make Our Lives Better"

In closing, Indigenous peoples facing successive waves of Euro-American colonization in California made strategic choices about how best to keep and modify aspects of their cultural traditions. They "persisted." Yet, in the forward-looking process of resisting and rebuilding, they remained resilient by drawing from memories and shared experiences, plugging into powerful cultural places, and remaining mobile. For Coast Miwok peoples, an indelible sense of relevance and belonging derives from a sense of place as well as the effort and skill required to continually make a home during times of enormous uncertainty.

The precarity I have described continues today. As an employee of UC Santa Cruz and guest in the unceded lands of the Uypi tribe of Awaswas-speaking Ohlone peoples, I am daily reminded of the injustices that California Indians continue to face. The Amah Mutsun Tribal Band (Awaswas and Mutsun descendants and stewards of the land where I live, work, and write) is one of more than one hundred tribes throughout California that remain "unacknowledged" by the United States government. Consequently, resources for elder and child care, pathways to a college education, access to healthcare, the ability to protect cultural sites and natural resources, and rights to safeguard and repatriate the remains of ancestors hang in the balance. And yet, the Amah Mutsun have been creative and deliberate in asserting their culture and authority, as well as resilient in their efforts to access, protect, and manage their homeland in keeping with a mandate from Creator. On a national stage, chilling rhetoric from the termination-era (i.e., federal policy of assimilation applied to Native American tribes, including Graton Rancheria, between the 1940s to 1960s) is resurfacing, and some elected representatives have felt empowered to use their status and office to openly question the legitimacy of Native American identities, Indigenous sovereignty, and decolonial reads of American history (Balingit and Meckler 2020; Shepard 2016). For Marin and Sonoma Counties, a rising sea attributed to global climate change continues to carry away sections of coastline and, with them, Coast Miwok sites and burials. Wildfires are laying waste to incomprehensibly large swaths of north bay lands with more conflagrations like the Tubbs, Nuns, Kincade, LNU Lightning Complex, and Glass wildfires and associated impacts to tribal heritage sites and resources likely to occur in the years ahead. Across the San Francisco Bay Area, still other erasures stem from basic misunderstandings about California Indian history and structural "unknowing" of living California Indian communities. In light of these and other challenges, California tribes will continue to resist, rebuild, and remain relevant, and archaeologists must also pursue research that is equally relevant and responsive to tribal directives.

In the years that have passed since beginning my research at China Camp State Park and pursuing new ways to theorize Native experiences of colonial power from the vantage of the places that mattered most to them, additional archaeological examples of refuge and Indigenous hinterlands in California have emerged. Yet, more than a simple matter of repositioning archaeological detective work to identify the countless places where Indigenous peoples sought refuge and found recourse, there remains a critical and much more basic need for knowing *how* to look and redesigning the intellectual apparatuses that inform archaeological method and theory (Schneider 2021). As part of this recalibration, there is continued work to be done in teaching archaeology, both in the classroom and by taking part in public-facing efforts to help transform misperceptions about Indigenous peoples (e.g., K. Schneider et al. 2019). There is also a vital need to continue crafting collaborative and community-oriented research in the service of social justice. In the field, lab, and museum archives, archaeologists should continue investigating the important role of continuity and change in the lives of Indigenous people; they must also document how Native people "learned to live with change" (Sarris 2017:230) and remained the authors of their own futures. This restructuring in archaeology and recentering of Indigenous worlds requires revisiting the categories archaeologists have created and deployed to divvy up time before and after contact.

To see resilience, archaeologists will also need to learn to think big. When researching and writing about California Indian experiences of colonialism, concepts like place, memory, and mobility take on new valences when two, four, or more sites are linked together. A broader landscape also takes shape. "Where do we stop? What is the last place in the territory we mark?" questions chairman of Graton Rancheria, Greg Sarris, when pondering the definition of sacred space. Eventually, he continues, "there would be so many places and connecting lines . . . that the map would finally look like a tightly woven, intricately designed Miwok basket. The patterns would circle around, endless, beautiful, so that the map would, in the end, designate the territory in its entirety as sacred" (Sarris 2003:5, 35). Extending the metaphor, closer inspection of the basket might also reveal a few holes that have worn through the meshwork, other gaps that have been mended with brand new wefts, and perhaps a few decorative clamshell disk beads mixed with colorful glass bead embellishments. In this landscape of Indigenous resilience, trading posts and shellmounds are interconnected and span space and time; obsidian projectile points comingle with flaked bottle glass tools; and gas-powered fishing boats and seasonal trips to Tomales Bay clam beds reflect the ongoing histories and resilient futures of Coast Miwok people.

References

Adelman, Jeremy, and Stephen Aron. 1999. From Borderlands to Borders: Empires, Nation-States, and the Peoples in Between in North American History. *American Historical Review* 104(3):814–41.

Ainis, Amira F., Richard B. Guttenberg, René L. Vellanoweth, Jon M. Erlandson, William E. Kendig, Jessica Colston, and Lisa Thomas. 2017. A Cache Within a Cache: Description of an Abalone "Treasure-Box" from the CA-SNI-14 Redwood Box Cache, San Nicolas Island, Alta California. *California Archaeology* 9(1):79–105.

Allen, Rebecca. 1998. *Native Americans at Mission Santa Cruz, 1791–1834: Interpreting the Archaeological Record.* Perspectives in California Archaeology, Vol. 5. Institute of Archaeology, University of California, Los Angeles.

Anonymous. 1940. Archaeological Site Survey Record for CA-MRN-202. On file at the Northwest Archaeological Information Center, Sonoma State University, Rohnert Park, California.

Anonymous. 1989. "Miwok Descendent Recalls Attending Marshall School." *Point Reyes Light* 42(3). Point Reyes National Seashore Archives, Point Reyes Station, California.

Anonymous. 2000. Ask Doctor Coyote. *News from Native California* 13(4):14.

Apodaca, Alec J. 2017. Selective Harvesting of Pacific Gaper Clams (*Tresus nuttallii*): An Eco-Archaeological Study of Indigenous Clam Bed Management at Colonial Period Toms Point (CA-MRN-202), Tomales Bay, California. Honor's thesis, Department of Anthropology, University of California, Santa Cruz.

Appadurai, Arjun. 1986. Introduction: Commodities and the Politics of Value. In *The Social Life of Things: Commodities in Cultural Perspective*, edited by Arjun Appadurai, pp. 3–63. Cambridge University Press, Cambridge, United Kingdom.

Arkush, Brooke S. 2011. Native Responses to European Intrusion: Cultural Persistence and Agency Among Mission Neophytes in Spanish Colonial California. *Historical Archaeology* 45(4):62–90.

Arndt, Katherine L. 2015. Transplanted to a Northern Clime: Californian Wives and Children in Russian Alaska. *Alaska Journal of Anthropology* 13(2):1–20.

Ashcroft, Lionel. 1992. Miwoks, Missions and Myths: Part 3 of a 3-part Series. *Sausalito Marin Scope*, 12 May 1992:6.

Ashley, Beth. 2007. Retired Bishop Apologizes for Mistreating the Miwoks. *Marin Independent Journal* 26 December. Electronic document, http://www.marinij.com/life styles/ci_7816920, accessed October 1, 2013.

Atalay, Sonya. 2006. Indigenous Archaeology as Decolonizing Practice. *American Indian Quarterly* 30(3/4):280–310.

Atalay, Sonya. 2012. *Community-Based Archaeology: Research with, by, and for Indigenous and Local Communities.* University of California Press, Berkeley.

Avery, Christy. 2009. *Tomales Bay Environmental History and Historic Resource Study: Point Reyes National Seashore*. United States Department of the Interior National Park Service, Pacific West Region, San Francisco.

Axtell, James. 1982. Some Thoughts on the Ethnohistory of Missions. *Ethnohistory* 29(1): 35–41.

Baker, Rob. 1992. The Clam "Gardens" of Tomales Bay. *News from Native California* 6(2):28–29.

Bancroft, Hubert H. 1884. *History of California: Volume 1, 1542–1800*. A. L. Bancroft & Company, San Francisco.

Bancroft, Hubert H. 1886. *History of California: Volume 3, 1825–1840*. History Company, San Francisco.

Bancroft Library. 184?a. "Diseño de Monte del Diablo solicitado por Salbio Pacheco." Land Case Maps, University of California, Berkeley. https://calisphere.org/item/ark:/13030/hb4g500571/, accessed August 13, 2019.

Bancroft Library. 184?b. "Diseño del Rancho San Pedro, Santa Margarita y Las Gallinas." Land Case Maps, University of California, Berkeley. https://oac.cdlib.org/ark:/13030/hb4870050 3/?brand=oac4, accessed August 13, 2019.

Bancroft Library. 1849. "Diseño del terreno del Rancho de Ynigo." Land Case Maps, University of California, Berkeley. https://calisphere.org/item/ark:/13030/hb4x0nb29j/, accessed August 13, 2019.

Bancroft Library. 1858a. "Diseño del Rancho Cañada de Jonive." Land Case Maps, University of California, Berkeley. https://calisphere.org/item/ark:/13030/hb129002q8/, accessed September 18, 2019.

Bancroft Library. 1858b. "Diseño del Rancho Estero Americano." Land Case Maps, University of California, Berkeley. https://calisphere.org/item/ark:/13030/hb1m3nb022/, accessed September 18, 2019.

Bancroft Library. 1858c. "Mapa del Rancho de Santiago Dawson." Land Case Maps, University of California, Berkeley. https://calisphere.org/item/ark:/13030/hb4199n83p/, accessed September 18, 2019.

Banks, Peter M., and Robert I. Orlins. 1981. Investigation of Cultural Resources within the Richmond Harbor Redevelopment Project 11-A, Richmond, Contra Costa County, California. Report prepared for the City of Richmond, California. California Archaeological Consultants, Oakland. On file at the Northwest Archaeological Information Center, Sonoma State University, Rohnert Park, California.

Barr, Juliana. 2009. *Peace Came in the Form of a Woman: Indians and Spaniards in the Texas Borderlands*. University of North Carolina Press, Chapel Hill.

Barr, Juliana. 2011. Geographies of Power: Mapping Indian Borders in the "Borderlands" of the Early Southwest. *The William and Mary Quarterly* 68(1):5–46.

Barrett, John C. 2001. Agency, the Duality of Structure, and the Problem of the Archaeological Record. In *Archaeological Theory Today*, edited by Ian Hodder, pp. 141–64. Polity Press, Cambridge, Massachusetts.

Barrett, Samuel A. 1908. The Ethno-Geography of the Pomo and Neighboring Indians. *University of California Publications in American Archaeology and Ethnology* 6(1):1–332.

Basso, Keith H. 1996. *Wisdom Sits in Places: Landscape and Language Among the Western Apache*. University of New Mexico Press, Albuquerque.

Bauer, William J., Jr. 2009. *'We Are All Like Migrant Workers Here': Work, Community, and Memory on California's Round Valley Reservation, 1850–1941*. University of North Carolina Press, Chapel Hill.

Bauer, William J., Jr. 2016. *California through Native Eyes: Reclaiming History*. University of Washington Press, Seattle.

Bean, Lowell J., and Thomas C. Blackburn (editors). 1976. *Native Californians: A Theoretical Retrospective*. Ballena Press, Menlo Park, California.

Beardsley, Richard K. 1948. Culture Sequences in Central California Archaeology. *American Antiquity* 14(1):1–28.

Beardsley, Richard K. 1954. Temporal and Areal Relationships in Central California Archaeology. *Reports of the University of California Archaeological Survey*, Vol. 24. University of California, Berkeley.

Bender, Barbara. 2001a. Introduction. In *Contested Landscapes: Movement, Exile, and Place*, edited by Barbara Bender and Margot Winer, pp. 1–18. Berg Publishers, London.

Bender, Barbara. 2001b. Landscapes On-the-Move. *Journal of Social Archaeology* 1(1):75–89.

Bennyhoff, James A., and Richard E. Hughes. 1987. Shell Bead and Ornament Exchange Networks between California and the Western Great Basin. *Anthropological Papers of the American Museum of Natural History* 64(2):79–175.

Bernard, Julienne. 2008. An Archaeological Study of Resistance, Persistence, and Culture Change in the San Emigdio Canyon, Kern County, California. PhD dissertation, Department of Anthropology, University of California, Los Angeles.

Bernard, Julienne, and David Robinson. 2018. Contingent Communities in a Region of Refuge. In *Forging Communities in Colonial Alta California*, edited by Kathleen L. Hull and John G. Douglas, pp. 113–32. University of Arizona Press, Tucson.

Bernard, Julienne, David Robinson, and Fraser Sturt. 2014. Points of Refuge in the South Central California Hinterlands. In *Indigenous Landscapes and Spanish Missions: New Perspectives from Archaeology and Ethnohistory*, edited by Lee M. Panich and Tsim D. Schneider, pp. 154–71. University of Arizona Press, Tucson.

Bolton, Herbert E. 1917. The Mission as a Frontier Institution in the Spanish-American Colonies. *The American Historical Review* 23(1):42–61.

Balingit, Moriah, and Laura Meckler. 2020. Trump Alleges "Left-Wing Indoctrination" in Schools, Says He Will Create National Commission to Push More "Pro-American" History. *Washington Post* September 17. Electronic document, https://www.washingtonpost.com/education/trump-history-education/2020/09/17/f405 35ec-ee2c-11ea-ab4e-581edb849379_story.html, accessed September 17, 2020.

Bourdieu, Pierre. 1977. *Outline of a Theory of Practice*. Cambridge University Press, Cambridge, United Kingdom.

Briones, Marvin. 1983. *China Camp and the San Francisco Bay Shrimp Fishery*. Office of Interpretive Services, California Department of Parks and Recreation, Sacramento.

Brooks, James F. 2002. *Captives and Cousins: Slavery, Kinship, and Community in the Southwest Borderlands*. University of North Carolina Press, Chapel Hill.

Brown, Kaitlin M. 2018. Crafting Identity: Acquisition, Production, Use, and Recycling of Soapstone during the Mission Period in Alta California. *American Antiquity* 83(2):244–62.

Brown, Kaitlin M., Jan Timbrook, and Dana N. Bardolph. 2018. "A Song of Resilience": Exploring Communities of Practice in Chumash Basket Weaving in Southern California. *Journal of California and Great Basin Anthropology* 38(2):143–62.

Byram, Scott. 2009. Shell Mounds and Shell Roads: The Destruction of Oregon Coast Middens for Early Road Surfacing. *Current Archaeological Happenings in Oregon* 34(1):6–14.

Byram, Scott. 2013. *Triangulating Archaeological Landscapes: The US Coast Survey in California, 1850–1895*. Contributions of the Archaeological Research Facility, No. 65. University of California, Berkeley.

Byrd, Brian, Adrian R. Whitaker, Patricia J. Mikkelsen, and Jeffrey S. Rosenthal. 2017. San Francisco Bay-Delta Regional Context and Research Design for Native American Archaeological Resources, Caltrans District 4. Far Western Anthropological Research Group, Davis, California. Submitted to the California Department of Transportation. On file at the Northwest Archaeological Information Center, Sonoma State University, Rohnert Park, California.

Byrd, Brian F., Shannon Dearmond, and Laurel Engbring. 2018. Re-visualizing Indigenous Persistence during Colonization from the Perspective of Traditional Settlements in the San Francisco Bay-Delta Area. *Journal of California and Great Basin Anthropology* 38(2):163–90.

Byrne, Dennis R. 2003. Nervous Landscapes: Race and Space in Australia. *Journal of Social Archaeology* 3(2):169–93.

Callaghan, Catherine A. 1970. Bodega Miwok Dictionary. University of California Publications in Linguistics, Vol. 60. University of California Press, Berkeley.

Callaghan, Catherine A. 2004. *Tamal Machchawko: Normalized Coast Miwok Dictionary*. Unpublished manuscript. Federated Indians of Graton Rancheria, Rohnert Park, California.

Carlson, Pamela McGuire, and E. Breck Parkman. 1986. An Exceptional Adaptation: Camillo Ynitia the Last Headman of the Olompalis. *California History* 238–47, 309–10.

Casey, Edward S. 1996. How to Get from Space to Place in a Fairly Short Stretch of Time: Phenomenological Prolegomena. In *Senses of Place*, edited by Steven Feld and Keith H. Basso, pp. 13–52. School of American Research Press, Santa Fe, New Mexico.

Ceci, Lynn. 1984. Shell Midden Deposits as Coastal Resources. *World Archaeology* 16(1): 62–74.

Chang, David A. 2011. Borderlands in a World at Sea: Concow Indians, Native Hawaiians, and South Chinese in Indigenous, Global, and National Spaces. *The Journal of American History* 98(2):384–403.

Cohen, Roger. 2017. Confederate Statues and American Memory. *New York Times* 6 September. Electronic document, https://www.nytimes.com/2017/09/06/opinion/confederate-statues-trump.html, accessed August 21, 2018.

Colley, Charles C. 1970. The Missionization of the Coast Miwok Indians of California. *California Historical Society Quarterly* 49(2):143–62.

Collier, Mary E. T., and Sylvia B. Thalman (editors). 1996. *Interviews with Tom Smith and Maria Copa: Isabel Kelly's Ethnographic Notes on the Coast Miwok Indians of Marin and Southern Sonoma Counties, California*. Miwok Archaeological Preserve of Marin Occasional Paper, No. 6. Miwok Archaeological Preserve of Marin, San Rafael, California.

Compass, Lynn. 1998. Research Design, Case Study, and Proposed Management Plan: Post-Contact Coast Miwok Settlement Patterns and Resource Procurement Strategies in Point Reyes National Seashore. Master's thesis, Department of Anthropology, Sonoma State University, Rohnert Park, California.

Connerton, Paul. 1989. *How Societies Remember*. Cambridge University Press, Cambridge, United Kingdom.

Connerton, Paul. 2008. Seven Types of Forgetting. *Memory Studies* 1(1):59–71.

Cook, Sherburne F. 1960. Colonial Expeditions to the Interior of California, Central Valley, 1800–1820. *University of California Anthropological Records* 16(6):239–92.

Cook, Sherburne F. 1976. *The Conflict between the California Indian and White Civilization*. University of California Press, Berkeley.

Cook, Sherburne F., and Adan E. Treganza. 1947. The Quantitative Investigation of Aboriginal Sites: Comparative Physical and Chemical Analysis of Two California Indian Mounds. *American Antiquity* 13(2):135–41.

Costello, Julia G., and Mary L. Maniery. 1987. *Rice Bowls in the Delta: Artifacts Recovered from the 1915 Asian Community of Walnut Grove, California*. Occasional Paper 16. Institute of Archaeology, University of California, Los Angeles.

Coté, Charlotte. 2010. *Spirits of Our Whaling Ancestors: Revitalizing Makah and Nuu-chah-nulth Traditions*. University of Washington Press, Seattle.

Cruikshank, Julie. 2005. *Do Glaciers Listen? Local Knowledge, Colonial Encounters, and Social Imagination*. University of British Columbia Press, Vancouver.

Cuthrell, Rob Q., Lee M. Panich, and Oliver R. Hegge. 2016. Investigating Native Californian Tobacco Use at Mission Santa Clara, California, through Morphometric Analysis of Tobacco (*Nicotiana* spp.) Seeds. *Journal of Archaeological Science: Reports* 6:451–62.

Daehnke, Jon D. 2017. *Chinook Resilience: Heritage and Cultural Revitalization on the Lower Columbia River*. University of Washington Press, Seattle.

Daily Alta California (DAC). 1849. Speech of Mr. Benton of Missouri: On the Adjudication of Land Titles, and Sale of Gold Mines in New Mexico and California. 6 September:2. California Digital Newspaper Collection, Center for Bibliographic Studies and Research, University of California, Riverside, https://cdnc.ucr.edu, accessed September 20, 2018.

Daily Alta California (DAC). 1852a. Shipping Intelligence. 14 July:2. California Digital Newspaper Collection, Center for Bibliographic Studies and Research, University of California, Riverside, https://cdnc.ucr.edu, accessed September 20, 2018.

Daily Alta California (DAC). 1852b. Loss of the Ship Oxford—Later Intelligence from the Wreck. 17 July:2. California Digital Newspaper Collection, Center for Bibliographic Studies and Research, University of California, Riverside, https://cdnc.ucr.edu, accessed September 20, 2018.

Dana, Richard Henry, Jr. 1937. *Two Years Before the Mast and Twenty-Four Years After*. P. F. Collier & Son Corporation, New York.

Deetz, James. 1963. Archaeological Investigations at La Purisima Mission. *Archaeological Survey Annual Report* 5:161–41.

DeGeorgey, Alex. 2007. Final Report on Archaeological Investigations at CA-MRN-44/H, Angel Island State Park, Marin County, California. Sentinel Archaeological Research, LLC, Geyserville, California. Submitted to the California Department of Parks and Recreation. On file at the Northwest Archaeological Information Center, Sonoma State University, Rohnert Park, California.

DeGeorgey, Alex. 2013. Final Report on Archaeological Investigations at a Stege Mound (CA-CCO-297), Contra Costa County, California. North Coast Resource Management, Santa Rosa, California. Submitted to Pacific Gas and Electric Company. On file at the Northwest Archaeological Information Center, Sonoma State University, Rohnert Park, California.

Deloria, Philip J. 2004. *Indians in Unexpected Places*. University Press of Kansas, Lawrence.

Deloria, Vine, Jr. 1973. Some Criticisms and a Number of Suggestions. In *Anthropology and the American Indian: A Symposium*, edited by James E. Officer, pp. 93–99. The Indian Historian Press, San Francisco, California.

Dickinson, A. Bray. 1957. Ever Tried Tasty Caterpillar Stew? *Daily Independent Journal* 1 June:15. https://www.newspapers.com/image/87923902/, accessed January 29, 2020.

Dietz, Stephen Alan. 1976. Echa-Tamal: A Study of Coast Miwok Acculturation. Master's thesis, Department of Anthropology, San Francisco State University, San Francisco.

Driver, Harold E. 1936. Wappo Ethnography. *University of California Publications in American Archaeology and Ethnology* 36(3):179–220.

DuVal, Kathleen. 2006. *The Native Ground: Indians and Colonists in the Heart of the Continent*. University of Pennsylvania Press, Philadelphia.

Edwards, Clinton R. 1964. Wandering Toponyms: El Puerto de la Bodega and Bodega Bay. *Pacific Historical Review* 33(3):253–72.

Eerkens, Jelmer W., and Eric J. Bartelink. 2019. New Radiocarbon Dates from CA-CCO-138 (Hotchkiss Mound) and CA-CCO-139 (Simone Mound) and Insights into Mounds, Settlement Patterns, and Culture History in the California Delta. *California Archaeology* 11(1):45–63.

Emberson, Geri, Sylvia Thalman, and Tim Campbell. 1999. *Point Reyes National Seashore Cultural Affiliation Report*. Report prepared by the Federated Coast Miwok Cultural Preservation Association, Novato, California. United States Department of the Interior National Park Service, San Francisco.

Essig, E. O., A. Ogden, and C. J. DuFour. 1933. The Russians in California. California Historical Society Special Publication No. 7. *Quarterly of the California Historical Society* 12(3). California Historical Society, San Francisco.

Fabian, Johannes. 1983. *Time and the Other: How Anthropology Makes Its Object*. Columbia University Press, New York.

Farris, Glenn J. 1989. The Russian Imprint on the Colonization of California. In *Columbian Consequences, Volume 1: Archaeological and Historical Perspectives on the Spanish Borderlands West*, edited by David Hurst Thomas, pp. 481–98. Smithsonian Institution Press, Washington, DC.

Farris, Glenn J. 1998. The Bodega Miwok as Seen by Mikhail Tikhonovich Tikhanov in 1818. *Journal of California and Great Basin Anthropology* 20(1):2–12.

Farris, Glenn J. (editor). 2012. *So Far from Home: Russians in Early California*. Heyday, Berkeley, California.

Felton, David L., Frank Lortie, and Peter D. Schulz. 1984. *The Chinese Laundry on Second Street: Papers on the Archaeology at the Woodland Opera House Site*. California Archaeological Reports, No. 24. California Department of Parks and Recreation, Sacramento.

Ferris, Neal. 2009. *The Archaeology of Native-Lived Colonialism: Challenging History in the Great Lakes*. University of Arizona Press, Tucson.

Fike, Richard E. 2006 [1987]. *The Bottle Book: A Comprehensive Guide to Historic, Embossed Medicine Bottles*. The Blackburn Press, Caldwell, New Jersey.

Finstad, Kari M., B. Lynn Ingram, Peter Schweikhardt, Kent G. Lightfoot, Edward M. Luby, and George R. Coles. 2013. New Insights about the Construction and Use of Shell Mounds from the Geochemical Analysis of Mollusks: An Example from the Greater San Francisco Bay. *Journal of Archaeological Science* 40:2648–58.

Fixico, Donald L. 2013. *Indian Resilience and Rebuilding: Indigenous Nations in the Modern American West*. University of Arizona Press, Tucson.

Fracassa, Dominic. 2018. SF's Board of Appeals says Civic Center Statue Many See as Offensive Stays Put. *San Francisco Chronicle* 19 April. Electronic document, https://www.sfchronicle.com/bayarea/article/SF-s-Board-of-Appeals-says-Civic-Center-statue-12849291.php, accessed August 21, 2018.

French, Harold. 1907. Chief Marin of Tamalpais Who Terrorized the Spanish Nearly a Century Ago. *San Francisco Chronicle*, 26 May:A2. https://www.proquest.com, accessed September 14, 2017.

Gallivan, Martin, Danielle Moretti-Langholtz, and Buck Woodard. 2011. Collaborative Archaeology and Strategic Essentialism: Native Empowerment in Tidewater Virginia. *Historical Archaeology* 45(1):10–23.

Gamble, Lynn H., and Irma Carmen Zepeda. 2002. Social Differentiation and Exchange among the Kumeyaay Indians during the Historic Period in California. *Historical Archaeology* 36(2):71–91.

Geiger, Maynard J., and Clement W. Meighan (editors). 1976. *As the Padres Saw Them: California Indian Life and Customs as Reported by the Franciscan Missionaries, 1813–1815*. Santa Barbara Mission Archive-Library, Santa Barbara, California.

Gerkin, Agnes S. 1967. *MRN-S-297: An Intertidal Site on Tom's Point in Three Volumes and Five Apple Cartons*. On file at the Northwest Archaeological Information Center, Sonoma State University, Rohnert Park, California.

Giddens, Anthony. 1979. *Central Problems in Social Theory: Action, Structure, and Contradiction in Social Analysis*. University of California Press, Berkeley.

Gifford, Edward W. 1916. Composition of California Shellmounds. *University of California Publications in American Archaeology and Ethnology* 12(1):1–29.

Gifford, Edward W. 1946. A Reconsideration of Shellmounds with Respect to Population and Nutrition. *American Antiquity* 12(1):50–53.

Gifford, Edward W. 1947. Californian Shell Artifacts. *University of California Anthropological Records* 9(1):1–132.

Goerke, Betty. 2007. *Chief Marin: Leader, Rebel, and Legend.* Heyday Books, Berkeley, California.

Goerke, Betty (editor). 1994. Uncovering the Past at College of Marin. *MAPOM Occasional Paper*, No. 7. Miwok Archaeological Preserve of Marin, San Rafael, California.

Golla, Victor. 2011. *California Indian Languages.* University of California Press, Berkeley.

Gould, Corrina. 2018. Opinion: Desecrating the Ohlone Village Site at West Berkeley Shellmound Won't Solve Housing Crisis. *Berkeleyside* 23 May. Electronic document, https://www.berkeleyside.com/2018/05/23/opinion-desecrating-the-ohlone-village-site-at-west-berkeley-shellmound-wont-solve-housing-crisis, accessed November 26, 2019.

Greengo, Robert E. 1951. Molluscan Species in California Shell Middens. *Reports of the University of California Archaeological Survey*, Vol. 13. University of California, Berkeley.

Greenwood, Roberta S. 1978. Obispeño and Purisimeño Chumash. In *California*, edited by Robert F. Heizer, pp. 520–23. Handbook of North American Indians, Vol. 8, William C. Sturtevant, general editor. Smithsonian Institution, Washington, DC.

Grove, Karen, and Tina M. Niemi. 1999. The San Andreas Fault Zone Near Point Reyes: Late Quaternary Deposition, Deformation, and Paleoseismology. In *Geologic Field Trips in Northern California: California Geological Survey Special Publication* 119, edited by David L. Wagner and Stephan A. Graham, pp. 176–87. Department of Conservation, Division of Mines and Geology, Sacramento, California.

Groza, Randall G., Jeffrey Rosenthal, John Southon, and Randall Milliken. 2011. A Refined Shell Bead Chronology for Late Holocene Central California. *Journal of California and Great Basin Anthropology* 31(2):135–54.

Guest, Francis F. 1973. *Fermín Francisco de Lasuén (1736–1803): A Biography.* Academy of American Franciscan History, Washington, DC.

Guest, Francis F. 1979. An Examination of the Thesis of S. F. Cook on the Forced Conversion of Indians in the California Missions. *Southern California Quarterly* 61(1):1–77.

Haas, Lisbeth. 2014. *Saints and Citizens: Indigenous Histories of Colonial Missions and Mexican California.* University of California Press, Berkeley.

Hackel, Steven W. 1998. Land, Labor, and Production: The Colonial Economy of Spanish and Mexican California. In *Contested Eden: California Before the Gold Rush*, edited by Ramón A. Gutiérrez and Richard J. Orsi, pp. 111–46. University of California Press, Berkeley.

Hackel, Steven W. 2005. *Children of Coyote: Missionaries of Saint Francis: Indian-Spanish Relations in Colonial California, 1769–1850.* University of North Carolina Press, Chapel Hill.

Halbwachs, Maurice. 1980. *The Collective Memory*. Translated by Francis J. Ditter, Jr. and Vida Yazdi Ditter. Harper & Row, New York.

Hämäläinen, Pekka. 2008. *The Comanche Empire*. Yale University Press, New Haven, Connecticut.

Hämäläinen, Pekka, and Samuel Truett. 2011. On Borderlands. *Journal of American History* 98(2):338–61.

Hammond, Laura C. 2004. *This Place Will Become Home: Refugee Repatriation to Ethiopia*. Cornell University Press, Ithaca, New York.

Harlan, Theresa. 2006. Bertha Felix Campigli (Coast Miwok, 1882–1949). In *Our People, Our Land, Our Images: International Indigenous Photographers*, pp. 10–12, edited by Hulleah J. Tsinhnahjinnie and Veronica Passalacqua. Heyday Books, Berkeley, California.

Harrington, John P. 1942. John Peabody Harrington Papers: Coast Miwok. In *The Papers of John Peabody Harrington in the Smithsonian Institution, 1907–1957, Volume 2: Northern and Central California*, transcribed and coded by the J. P. Harrington Database Project, Martha J. Macri, Victor K. Golla, and Lisa Woodward, Reel 5, Frames 1–158. University of California, Davis.

Harrington, Mark R. 1945. Shell Lime at Carmel Mission. *The Masterkey* 19(2):70.

Harrison, Rodney. 2000. "Nowadays with Glass": Regional Variation in Aboriginal Bottle Glass Artefacts from Western Australia. *Archaeology in Oceania* 35(1):34–47.

Harrison, Rodney. 2002. Archaeology and the Colonial Encounter: Kimberley Spearpoints, Cultural Identity and Masculinity in the North of Australia. *Journal of Social Archaeology* 2(3):352–77.

Harrison, Rodney. 2003. "The Magical Virtue of These Sharp Things": Colonialism, Mimesis and Knapped Bottle Glass Artefacts in Australia. *Journal of Material Culture* 8(3):311–36.

Hauser, Mark W., and Douglas V. Armstrong. 2012. The Archaeology of Not Being Governed: A Counterpoint to a History of Settlement of Two Colonies in the Eastern Caribbean. *Journal of Social Archaeology* 12:310–33.

Hayes, Katherine F. H. 2008. Memory's Materiality. *The SAA Archaeological Record* 8(1):22–25.

Hayes, Katherine H., and Craig N. Cipolla. 2015. Introduction: Re-Imagining Colonial Pasts, Influencing Colonial Futures. In *Rethinking Colonialism: Comparative Archaeological Approaches*, edited by Craig N. Cipolla and Katherine Howlett Hayes, pp. 1–13. University Press of Florida, Gainesville.

Heizer, Robert F. 1941a. Archaeological Evidence of Sebastian Rodríguez Cermeño's California Visit in 1595. *California Historical Society Quarterly* 20(4):5–22.

Heizer, Robert F. 1941b. The Direct-Historical Approach in California Archaeology. *American Antiquity* 7(2):98–122.

Heizer, Robert F. 1947. Francis Drake and the California Indians, 1579. *University of California Publications in American Archaeology and Ethnology* 42(3):251–302.

Heizer, Robert F. 1949. The California Archaeological Survey. *American Antiquity* 14(3):222–23.

Hildebrandt, William R., and Terry L. Jones. 1992. Evolution of Sea Mammal Hunting: A View from the California and Oregon Coasts. *Journal of Anthropological Archaeology* 11(4):360–401.

Holland-Lulewicz, Jacob, Victor D. Thompson, James Wettstaed, and Mark Williams. 2020. Enduring Traditions and the (Im)materiality of Early Colonial Encounters in the Southeastern United States. *American Antiquity* 85(4):694–714.

Hollimon, Sandra E. 2004. Bear Shamanism and Social Control in Native California Societies. *Society for California Archaeology Newsletter* 38(3):26–31.

Hudson, Travis, and Craig Bates. 2015. *Treasures from Native California: The Legacy of Russian Exploration.* Edited by Thomas Blackburn and John R. Johnson. Left Coast Press, Walnut Creek, California.

Hughes, Richard E. 2018. Obsidian Studies in California Archaeology. *Quaternary International* 482:67–82.

Hull, Kathleen L. 2009. *Pestilence and Persistence: Yosemite Indian Demography and Culture in Colonial California.* University of California Press, Berkeley.

Hull, Kathleen L. 2011. Death and Sex: Procreation in the Wake of Fatal Epidemics within Indigenous Communities. In *The Archaeology of Colonialism: Intimate Encounters and Sexual Effects,* edited by Barbara L. Voss and Eleanor Conlin Casella, pp. 122–37. Cambridge University Press, Cambridge.

Hull, Kathleen L., and Barbara L. Voss. 2016. Native Californians at the Presidio of San Francisco: Analysis of Lithic Specimens from El Polín Spring. *International Journal of Historical Archaeology* 20(2):264–88.

Hull, Kathleen L., and John G. Douglas (editors). 2018. *Forging Communities in Colonial Alta California.* University of Arizona Press, Tucson.

Hunter, Ryan, Stephen W. Silliman, and David B. Landon. 2014. Shellfish Collection and Community Connections in Eighteenth-Century Native New England. *American Antiquity* 79(4):712–29.

Huntington Library. 2006. Early California Population Project Database. Online database, https://www.huntington.org/information/ECPPmain.htm, accessed July 9, 2019.

Ingold, Tim. 2012. No More Ancient; No More Human: The Future Past of Archaeology and Anthropology. In *Archaeology and Anthropology: Past, Present and Future,* edited by David Shankland, pp. 77–89. Berg Publishers, London.

Jackson, Robert H. 1983. Intermarriage at Fort Ross: Evidence from the San Rafael Mission Baptismal Register. *Journal of California and Great Basin Anthropology* 5(2):240–41.

Jackson, Robert H. 1994. *Indian Population Decline: The Missions of Northwestern New Spain, 1687–1840.* University of New Mexico Press, Albuquerque.

Jackson, Robert H., and Edward Castillo. 1995. *Indians, Franciscans, and Spanish Colonization: The Impact of the Mission System on California Indians.* University of New Mexico Press, Albuquerque.

Jackson, Thomas L. 1974. San Jose Village: A Northern Marin County Site: A Preliminary Report on 1972 Excavations. *MAPOM Occasional Paper,* No. 1. Miwok Archaeological Preserve of Marin, San Rafael, California.

Jackson, Thomas L. 1986. Late Prehistoric Obsidian Exchange in Central California. PhD dissertation, Department of Anthropology, Stanford University, Stanford, California.

Johnson, John R. 1984. Indian History in the Santa Barbara Back Country. *Los Padre Notes* 3:12.

Johnson, John R. 2006. On the Ethnolinguistic Identity of the Napa Tribe: The Implications of Chief Constancio Occaye's Narratives as Recorded by Lorenzo G. Yates. *Journal of California and Great Basin Anthropology* 26(2):193–204.

Joyce, Rosemary A. 2012. Life with Things: Archaeology and Materiality. In *Archaeology and Anthropology: Past, Present and Future*, edited by David Shankland, pp. 119–32. Berg Publishers, London.

Justice, Daniel Heath. 2016. A Better World Becoming: Placing Critical Indigenous Studies. In *Critical Indigenous Studies: Engagements in First World Locations*, edited by Aileen Moreton-Robinson, pp. 19–32. University of Arizona Press, Tucson.

Justice, Noel D. 2002. *Stone Age Spear and Arrow Points of California and the Great Basin*. Indiana University Press, Bloomington.

Karklins, Karlis. 2012 [1970]. Guide to the Description and Classification of Glass Beads Found in the Americas. *Beads* 24:62–90.

Kelly, Isabel. 1978. Coast Miwok. In *California*, edited by Robert F. Heizer, pp. 414–35. Handbook of North American Indians, Vol. 8, William C. Sturtevant, general editor. Smithsonian Institution, Washington, DC.

Kenneally, Finbar (editor). 1965. *Writings of Fermín Francisco de Lasuén*, Vol. 2. Translated by Finbar Kenneally. Academy of American Franciscan History, Washington, DC.

Kerr, D. 1862. *Part of Tomales Bay California*. T-sheet map T00849. United States Coast Survey, Washington, DC.

Kidd, Kenneth E., and Martha Ann Kidd. 2012 [1970]. A Classification System for Glass Beads for the Use of Field Archaeologists. *Beads* 24:39–61.

King, Thomas F. 1970a. Archaeology of the Coast Miwok to 1970. In *Contributions to the Archaeology of Point Reyes National Seashore: A Compendium in Honor of Adan E. Treganza*, edited by Robert E. Schenk, pp. 275–87. Treganza Museum Papers, No. 6. San Francisco State College, San Francisco, California.

King, Thomas F. 1970b. The Dead at Tiburon. *Northwestern California Archaeological Society Occasional Paper*, No. 2. Petaluma, California.

King, Thomas F., and Ward F. Upson 1970. Protohistory on Limantour Sandspit: Archaeological Investigations at 4-Mrn-216 and 4-Mrn-298. In *Contributions to the Archaeology of Point Reyes National Seashore: A Compendium in Honor of Adan E. Treganza*, edited by Robert E. Schenk, pp. 115–94. Treganza Museum Papers, No. 6. San Francisco State College, San Francisco, California.

Kroeber, Alfred L. 1925. *Handbook of the Indians of California*. Bureau of American Ethnology Bulletin 78. Smithsonian, Washington, DC.

Kroeber, Alfred L. 1955. Nature of the Land-holding Group. *Ethnohistory* 2(4):303–14.

Kryder-Reid, Elizabeth. 2016. *California Mission Landscapes: Race, Memory, and the Politics of Heritage*. University of Minnesota Press, Minneapolis.

LaFramboise, Teresa D., Dan R. Hoyt, Lisa Oliver, and Les B. Whitbeck. 2006. Family, Community, and School Influences on Resilience among American Indian Adolescents in the Upper Midwest. *Journal of Community Psychology* 34(2):193–209.

Lauff, Charles. 2016 [1916]. *Reminiscences of Charles Lauff: Memories of an Early Marin County Pioneer*. Edited by Laurie Thompson and Brian K. Crawford. Anne T. Kent California Room, Marin County Free Library, San Rafael, California.

Law Pezzarossi, Heather. 2015. Native Basketry and the Dynamics of Social Landscapes in Southern New England. In *Things in Motion: Object Itineraries in Anthropological Practice*, edited by Rosemary A. Joyce and Susan D. Gillespie, pp. 179–99. School for Advanced Research Press, Santa Fe, New Mexico.

Layton, Thomas N. 1990. *Western Pomo Prehistory: Excavations at Albion Head, Nightbirds' Retreat, and Three Chop Village, Mendocino County, California*. Monograph, No. 32. Institute of Archaeology, University of California, Los Angeles.

LeBaron, Gaye, Young Smith, and Kathleen Smith. 2011. "Smith Brothers Fishing in Tomales and Bodega Bays." Digital recording of presentation at Point Reyes National Seashore, November 11, 2011. Point Reyes National Seashore Museum and Archives, Point Reyes Station, California.

Lelièvre, Michelle A. 2017. *Unsettling Mobility: Mediating Mi'kmaw Sovereignty in Post-Contact Nova Scotia*. University of Arizona Press, Tucson.

Leventhal, Alan. 1993. A Reinterpretation of Some Bay Area Shellmound Sites: A View from the Mortuary Complex from CA-ALA-329, the Ryan Mound. Master's thesis, Department of Anthropology, San José State University, San José, California.

Levin, Rachel. 2015. How Was Your Day . . . Last Coast Miwok on Tomales Bay? *OZY* 25 July. Electronic document, https://www.ozy.com/true-story/how-was-your-day-last-coast-miwok-on-tomales-bay/39544/, accessed November 21, 2019.

Libby, Willard F. 1955. *Radiocarbon Dating*. 2nd ed. University of Chicago Press, Chicago.

Liebmann, Matthew, and Melissa J. Murphy. 2011. Rethinking the Archaeology of "Rebels, Backsliders, and Idolaters." In *Enduring Conquests: Rethinking the Archaeology of Resistance to Spanish Colonialism in the Americas*, edited by Matthew Liebmann and Melissa S. Murphy, pp. 3–18. School for Advanced Research Press, Santa Fe, New Mexico.

Lightfoot, Kent G. 1992. Coastal Hunter-Gatherer Settlement Systems in the Southern North Coast Ranges. In *Essays on the Prehistory of Maritime California*, edited by Terry L. Jones, pp. 39–53. Center for Archaeological Research at Davis Publication, No. 10. University of California, Davis.

Lightfoot, Kent G. 1995. Culture Contact Studies: Redefining the Relationship between Prehistoric and Historical Archaeology. *American Antiquity* 60(2):199–17.

Lightfoot, Kent G. 1997. Cultural Construction of Coastal Landscapes: A Middle Holocene Perspective from San Francisco Bay. In *Archaeology of the California Coast during the Middle Holocene*, edited by Jon M. Erlandson and Michael A. Glassow, pp. 129–41. Perspectives in California Archaeology, Vol. 4. Cotsen Institute of Archaeology, University of California, Los Angeles.

Lightfoot, Kent G. 2001. Traditions as Cultural Production: Implications for Contemporary Archaeological Research. In *The Archaeology of Traditions: Agency and History Before and After Columbus*, edited by Timothy R. Pauketat, pp. 237–52. University Press of Florida, Gainesville.

Lightfoot, Kent G. 2005. *Indians, Missionaries, and Merchants: The Legacy of Colonial Encounters on the California Frontiers*. University of California Press, Berkeley.

Lightfoot, Kent G., and Ann E. Danis. 2018. Franciscans, Russians, and Indians on the International Borders of Alta California. In *Franciscans and American Indians in Pan-Borderlands Perspective: Adaptation, Negotiation, and Resistance*, edited by Jeffrey M. Burns and Timothy J. Johnson, pp. 281–94. Academy of American Franciscan History, Oceanside, California.

Lightfoot, Kent G., and Antoinette Martinez. 1995. Frontiers and Boundaries in Archaeological Perspective. *Annual Review of Anthropology* 24:471–92.

Lightfoot, Kent G., and Edward M. Luby. 2002. Late Holocene in the San Francisco Bay Area: Temporal Trends in the Use and Abandonment of Shell Mounds in the East Bay. In *Catalysts to Complexity: Late Holocene Societies of the California Coast*, edited by Jon M. Erlandson and Terry L. Jones, pp. 263–81. Perspectives in California Archaeology, Vol. 6. Cotsen Institute of Archaeology, University of California, Los Angeles.

Lightfoot, Kent G., and Otis Parrish. 2009. *California Indians and Their Environment*. University of California Press, Berkeley.

Lightfoot, Kent G., and Sara L. Gonzalez. 2018. *Metini Village: An Archaeological Study of Sustained Colonialism in Northern California*. Contributions of the Archaeological Research Facility, No. 69. Archaeological Research Facility, University of California, Berkeley.

Lightfoot, Kent G., and William S. Simmons. 1998. Culture Contact in Protohistoric California: Social Contexts of Native and European Encounters. *Journal of California and Great Basin Anthropology* 20(2):138–70.

Lightfoot, Kent G., Antoinette Martinez, and Ann M. Schiff. 1998. Daily Practice and Material Culture in Pluralistic Social Settings: An Archaeological Study of Culture Change and Persistence from Fort Ross, California. *American Antiquity* 63(2):199–222.

Lightfoot, Kent G., Lee M. Panich, Tsim D. Schneider, and K. Elizabeth Soluri. 2009. California Indian Uses of Natural Resources. In *California Indians and Their Environment*, by Kent G. Lightfoot and Otis Parrish, pp. 183–363. University of California Press, Berkeley.

Lightfoot, Kent G., Lee M. Panich, Tsim D. Schneider, and Sara L. Gonzalez. 2013. European Colonialism and the Anthropocene: A View from the Pacific Coast of North America. *Anthropocene* 4:101–15.

Lindsay, Brendan C. 2012. *Murder State: California's Native American Genocide, 1846–1873*. University of Nebraska Press, Lincoln.

Lindsey, Bill. 2019. Historic Glass Bottle Identification & Information Website. Society for Historical Archaeology. https://sha.org/bottle/, accessed October 14, 2019.

London, Jack. 2001 [1905]. *Tales of the Fish Patrol*. Quiet Vision Publishing, Sandy, Utah.

Loud, Llewellyn L. 1912. Notes on Castro Mound #356. *University of California Archaeological Survey Manuscripts*, No. 361-B. Phoebe A. Hearst Museum of Anthropology, University of California, Berkeley.

Loud, Llewellyn L. 1913. Walnut Creek Mounds #419–28, (CA-CCO-239, CA-CCO-240). *University of California Archaeological Survey Manuscripts*, No. 365. Phoebe A. Hearst Museum of Anthropology, University of California, Berkeley.

Luby, Edward M., and Mark F. Gruber. 1999. The Dead Must be Fed: Symbolic Meanings of the Shellmounds of the San Francisco Bay Area. *Cambridge Archaeological Journal* 9(1):95–108.

Luby, Edward M., Clayton D. Drescher, and Kent G. Lightfoot. 2006. Shell Mounds and Mounded Landscapes in the San Francisco Bay Area: An Integrated Approach. *Journal of Island and Coastal Archaeology* 1(2):191–214.

Lycett, Mark T. 2004. Archaeology under the Bell: The Mission as Situated History in Seventeenth Century New Mexico. *Missionalia* 32:357–79.

Mahr, August C. (editor). 1932. The Visit of the "Rurik" to San Francisco in 1816. Translated by August C. Mahr. *Stanford University Publications University Series: History, Economics, and Political Science* 11(2):1–194. Stanford University Press, Palo Alto, California.

Mann, Rob. 2005. Intruding on the Past: The Reuse of Ancient Earthen Mounds by Native Americans. *Southeastern Archaeology* 24(1):1–10.

Marin County Journal (MCJ). 1866. A New Summer Resort. 14 April:2. California Digital Newspaper Collection, Center for Bibliographic Studies and Research, University of California, Riverside, https://cdnc.ucr.edu, accessed September 20, 2018.

Marin County Journal (MCJ). 1872a. The Oldest Pioneer. 2 March:3. California Digital Newspaper Collection, Center for Bibliographic Studies and Research, University of California, Riverside, https://cdnc.ucr.edu, accessed September 20, 2018.

Marin County Journal (MCJ). 1872b. The Court House. 16 March:3. California Digital Newspaper Collection, Center for Bibliographic Studies and Research, University of California, Riverside, https://cdnc.ucr.edu, accessed September 20, 2018.

Marin County Journal (MCJ). 1877. Letter from Marshall. 14 June:3. California Digital Newspaper Collection, Center for Bibliographic Studies and Research, University of California, Riverside, https://cdnc.ucr.edu, accessed September 20, 2018.

Marin County Tocsin (MCT). 1907. Was it a Murder How Santos Soza Died: Details of Some Recent Events at Marshall's and Conditions There. 17 August:1, 4. California Digital Newspaper Collection, Center for Bibliographic Studies and Research, University of California, Riverside, https://cdnc.ucr.edu, accessed October 20, 2019.

Marin Independent Journal. 1952. U.C. Anthropologists Uncover Indian Burial Mounds at Ignacio. 25 October:M9. Phoebe A. Hearst Museum of Anthropology, University of California, Berkeley.

Marin Journal. 1907. Indian Remains Are Plowed Up. 10 January:6. California Digital Newspaper Collection, Center for Bibliographic Studies and Research, University of California, Riverside, https://cdnc.ucr.edu, accessed September 20, 2018.

Marin Journal. 1922. Marin's Old Days. 13 April:7. California Digital Newspaper Collection, Center for Bibliographic Studies and Research, University of California, Riverside, https://cdnc.ucr.edu, accessed September 20, 2018.

Marquínez, Marcelino, and Jayme Escudé. 1814. "Preguntas y Respuestas, Misión de Santa Cruz, 30 Abril 1814." Preguntas y Respuestas Collection, PRA-106, Santa Barbara Mission Archive-Library, Santa Barbara, California.

Martindale, Andrew, and Irena Jurakic. 2006. Identifying Expedient Glass Tools from a Post-Contact Tsimshian Village Using Low Power (10–100x) Magnification. *Journal of Archaeological Science* 33:414–27.

Mason, Jack. 1976a. *Earthquake Bay: A History of Tomales Bay, California.* North Shore Books, Inverness, California.

Mason, Jack. 1976b. The Man from Pierce Point. *Pt. Reyes Historian* 1(3):78–84, 91.

Mason, J. Alden. 1966. Nels Christian Nelson, 1875–1964. *American Antiquity* 31(3): 393–97.

Mason, Roger D., Mark L. Peterson, and Joseph A. Tiffany. 1998. Weighing vs. Counting: Measurement Reliability and the California School of Midden Analysis. *American Antiquity* 63(2):303–24.

Mathes, W. Michael. 2008. *The Russian-Mexican Frontier: Mexican Documents Regarding the Russian Establishments in California 1808–1842.* Fort Ross Interpretive Association, Jenner, California.

Matthewson, R. C. 1858. "Rancho Punta de los Reyes Sobrante." Manuscript map on file at the Point Reyes National Seashore Museum and Archives, Point Reyes Station, California.

McGeein, D. J., and W. C. Mueller. 1955. A Shellmound in Marin County, California. *American Antiquity* 21(1):52–62.

Meehan, Betty. 1982. *From Shell Bed to Shell Midden.* Australian Institute of Aboriginal Studies, Canberra City.

Meighan, Clement W. 1950. Observations on the Efficiency of Shovel Archaeology. *Reports of the University of California Archaeological Survey*, Vol. 7. University of California, Berkeley.

Meighan, Clement W. 1952. Archaeological Sites Survey Record for P-21–000270 (CA-MRN-284/H). On file at the Northwest Archaeological Information Center, Sonoma State University, Rohnert Park, California.

Meighan, Clement W. 1953. Preliminary Excavations at the Thomas Site, Marin County. *Reports of the University of California Archaeological Survey*, No. 19. University of California, Berkeley.

Menzies, Charles R. 2015. Revisiting "Dm Sibilhaa'nm da Laxyuubm Gitxaała (Picking Abalone in Gitxaała Territory)": Vindication, Appropriation, and Archaeology. *BC Studies: The British Columbian Quarterly*, No. 187, pp. 129–53.

Merriam, C. Hart. 1907. Distribution and Classification of the Mewan Stock of California. *American Anthropologist* 9(2):338–57.

Merriam, C. Hart. 1967. Ethnographic Notes on California Indian Tribes III: Ethnological Notes on Central California Indian Tribes, compiled and edited by Robert F. Heizer.

Reports of the University of California Archaeological Survey, No. 68, Part III. University of California, Berkeley.

Meskell, Lynn. 2008. Memory Work and Material Practices. In *Memory Work: Archaeologies of Material Practices*, edited by Barbara J. Mills and William H. Walker, pp. 233–43. School for Advanced Research Press, Santa Fe, New Mexico.

Milliken, Randall. 1995. *A Time of Little Choice: The Disintegration of Tribal Culture in the San Francisco Bay Area, 1769–1810*. Ballena Press, Menlo Park, California.

Milliken, Randall. 2009. Ethnohistory and Ethnogeography of the Coast Miwok and Their Neighbors, 1783–1840. Report prepared for the National Park Service, Golden Gate National Recreational Area, Cultural Resources and Museum Management Division, San Francisco. Archaeological/Historical Consultants, Oakland, California.

Milliken, Randall, Richard T. Fitzgerald, Mark G. Hylkema, Randy Groza, Tom Origer, David G. Bieling, Alan Leventhal, Randy S. Wiberg, Andrew Gottsfield, Donna Gillette, Viviana Bellifemine, Eric Strother, Robert Cartier, and David A. Fredrickson. 2007. Punctuated Culture Change in the San Francisco Bay Area. In *California Prehistory: Colonization, Culture, and Complexity*, edited by Terry L. Jones and Kathryn Klar, pp. 99–123. Alta Mira Press/Rowman & Littlefield Publishers, Lanham, Maryland.

Moffitt, Mike. 2020. Sir Francis Drake Sculpture Removed from Larkspur Landing. *SFGate* 29 July. Electronic document, https://www.sfgate.com/bayarea/article/Sir -Francis-Drake-sculpture-removed-from-Larkspur-15443255.php, accessed September 1, 2020.

Montgomery, Lindsay M., and Chip Colwell. 2019. *Objects of Survivance: A Material History of the American Indian School Experience*. Denver Museum of Nature & Science and University Press of Colorado, Denver.

Morales, Laurie, and Beverly Ortiz. 2019. The Nicky D, Alcatraz Island, and a Tule Boat. *News from Native California* 33(1):10–14.

Moratto, Michael J. 1984. *California Archaeology*. Academic Press, New York.

Munro-Fraser, J.P. 1880. *History of Marin County, California*. Alley, Bowen & Co., San Francisco.

Nabokov, Peter. 2006. *Where the Lightning Strikes: The Lives of American Indian Sacred Places*. Penguin Books, New York.

Nelson, Nels C. 1907. San Francisco Bay Mounds. *University of California Archaeological Survey Manuscripts*, No. 349. Phoebe A. Hearst Museum of Anthropology, University of California, Berkeley.

Nelson, Nels C. 1909a. Shellmounds of the San Francisco Bay Region. *University of California Publications in American Archaeology and Ethnology* 7(4):309–56.

Nelson, Nels C. 1909b. *Transcript of Archaeological Reconnaissance Notes: The California Coast from the Russian River to the Golden Gate. June, 1909*. On file at the Northwest Archaeological Information Center, Sonoma State University, Rohnert Park, California.

Nelson, Nels C. 1910a. Sausalito Mound #3. *University of California Archaeological Survey Manuscripts*, No. 353. Phoebe A. Hearst Museum of Anthropology, University of California, Berkeley.

Nelson, Nels C. 1910b. The Ellis Landing Shellmound. *University of California Publications in American Archaeology and Ethnology* 7(5):357–426.

Nelson, Peter A. 2020. Refusing Settler Epistemologies and Maintaining an Indigenous Future for Tolay Lake, Sonoma County, California. *American Indian Quarterly* 44(2):221–242.

Newell, Quincy D. 2009. *Constructing Lives at Mission San Francisco: Native Californians and Hispanic Colonists, 1776–1821*. University of New Mexico Press, Albuquerque.

Nicholas, George P., and Thomas D. Andrews. 1997. Indigenous Archaeology in the Postmodern World. In *At a Crossroads: Archaeologists and First Peoples in Canada*, edited by George P. Nicholas and Thomas D. Andrews, pp. 1–18. Simon Fraser University, Archaeology Press, Burnaby, British Columbia, Canada.

Oakland Tribune. 1929. Four Killed, Six Near Death from Clams. 6 August:25. https://www.newspapers.com/image/95961565, accessed October 20, 2019.

O'Brien, Jean M. 2010. *Firsting and Lasting: Writing Indians Out of Existence in New England*. University of Minnesota Press, Minneapolis.

Origer, Thomas M. 1982. Temporal Control in the Southern North Coast Ranges of California: The Application of Obsidian Hydration Analysis. Master's thesis, Department of Anthropology, San Francisco State University, San Francisco.

Panich, Lee M. 2014. Native American Consumption of Shell and Glass Beads at Mission Santa Clara de Asís. *American Antiquity* 79(4):730–48.

Panich, Lee M. 2015. "Sometimes They Bury the Deceased's Clothes and Trinkets": Indigenous Mortuary Practices at Mission Santa Clara de Asís. *Historical Archaeology* 49(4):110–29.

Panich, Lee M. 2017. Indigenous Vaqueros in Colonial California: Labor, Identity, and Autonomy. In *Foreign Objects: Rethinking Indigenous Consumption in American Archaeology*, edited by Craig N. Cipolla, pp. 187–203. University of Arizona Press, Tucson.

Panich, Lee M. 2020. *Narratives of Persistence: Indigenous Negotiations of Colonialism in Alta and Baja California*. University of Arizona Press, Tucson.

Panich, Lee M., and Tsim D. Schneider. 2015. Expanding Mission Archaeology: A Landscape Approach to Indigenous Autonomy in Colonial California. *Journal of Anthropological Archaeology*. 40:48–58.

Panich, Lee M., and Tsim D. Schneider. 2019. Categorical Denial: Evaluating Post-1492 Indigenous Erasure in the Paper Trail of American Archaeology. *American Antiquity* 84(4):651–68.

Panich, Lee M., and Tsim D. Schneider (editors). 2014. *Indigenous Landscapes and Spanish Missions: New Perspectives from Archaeology and Ethnohistory*. University of Arizona Press, Tucson.

Panich, Lee M., Ben Griffen, and Tsim D. Schneider. 2018a. Native Acquisition of Obsidian in Colonial-Era Central California: Implications from Mission San José. *Journal of Anthropological Archaeology* 50:1–11.

Panich, Lee M., Rebecca Allen, and Andrew Galvan. 2018b. The Archaeology of Native American Persistence at Mission San José. *Journal of California and Great Basin Anthropology* 38(1):11–29.

Panich, Lee M., Tsim D. Schneider, and Paul Engel. 2018c. The Marine Radiocarbon Reservoir Effects in Tomales Bay, California. *Radiocarbon* 60(3):963–74.

Panich, Lee M., Tsim D. Schneider, and R. Scott Byram. 2018d. Finding Mid-Nineteenth Century Native Settlements: Cartographic and Archaeological Evidence from Central California. *Journal of Field Archaeology* 43(2):152–65.

Panich, Lee M., GeorgeAnn DeAntoni, and Tsim D. Schneider. 2020. "By the Aid of His Indians": Native Negotiations of Settler Colonialism in Marin County, California, 1840–1870. *International Journal of Historical Archaeology*. DOI: 10.1007/s10761-020-00549-5.

Parkman, E. Breck. 1994. The Bedrock Milling Station. In *The Ohlone Past and Present: Native Americans of the San Francisco Bay Region*, edited by Lowell J. Bean, pp. 43–63. Ballena Press, Menlo Park, California.

Pauketat, Timothy R. 2009. *Cahokia: Ancient America's Great City on the Mississippi.* Viking Books, New York.

Pawling, Micah. 2016. Wabanaki Homeland and Mobility: Concepts of Home in Nineteenth-Century Maine. *Ethnohistory* 63(4):621–43.

Peelo, Sarah. 2009. Baptism among the Salinan Neophytes of Mission San Antonio de Padua: Investigating the Ecological Hypothesis. *Ethnohistory* 56(4):589–24.

Peelo, Sarah. 2011. Pottery-Making in Spanish California: Creating Multi-Scalar Social Identity through Daily Practice. *American Antiquity* 76(4):642–66.

Peri, David W., Scott M. Patterson, and Susan L. McMurray. 1985. *The Makahmo Pomo: An Ethnographic Survey of the Cloverdale (Makahmo) Pomo.* Report prepared by the Warm Springs Cultural Resources Study, Sonoma State University Academic Foundation Inc., Rohnert Park, Calif. US Army Corps of Engineers, Sacramento District.

Petaluma Courier. 1879a. Santa Rosa Items. 14 May:3. https://www.newspapers.com/image/235796631/, accessed October 20, 2019.

Petaluma Courier. 1879b. Jottings. 21 May:3. https://www.newspapers.com/image/235796647/, accessed October 20, 2019.

Petaluma Daily Morning Courier (PDMC). 1902. Briefs. 12 May:1. https://www.newspapers.com/image/609021876/, accessed October 20, 2019.

Petaluma Daily Morning Courier (PDMC). 1915. Tomales Bay Co. Asks Injunction [sic]. 18 November:8. https://www.newspapers.com/image/609430766/, accessed October 20, 2019.

Peter, Jesse. 1921. *Site Survey of Tomales, Bodega Bay and Sonoma County Coast.* On file at the Northwest Archaeological Information Center, Sonoma State University, Rohnert Park, Calif.

Phillips, George Harwood. 1993. *Indians and Intruders in Central California, 1769–1849.* University of California Press, Berkeley.

Phillips, George Harwood. 2010. *Vineyards & Vaqueros: Indian Labor and the Economic Expansion of Southern California, 1771–1877.* University of Oklahoma Press, Norman.

Phillips, George Harwood. 2016. *Indians of the Tulares: Adaptation, Relocation, and Subjugation in Central California 1771–1917.* Great Oak Press, Pechanga, California.

Pilling, Arnold R., and Franklin Fenenga. 1950. Archaeological Notes on the Castro Mound, CA-SCL-1. *University of California Archaeological Survey Manuscripts*, No. 47. Phoebe A. Hearst Museum of Anthropology, University of California, Berkeley.

Popper, Virginia S. 2016. Change and Persistence: Mission Neophyte Foodways at Selected Colonial Alta California Institutions. *Journal of California and Great Basin Anthropology* 36(1):5–25.

Potter, Jeanne O. 1942. Men of Marin—Don Timoteo Murphy. *Mill Valley Record* 10 July:4. California Digital Newspaper Collection, Center for Bibliographic Studies and Research, University of California, Riverside, https://cdnc.ucr.edu, accessed September 16, 2020.

Powers, Stephen. 1976 [1877]. *Tribes of California*. Introduction and Annotations by Robert F. Heizer. University of California Press, Berkeley.

Preston, William. 1998. Serpent in the Garden: Environmental Change in Colonial California. In *Contested Eden: California Before the Gold Rush*, edited by Ramón A. Gutiérrez and Richard J. Orsi, pp. 260–98. University of California Press, Berkeley.

Reddy, Seetha N. 2015. Feeding Family and Ancestors: Persistence of Traditional Native American Lifeways during the Mission Period in Coastal Southern California. *Journal of Anthropological Archaeology* 37:48–66.

Reid, Joshua L. 2015. *The Sea Is My Country: The Maritime World of the Makahs*. Yale University Press, New Haven, Connecticut.

Reséndez, Andrés. 2016. *The Other Slavery: The Uncovered Story of Indian Enslavement in America*. Houghton Mifflin Harcourt, Boston.

Revere, Joseph Warren. 1947 [1849]. *Naval Duty in California*. Biobooks, Oakland, California.

Revere, Joseph Warren. 1872. *Keel and Saddle: A Retrospect of Forty Years of Military and Naval Service*. James R. Osgood and Company, Boston.

Richard, François G. 2012. Hesitant Geographies of Power: The Materiality of Colonial Rule in the Siin (Senegal), 1850–1960. *Journal of Social Archaeology* 13(1):54–79.

Rizzo, Martin. 2020. "If They Do Not Fulfill What They Have Promised, I Will Accuse Them": Locating Indigenous Women and Their Influence in the California Missions. *The Western Historical Quarterly* 51(3):291–313.

Robinson, David W., Kelly Brown, Moira McMenemy, Lynn Dennany, Matthew J. Baker, Pamela Allan, Caroline Cartwright, Julienne Bernard, Fraser Sturt, Elena Kotoula, Christopher Jazwa, Kristina M. Gill, Patrick Randolph-Quinney, Thomas Ash, Clare Bedford, Devlin Gandy, Matthew Armstrong, James Miles, and David Haviland. 2020. Datura Quids at Pinwheel Cave, California, Provide Unambiguous Confirmation of the Ingestion of Hallucinogens at a Rock Art Site. *PNAS* 117(49):31026–37.

Rubertone, Patricia J. 2000. The Historical Archaeology of Native Americans. *Annual Review of Anthropology* 29:425–46.

Ruby, Allika, and Adrian R. Whitaker. 2019. Remote Places as Post-Contact Refugia. *California Archaeology* 11(2):205–33.

Russell, Lynette. 2012. *Roving Mariners: Australian Aboriginal Whalers and Sealers in the Southern Oceans, 1790–1870*. State University of New York Press, Albany.

Russell, Matthew A. 2011. Encounters at *tamál-húye*: An Archaeology of Intercultural Engagement in Sixteenth-Century Northern California. PhD dissertation, Department of Anthropology, University of California, Berkeley.

Sahlins, Marshall. 1981. *Historical Metaphors and Mythical Realities: Structure in the Early History of the Sandwich Islands Kingdom*. Ann Arbor: University of Michigan Press.

Sandos, James A. 2004. *Converting California: Indians and Franciscans in the Missions*. Yale University Press, New Haven, Connecticut.

San Francisco Call (SFC). 1892. Graves of Aborigines. 10 September:8. California Digital Newspaper Collection, Center for Bibliographic Studies and Research, University of California, Riverside, https://cdnc.ucr.edu, accessed September 20, 2018.

San Francisco Call (SFC). 1893. Bones and Gold. 13 October:3. California Digital Newspaper Collection, Center for Bibliographic Studies and Research, University of California, Riverside, https://cdnc.ucr.edu, accessed September 20, 2018.

San Francisco Call (SFC). 1896. Graves of Old Sausalitans. 29 July:16. California Digital Newspaper Collection, Center for Bibliographic Studies and Research, University of California, Riverside, https://cdnc.ucr.edu, accessed September 20, 2018.

San Francisco Call (SFC). 1902. Digs Up Bones of Aborigines. 22 June:20. California Digital Newspaper Collection, Center for Bibliographic Studies and Research, University of California, Riverside, https://cdnc.ucr.edu, accessed September 20, 2018.

San Francisco Call (SFC). 1907. Digger Indians Lose Clam Beds in Quake: Shellfish Disappear and Disturbance of Earth Is Blamed. 30 November:11. California Digital Newspaper Collection, Center for Bibliographic Studies and Research, University of California, Riverside, https://cdnc.ucr.edu, accessed October 20, 2019.

San Francisco Call (SFC). 1910. Bones of Indians Show Death Fight. 3 October:1. California Digital Newspaper Collection, Center for Bibliographic Studies and Research, University of California, Riverside, https://cdnc.ucr.edu, accessed September 20, 2018.

San Francisco Chronicle (SFCr). 1879. Salvador Strangled: Execution of Paul Rieger's Murderer at San Rafael. 3 October:1. California Digital Newspaper Collection, Center for Bibliographic Studies and Research, University of California, Riverside, https://cdnc.ucr.edu, accessed September 20, 2018.

San Francisco Chronicle (SFCr). 1892. Indian Skeletons. 18 February:12. California Digital Newspaper Collection, Center for Bibliographic Studies and Research, University of California, Riverside, https://cdnc.ucr.edu, accessed September 20, 2018.

San Francisco Chronicle (SFCr). 1910. Finds Bone Whistles in Historic Mounds. 19 January:8. California Digital Newspaper Collection, Center for Bibliographic Studies and Research, University of California, Riverside, https://cdnc.ucr.edu, accessed September 20, 2018.

San Francisco Examiner. 1883. A Sunday Jaunt. 25 June:1. https://www.newspapers.com/image/457917450/, accessed October 20, 2019.

Santa Barbara Mission Archive-Library (SBMAL). 1800. "Fray Juan Cortés, O.F.M., and Fray Tapis, O.F.M., to Francisco Lasuén describing in the greatest detail the daily mode of life at the Indian mission and refuting certain misrepresentations of Goycoechea." California Mission Documents, CMD-497. Santa Barbara Mission Archive-Library, Santa Barbara, California.

Santa Rosa Press Democrat. 1925. Clam Diggers Fined Here for Heavy Catches: Game Warden Fears Prize Bivalves May Become Extinct. 26 May:9. California Digital Newspaper Collection, Center for Bibliographic Studies and Research, University of California, Riverside, https://cdnc.ucr.edu, accessed October 20, 2019.

Sarris, Greg. 2001. First Thoughts on Restoration: Notes from a Tribal Chairman. *News from Native California* 14(3):12–15.

Sarris, Greg. 2002. When My Great-Great-Grandfather Tom Smith Caused the 1906 Earthquake. In *The Dirt Is Red Here: Art and Poetry from Native California*, edited by Margaret Dubin, pp. 65. Heyday, Berkeley, California.

Sarris, Greg. 2003. On Sacred Places. *Bay Nature*, April–June:5, 35.

Sarris, Greg. 2013 [1994]. *Mabel McKay: Weaving the Dream*. University of California Press, Berkeley.

Sarris, Greg. 2017. *How a Mountain Was Made: Stories*. Heyday, Berkeley, California.

Sausalito News (SN). 1896. News from Mill Valley. 26 December:1. California Digital Newspaper Collection, Center for Bibliographic Studies and Research, University of California, Riverside, https://cdnc.ucr.edu, accessed September 20, 2018.

Sausalito News (SN). 1897a. Mill Valley Is Lively. 29 May:1. California Digital Newspaper Collection, Center for Bibliographic Studies and Research, University of California, Riverside, https://cdnc.ucr.edu, accessed September 20, 2018.

Sausalito News (SN). 1897b. Fables. 18 December:1. California Digital Newspaper Collection, Center for Bibliographic Studies and Research, University of California, Riverside, https://cdnc.ucr.edu, accessed September 20, 2018.

Sausalito News (SN). 1901. Terpsichore on Tomales Bay: An Indian Dance that Continued for Three Days and Nights. 16 March:3. California Digital Newspaper Collection, Center for Bibliographic Studies and Research, University of California, Riverside, https://cdnc.ucr.edu, accessed September 20, 2018.

Sausalito News (SN). 1903. Late Paragraphs Too Short for Heads, But Generally the First to be Read. 30 May:3. California Digital Newspaper Collection, Center for Bibliographic Studies and Research, University of California, Riverside, https://cdnc.ucr.edu, accessed September 20, 2018.

Sausalito News (SN). 1904. Finds Giant Bones in Mound. 9 January:1. California Digital Newspaper Collection, Center for Bibliographic Studies and Research, University of California, Riverside, https://cdnc.ucr.edu, accessed September 20, 2018.

Sausalito News (SN). 1928. What Would He Think of It Now. 21 January:3. California Digital Newspaper Collection, Center for Bibliographic Studies and Research, University of California, Riverside, https://cdnc.ucr.edu, accessed September 20, 2018.

Sayers, Daniel O. 2014. *A Desolate Place for a Defiant People: The Archaeology of Maroons, Indigenous Americans, and Enslaved Laborers in the Great Dismal Swamp*. University Press of Florida, Gainesville.

Schneider, Khal. 2010. Making Indian Land in the Allotment Era: Northern California's Indian Rancherias. *The Western Historical Quarterly* 41(4):429–50.

Schneider, Khal, Dale Allender, Margarita Berta-Avila, Rose Borunda, Gregg Castro, Amy Murray, and Jenna Porter. 2019. More Than Missions: Native Californians and Allies Changing the Story of California History. *Journal of American Indian Education* 58(3):58–77.

Schneider, Tsim D. 2007a. The Illusive Kostromitinov Ranch: A Russian-American Company Ranch in Sonoma County, California. *Journal of California and Great Basin Anthropology* 27(2):165–71.

Schneider, Tsim D. 2007b. The Role of Archived Photographs in Native California Archaeology. *Journal of Social Archaeology* 7(1):49–71.

Schneider, Tsim D. 2010. Placing Refuge: Shell Mounds and the Archaeology of Colonial Encounters in the San Francisco Bay Area, California. PhD dissertation, Department of Anthropology, University of California, Berkeley.

Schneider, Tsim D. 2015a. Envisioning Colonial Landscapes Using Mission Registers, Radiocarbon, and Stable Isotopes: An Experimental Approach from San Francisco Bay. *American Antiquity* 80(3):511–29.

Schneider, Tsim D. 2015b. Placing Refuge and the Archaeology of Indigenous Hinterlands in Colonial California. *American Antiquity* 80(4):695–713.

Schneider, Tsim D. 2018. Making and Unmaking Native Communities in Mission and Post-Mission Era Marin County, California. In *Forging Communities in Colonial Alta California*, edited by Kathleen L. Hull and John G. Douglas, pp. 88–109. University of Arizona Press, Tucson.

Schneider, Tsim D. 2019. Heritage In-Between: Seeing Native Histories in Colonial California. *The Public Historian* 41(1):51–63.

Schneider, Tsim D. 2021. "Dancing on the Brink of the World": Seeing Indigenous Dance and Resilience in the Archaeology of Colonial California. *American Anthropologist* 123(1):50–66.

Schneider, Tsim D., and Katherine Howlett Hayes. 2020. Epistemic Colonialism: Is It Possible to Decolonize Archaeology? *American Indian Quarterly* 44(2):127–48.

Schneider, Tsim D., and Lee M. Panich. 2008. Total Station Mapping: Practical Examples from Alta and Baja California. *Journal of California and Great Basin Anthropology* 28(2):166–83.

Schneider, Tsim D., and Lee M. Panich. 2019. Landscapes of Refuge and Resiliency: Native Californian Persistence at Tomales Bay, California, 1770s–1870s. *Ethnohistory* 66(1):21–47.

Schneider, Tsim D., Anneke Janzen, GeorgeAnn M. DeAntoni, Amanda M. Hill, Alec J. Apodaca, and Rob Q. Cuthrell. 2018. Indigenous Persistence and Foodways at the Toms Point Trading Post (CA-MRN-202), Tomales Bay, California. *Journal of California and Great Basin Anthropology* 38(1):51–73.

Schneider, Tsim D., John Holson, Lori D. Hager, Samantha S. Schell, and Lucian N. Schrader III. 2014. Obsidian Production and Mortuary Practices at CA-NAP-399, Napa Valley: Inferences from AMS Radiocarbon Assays. *California Archaeology* 6(2):191–218.

Schneider, Tsim D., Khal Schneider, and Lee M. Panich. 2020. Scaling Invisible Walls: Reasserting Indigenous Persistence in Mission-Era California. *The Public Historian* 42(4):97–120.

Scheiber, Laura L., and Mark D. Mitchell (editors). 2010. *Across a Great Divide: Continuity and Change in Native North American Societies, 1400–1900.* University of Arizona Press, Tucson.

Schenck, W. Egbert, and Elmer J. Dawson. 1929. Archaeology of the Northern San Joaquin Valley. *University of California Publications in American Archaeology and Ethnology* 25(4):289–413.

Schulz, Peter D. 1988. Excavations of a Brickwork Feature at a Nineteenth-Century Chinese Shrimp Camp on San Francisco Bay. *Northwest Anthropological Research Notes* 22(1):121–34.

Schulz, Peter D., and Frank Lortie. 1985. Archaeological Notes on a Chinese Shrimp Boiler. *Historical Archaeology* 19(1):86–95.

Schweikhardt, Peter, B. Lynn Ingram, Kent Lightfoot, and Edward Luby. 2011. Geochemical Methods for Inferring Seasonal Occupation of an Estuarine Shellmound: A Case Study from San Francisco Bay. *Journal of Archaeological Science* 38:2301–12.

Scott, James C. 1990. *Domination and the Arts of Resistance: Hidden Transcripts.* Yale University Press, New Haven.

Scott, James C. 2009. *The Art of Not Being Governed: An Anarchist History of Upland Southeast Asia.* Yale University Press, New Haven.

Seymour, Deni J. 2010. Contextual Incongruities, Statistical Outliers, and Anomalies: Targeting Inconspicuous Occupational Events. *American Antiquity* 75(1):158–76.

Seymour, Deni J. 2017. Perceiving the Protohistoric: When Weak Signatures Represent the Strongest Cases. In *The Strong Case Approach in Behavioral Archaeology*, edited by Michael Brian Schiffer, Charles R. Riggs, and J. Jefferson Reid, pp. 139–57. University of Utah Press, Salt Lake City.

Shackley, M. Steven. 2001. The Stone Tool Technology of Ishi and the Yana of North Central California: Inferences for Hunter-Gatherer Cultural Identity in Historic California. *American Anthropologist* 102(4):693–712.

Shackley, M. Steven. 2005. *Obsidian: Geology and Archaeology in the North American Southwest.* University of Arizona Press, Tucson.

Shangraw, Clarence, and Edward P. Von der Porten. 1981. *The Drake and Cermeño Expeditions' Chinese Porcelains at Drakes Bay, California, 1579 and 1595.* Santa Rosa Junior College and Drake Navigator Guild, Santa Rosa and Palo Alto, California.

Shanks, Ralph. 2006. *Indian Baskets of Central California: Art, Culture, and History: Native American Basketry from San Francisco Bay and Monterey Bay North to Mendocino and East to the Sierras.* MAPOM Publication, No. 8. Costaño Books in Association with Miwok Archaeological Preserve of Marin, Novato, California.

Shanks, Ralph. 2012. MAPOM Co-founder Sylvia Thalman (1927–2012). *The Acorn: Newsletter of the Miwok Archaeological Preserve of Marin* 43(1):1.

Shepard, Michael Alvarez. 2016. Could a Trump Presidency Bring Back the Termination Era? *Anthropology News* 57(11):57–61.

Shoup, Laurence H., and Randall T. Milliken. 1999. *Inigo of Rancho Posolmi: The Life and Times of a Mission Indian.* Ballena Press, Novato, California.

Silliman, Stephen W. 1997. European Origins and Native Destinations: Historical Artifacts from the Native Alaskan Village and Fort Ross Beach Sites. In *The Archaeology and Ethnohistory of Fort Ross, California, Volume 2: The Native Alaskan Neighborhood: A Multiethnic Community at Colony Ross*, edited by Kent G. Lightfoot, Ann M. Schiff, and Thomas A. Wake, pp. 136–78. Contributions of the University of California Archaeological Research Facility, No. 55. University of California, Berkeley.

Silliman, Stephen W. 2001a. Agency, Practical Politics and the Archaeology of Culture Contact. *Journal of Social Archaeology* 1(2):190–209.

Silliman, Stephen W. 2001b. Theoretical Perspectives on Labor and Colonialism: Reconsidering the California Missions. *Journal of Anthropological Archaeology* 20(4): 379–407.

Silliman, Stephen W. 2004. *Lost Laborers in Colonial California: Native Americans and the Archaeology of Rancho Petaluma*. University of Arizona Press, Tucson.

Silliman, Stephen W. 2009. Change and Continuity, Practice and Memory: Native American Persistence in Colonial New England. *American Antiquity* 74(2):211–30.

Silverman, David J. 2003. "We Chuse to be Bounded": Native American Animal Husbandry in Colonial New England. *The William and Mary Quarterly* 60(3):511–48.

Simons, Dwight D. 1992. Prehistoric Mammal Exploitation in the San Francisco Bay Area. In *Essays on the Prehistory of Maritime California*, edited by Terry L. Jones, pp. 73–103. Center for Archaeological Research at Davis Publication, No. 10. University of California, Davis.

Slaymaker, Charles M. 1972. *Cry for Olompali*. Privately printed.

Slaymaker, Charles M. 1974. Fidemo, the Twilight and Before: A Study of Coast Miwok Political Organization. Master's thesis, Department of Anthropology, San Francisco State University, San Francisco.

Slaymaker, Charles M. 1977. The Material Culture of Cotomko'tca: A Coast Miwok Tribelet in Marin County, California. *MAPOM Occasional Paper*, No. 3. Miwok Archaeological Preserve of Marin, San Rafael, California.

Slaymaker, Charles M. 1982. A Model for the Study of Coast Miwok Ethnogeography. PhD dissertation, Department of Anthropology, University of California, Davis.

Sloan, Doris. 2006. *Geology of the San Francisco Bay Region*. University of California Press, Berkeley.

Smith, Kathleen (editor). 1993. *We Are Still Here: A Coast Miwok Exhibit*. Booklet published in conjunction with the exhibition, "We Are Still Here: A Coast Miwok Exhibit," August 22–October 3, 1993. Bolinas Museum, Bolinas, California.

Smith, Kathleen Rose. 2014. *Enough for All: Foods of My Dry Creek Pomo and Bodega Miwuk People*. Heyday, Berkeley, California.

Sousa, Ashley Riley. 2015. "An Influential Squaw": Intermarriage and Community in Central California, 1839–1851. *Ethnohistory* 62(4):707–27.

Starn, Orin. 2003. Ishi's Spanish Words. In *Ishi in Three Centuries*, edited by Karl Kroeber and Clifton Kroeber, pp. 201–7. University of Nebraska Press, Lincoln.

Stein, Julie K. (editor). 1992. *Deciphering a Shell Midden*. Academic Press, New York.

Stewart, Suzanne B., and Adrian Praetzellis (editors). 2003. *Archaeological Research Issues for the Point Reyes National Seashore—Golden Gate National Recreation Area: 2. An Overview of Research Issues for Indigenous Archaeology for the PRNS—GGNRA*. Report prepared for National Park Service, Golden Gate National Recreation Area, San Francisco. Report prepared by the Anthropological Studies Center, Sonoma State University, Rohnert Park, California.

Stuiver, M., P. J. Reimer, and R. W. Reimer. 2020. CALIB 7.1 (WWW program). http://calib.org/calib/, accessed February 26, 2020.

Sunseri, Charlotte K. 2017. Capitalism as Nineteenth-Century Colonialism and Its Impacts on Native Californians. *Ethnohistory* 64(4):471–95.

Supernant, Kisha, Jane Eva Baxter, Natasha Lyons, and Sonya Atalay (editors). 2020. *Archaeologies of the Heart*, Springer Nature Switzerland AG, Cham, Switzerland.

Taylor, Dennis. 2012. Monterey Bishop Offers Apology to Amah Mutsun Tribe for Past Abuses. *Monterey County Herald* 22 December. Electronic document, http://www.montereyherald.com/christmascheer/ci_22247499/monterey-bishop-offers-apology-amah-mutsun-tribe-past, accessed October 1, 2013.

Taylor, Thomas. 1872. Report of the Commissioner of Agriculture for the Year 1871: Report on Fungoid Diseases of Plants. In *Executive Documents Printed by Order of the House of Representatives during the Second Session of the Forty-Second Congress, 1871–72*, pp. 110–22. Government Printing Office, Washington, DC.

Thomas, Nicholas. 1994. *Colonialism's Culture: Anthropology, Travel, and Government*. Princeton University Press, Princeton, New Jersey.

Thrush, Coll. 2007. *Native Seattle: Histories from the Crossing-Over Place*. University of Washington Press, Seattle.

Tibesar, Antonine (editor). 1955. *Writings of Junípero Serra*, Vol. 3. Translated by Antonine Tibesar. Academy of American Franciscan History, Washington, DC.

Tikhmenev, P. A. 1978 [1862]. *A History of the Russian-American Company*. Translated by R. A. Pierce and A. S. Donnelly. University of Washington Press, Seattle.

Tovell, Freeman M. 2008. *At the Far Reaches of Empire: The Life of Juan Francisco de la Bodega y Quadra*. University of British Columbia Press, Vancouver.

Treganza, Adan F. 1959. *The Examination of Indian Shellmounds in the Tomales and Drake's Bay Areas with Reference to Sixteenth Century Historic Contacts*. California Department of Parks and Recreation, Sacramento.

Treganza, Adan F., and Sherburne F. Cook. 1948. The Quantitative Investigation of Aboriginal Sites: Complete Excavation with Physical and Archaeological Analysis of a Single Mound. *American Antiquity* 13(4):287–97.

Trigger, Bruce G. 1980. Archaeology and the Image of the American Indian. *American Antiquity* 45(4):662–76.

Trigger, Bruce G. 1986. *Native Shell Mounds of North America: Early Studies*. Garland, New York.

Trigger, Bruce G. 2006. *A History of Archaeological Thought*. 2nd ed. Cambridge University Press, Cambridge.

Uhle, Max. 1907. The Emeryville Shellmound. *University of California Publications in American Archaeology and Ethnology* 7:1–107.

United States Census Bureau. 1880. Tenth Manuscript Census of the United States. Population schedules for Nicasio and Point Reyes Townships, Marin County, California.

United States Census Bureau. 1900. Twelfth Manuscript Census of the United States. Indian population schedules for Bodega Township, Sonoma County, California.

Vaughn, Chelsea K. 2011. Locating Absence: The Forgotten Presence of Monjeríos in Alta California Missions. *Southern California Quarterly* 93(2):141–74.

Vaux, William S. W. (editor). 1854. *The World Encompassed by Sir Francis Drake*. The Hakluyt Society, London.

Vigness, Paul G. 1952. *Alameda Community Book*. A. H. Cawston, Alameda, California.

Von der Porten, Peter, and Alex DeGeorgey. 2015. Historical Insights into Abandonment of a San Francisco Bay Shellmound (CA-CCO-297). *Proceedings of the Society for California Archaeology* 29:99–114.

Voss, Barbara L. 2005. From *Casta* to *Californio*: Social Identity and the Archaeology of Culture Contact. *American Anthropologist* 107(3):461–74.

Voss, Barbara L. 2008. *The Archaeology of Ethnogenesis: Race and Sexuality in Colonial San Francisco*. University of California Press, Berkeley.

Wade, Mariah F. 2008. *Missions, Missionaries, and Native Americans: Long-Term Processes and Daily Practices*. University Press of Florida, Gainesville.

Wade, Mariah F. 2013. The Missionary Predicament: Conversion Practices in Texas, New Mexico, and the Californias. In *From La Florida to La California: Franciscan Evangelization in the Spanish Borderlands*, edited by Timothy J. Johnson and Gert Melville, pp. 285–96. Academy of American Franciscan History, Berkeley, California.

Wagner, Henry R. 1924. The Voyage to California of Sebastian Rodriguez Cermeño in 1595. *California Historical Society Quarterly* 3(1):3–24.

Wagner, Henry R. 1931. The Last Spanish Exploration of the Northwest Coast and the Attempt to Colonize Bodega Bay. *California Historical Society Quarterly* 10(4):313–45.

Wake, Thomas A. 1997. Bone Artifacts and Tool Production in the Native Alaskan Neighborhood. In *The Archaeology and Ethnohistory of Fort Ross, California, Volume 2: The Native Alaskan Neighborhood: A Multiethnic Community at Colony Ross*, edited by Kent G. Lightfoot, Ann M. Schiff, and Thomas A. Wake, pp. 248–78. Contributions of the University of California Archaeological Research Facility, No. 55. University of California, Berkeley.

Walshe, Keryn, and Tom Loy. 2004. An Adze Manufactured from a Telegraph Insulator, Harvey's Return, Kangaroo Island. *Australian Archaeology* 58(1):38–40.

Waselkov, Gregory A. 1987. Shellfish Gathering and Shell Midden Archaeology. *Advances in Archaeological Method and Theory* 10:93–210.

Watkins, Joe. 2000. *Indigenous Archaeology: American Indian Values and Scientific Practice*. AltaMira Press, Walnut Creek, California.

Weber, David J. 1982. *The Mexican Frontier, 1821–1846: The American Southwest Under Mexico*. University of New Mexico Press, Albuquerque.

Weekly Alta California. 1849. Marine Journal. 26 July:2. California Digital Newspaper Collection, Center for Bibliographic Studies and Research, University of California, Riverside, https://cdnc.ucr.edu, accessed September 20, 2018.

Weik, Terry. 1997. The Archaeology of Maroon Societies in the Americas: Resistance, Cultural Continuity, and Transformation. *Historical Archaeology* 31(2):81–92.

White, John R. 1977. Aboriginal Artifacts on Non-Traditional Material: Six Specimens from Fort Ross, California. *Northwest Anthropological Research Notes* 11(2):240–47.

Wilbur, Marguerite Eyer (editor). 1953. *Vancouver in California, 1792–1794: The Original Account of George Vancouver*, Vol. 1. Glen Dawson, Los Angeles.

Wilkins, James H. 1918. *The Days of the Dons: Reminiscences of California's Oldest Native Son.* Anne T. Kent California Room, Marin County Free Library, San Rafael, California.

Wrangell, Baron Ferdinand Petrovich von. 1974. Some Remarks on the Savages on the Northwest Coast of America: The Indians of Upper California. In *Ethnographic Observations on the Coast Miwok and Pomo by Contre-Admiral F.P. von Wrangell and P. Kostromitinov of the Russian Colony Ross, 1839*, translated and edited by Fred Stross and Robert H. Heizer, pp. 1–20. Archaeological Research Facility, University of California, Berkeley.

Zappia, Natale A. 2014. *Raiders and Traders: The Indigenous World of the Colorado Basin, 1540–1859*. University of North Carolina Press, Chapel Hill.

Index

About the Author

Tsim D. Schneider is an assistant professor of anthropology at the University of California, Santa Cruz. He is the co-editor with Lee M. Panich of *Indigenous Landscapes and Spanish Missions: New Perspectives from Archaeology and Ethnohistory* and his research has also appeared in publications such as *American Antiquity*, *American Indian Quarterly*, *Ethnohistory*, and *The Public Historian*.